REMETZ

RESISTANCE FIGHTER AND SURVIVOR OF THE
WARSAW GHETTO

JAN YOHAY REMETZ

ap

ISBN: 9789493276048 (ebook)

ISBN: 9789493276024 (paperback)

ISBN: 9789493276031 (hardcover)

Publisher: Amsterdam Publishers, The Netherlands

info@amsterdampublishers.com

Remetz. Resistance Fighter and Survivor of the Warsaw Ghetto is **Book 14 in the Series Holocaust Survivor Memoirs WWII**

CONTENTS

PROLOGUE

Jan Yohay Remetz

My father was born by the name of Tadeusz Grauzalc on December 25, 1923. The stories of his survival and that of his family throughout WWII are detailed in this book, originally also named *Remetz*. The book was published first in Poland in 2002, in the Polish language, and later translated and published in Hebrew in 2006 by Yad Vashem, The World Holocaust Remembrance Center.

We changed my father's cover name, Piechocki, before going on an official mission abroad in 1978 since it was obligatory then to carry a Hebrew last name. My father chose the name Remetz, which in Hebrew means "cinder" or "burning ash," attributed to us being the only relic of both my mother's name, Brenner, and my father's name, Grauzalc, both large and thriving families.

Barbara Engelking, a renowned Holocaust researcher and a friend of my father's, wrote:

"Survival was possible if you had a number of resources—and not just material ones, such as money and possessions to sell. Nonmaterial resources included psychological wherewithal such as courage, determination, and awareness of danger, and quick reactions; biological assets (a "good appearance"); cultural basics, such as a very good command of Polish, knowledge of customs and the Catholic religion; a social network, such as family, friends, and contacts. Survival did not depend on having all of these resources, or even most of them, but survivors' accounts usually relate to a combination of some of them."

Apparently, my father had been endowed with several of these resources—first and foremost, his determination and courage.

After having survived the Holocaust, keeping his Polish identity under the name Jan Piechocki, my father had served as an officer (major) in the Polish army, cavalry corps, and had graduated from the communist Polish military academy. After being forced to leave the military for political reasons (due to his father's return to Poland following a decade in a gulag in Siberia, in which he had been imprisoned for his Zionist background), he remained in Poland and worked for the government tourist administration. In 1957, after Wladyslaw Gomulka came into power in Poland, it became possible for Polish

Jews to relocate to Israel. Leaving Poland was not officially mandatory for Jews in that period, but a rise in antisemitism and disappointment with the communist regime led many Polish Jews to make the decision to emigrate. That immigration wave was named the "*Gomulka Aliya*" between 1956 and 1960, among whom was my father. His father and brother immigrated to Israel as well in this time frame, his brother continuing onward to the United States a few years later.

At the beginning of the 1960s, he studied economics in Paris and, upon returning to Israel, took part in establishing the Timna copper mines while based in the city of Eilat. Later, he joined the Israeli Aircraft Industries (IAI), from which he retired in 1986. He married my mother, Helen Brenner, in 1963.

My mother was born on September 26, 1933. She survived the Holocaust years with her mother and brother, who had perished toward the end of the war. The three had managed to flee the Warsaw Ghetto shortly before the uprising, and were hidden in the house of Eva Woidat, her mother's sister, who had converted to Catholicism at the beginning of the 1930s after marrying a Catholic community leader. My mother's father had been taken by the Germans in the early stages of the Warsaw occupation. According to witnesses who spoke with Helen's mother after the war, he managed to escape from either Treblinka or the transport to Treblinka, made his way to the family's hometown of Wysokie Mazowieckie, in the outskirts of which he was intercepted by local residents who had known him as a wealthy industrialist before the war. After having failed to blackmail him for money, they simply murdered him with axes.

Following the Warsaw uprising, my mother, along with her mother and brother, fled to the countryside, living with local villagers under Christian identities. By the end of the war, Helen had been taken into a postwar Jewish children's home in Otwock, near Warsaw. In 1950, she and her mother immigrated to Israel as part of the

Hashomer Hatzair socialist-Zionist youth movement. She worked as an operating-room nurse for many years.

Both my parents were among the few survivors of their large families. Both their families had perished in the Treblinka extermination camp.

There is an epilogue added to the book, written in the past few years by my father. He recalled a specific affair that had been omitted from the original book and asked me to add it to the English translation.

The epilogue contains some impressions of my parents' first visit to Poland more than 40 years after they had left it. That took place in 1991, enabled by the fall of the Iron Curtain. Beforehand, such a visit would have been impossible since most Soviet bloc countries broke diplomatic ties with Israel after the Six-Day War and had sided with its Arab enemies. My father wrote down his impressions of post-Iron Curtain Poland, including the concentration camps they had visited for the first time.

My father mentions his close friend Leszek Koter. They had worked together after the war, became close friends, and kept in touch through letters after my father had left for Israel. In 1960, my grandfather asked him to check out the site of the Treblinka extermination camp. Koter went there and was horrified to find an open field, covered by shrubs and bushes and mass graves repeatedly dug open by the local population looking for gold teeth and other "treasures." He initiated a long correspondence with the local authorities, which eventually brought about the rehabilitation of the site and its designation as a national memorial site. The story (in Hebrew) and the photos he took at the site are listed on the Yad Vashem website.[1]

I joined my parents on a visit to Poland in 1999 and later in 2011 when my two older boys joined my father on another special "roots" visit. On that trip, we visited the various locations where my father had roamed during the war in Warsaw and its surrounding, as well as, of course, the Treblinka and Auschwitz-Birkenau sites. It was a very moving and emotional trip for all. We also found the Warsaw house in which my mother had lived at the beginning of the war and their hideout in Eva's house in the Mokotow neighborhood.

The following is a web page by Yad Vashem dedicated to my father and his story of survival, in Hebrew: https://www.yadvashem.org/he/remembrance/survivors/remetz.html

I have enclosed explanatory footnotes to the translated texts, as well as some of its original photos and other explanatory photos and maps, in order to clarify some of the historical background of events and locations mentioned in the book.

Eva Tidhar

Israel

To my mother

I needed time to struggle with many thoughts and clear my head.

For many years I saw this mission as clear and obvious: to tell what I went through, what everyone went through.

I didn't write. First, because the circumstances were not right, and later for the simple reason that I had to build my life again.

Throughout the years, many memoires were published by people who survived thanks to an extraordinary luck, a miracle. Sensational stories became common. Nevertheless, the question kept coming up— where do my experiences stand in all this?

This story is intended firstly for my grandchildren; once they have read it, I will see my mission as accomplished.

I hope the descendants of Holocaust survivors will continue the effort of learning of their forefathers' past.

MY FAMILY

Our house was humble, even very humble. But my parents aspired to live cultural lives and to grant their sons an education. It wasn't easy. During the economic depression, my father was unemployed for a long time. Had it not been for my aunts' help, my mother's sisters, surely my brother and I wouldn't have finished high school. Our house can be described as secular, progressive, all ideals' catchphrases taken most seriously—secularism based on Jewish assimilation. Polish was the spoken language at home: Polish books, newspapers, and theater. My parents loved music and dedicated time and interest to it. My mother learned singing for some years but ceased once she married. We heard her sing *Solveigh* at home and *Tosca Prayer*, *Delilah*'s aria, and that's how I learned to love many Polish songs. After the war, I searched for the performance of one song, *Kalina* (Viburnum, a flower), until I managed to find an original one on tape. I felt my mom's performance was more beautiful.

To the amazement of some of my friends and my father's parents, my mother did not know Yiddish. Neither did my brother and me. Nevertheless, since our father was a Zionist activist, our house preserved a Jewish character but lacked almost any religious characteristics. We attended synagogue twice a year, and my brother and I celebrated our bar mitzvahs. I think that emphasizing ourselves as Jews on the outside was mainly "to prove to the Poles that we are not ashamed of our Judaism." Not that it was easy. We were Poles in our everyday lives, although, amid the growing violence around us, Polish society looked upon Catholicism and nationality as one inseparable entity. Part of the Jewish intelligentsia, of which my mother's family was part, looked upon themselves as "Poles of the Mosaic descent."[1] My parents did not declare themselves as such, but in practice, like many others, were drawn into it.

Father tried to influence us with his Zionist inclinations, but without much success. He worked hard to make a living but did not succeed in filling all our needs. If not for the help of our aunts, who were all childless... They saw us as their sons. The elder, Stella, had a Dutch Catholic husband, and they both lived in the Netherlands. The other two, Basia and Stefa, who lived in Poland, were rich and influenced our assimilation—something that my father was unhappy about.

Our lives until 1939 were divided into two: Kalisz and Warsaw.

I was born in Kalisz and went to a Jewish primary school there, which was secular and Zionist. Kalisz was a rather large district center. The Jews constituted a third of its population—far too big a proportion claimed the Poles with unhidden concern. The city operated as the commercial-industrial center of an agricultural region. A significant part of both industry and commerce were held by Jews, which caused envy and antisemitism. Compared to other district cities, Kalisz was elegant. Its residents were proud of their "chic" town. It had a large park; in many places, it was separated by a river whose banks were joined by a dozen bridges. At the edge of the park was the theater, housed in a classical building with a wide veranda—the city's pride. A few years before the war, it had a steady group of actors—all young, ambitious, and talented. Many of them moved to the country's more central theaters and had prosperous careers. We would visit this theater when we came to visit our aunts during the winter break. At times, we managed to see up to three plays in one week.

In the city's central boulevard was an elegant café with excellent pastries. When we were allowed to join our mother and aunts, they would seat us at a separate table. We sat at the marble table, enjoying the pastries, reading the comical magazines. The comics— *"shmontzes,"* about two Jews—taught us that Jews could make fun of themselves.[2] We were told at home that a joke does not mock; it's all about circumstances, tone, and intent. We were too young to understand this complexity.

Kalisz's main traffic road, named after Josef Piłsudski, was a vibrant commercial street. It led to a square with the city's huge municipal building and extended up to the big church with a well in its yard: the street and the well-won fame in a book by Maria Dąbrowska. Kalisz had many churches. The city's life rhythm was dictated by the church bells ringing every half-hour all day. The ringing did not bother; on the contrary, they were integrated into the city's life and scenery. The city was mostly sleepy except for its vibrant center, and there, too, everything stopped in the early evening hours.

The youth studied in three state high schools: two for boys and one for girls. Among their students were many children of progressive, assimilating Jewish families—two concepts that are often thought of jointly. The only Jewish high school was for both girls and boys, in the Polish language, dedicating five hours a week for Hebrew lessons. This high school was well known for its high-level studies. Next to it was a Jewish primary school, where I spent my first years. Its teachers were the high-school teachers, most of them with PhD degrees or PhD students from Galicia, who, during the Great Depression, preferred a steady income instead of research jobs at the university.

In order to keep the students busy, they organized afternoon activities. The Polish schools had the Scouts movement, which did not accept Jews as members. There were also some clerical movements. Despite the prohibition on political activity, many of the Jewish high school students were active in Jewish youth movements. Yet, when during the Polish National Day parade, my brother marched with the *"Beitar"* movement, he was immediately suspended from school, and Father was required to promise this will not happen again.

The majority of the Jewish population identified politically mostly as left-wing. The fact that most kids were part of the leftist *"Ha-Shomer"* youth movement caused tension at times between the kids and the traditional Jewish parents.

The national holidays were celebrated at schools with grand ceremonies. The Polish schools held formal masses at church, while the Jewish students held special prayers at the great synagogue at the city's center. For the ceremony, we all crossed the city marching in fours with the high school's flag up front.

My father was destined to become a lawyer. He married my mother at 21, a very young age. She was barely 18. She was an orphan raised by her older sisters. The young couple first lived in Warsaw, but a year later, my brother was born, and the student-father had to start working as a clerk. He continued studying in college, but that was disrupted as well due to my aunt's decision to move the family to Kalisz.

My father changed several jobs. For a long time, he had worked as an editor, wrote a column and articles in the local newspaper *Gazeta Kaliszka*. As the editor's family, we had free entry into all the city events, plays, concerts, even the cinema. At some moment, father resumed his Zionist activity, which he interrupted as we left Warsaw.

In Kalisz, a city of three rivers (actually one river, Prosna, flowing in three canals), Jews were refused membership in the water-sports club. My father, who was one of the founders of *Maccabi Warsaw*, initiated the establishment of a Jewish rowing club. This is how the Jewish Rowing Association came to be. The town allocated a lot on the riverbank, and a trainer was hired. After only a month, they found out that in order to participate in tournaments, they had to be part of the rowing teams' association, but that it did not accept any club with the word "Jewish" in its title. After much discussion, it was decided to change the club's title to Rowers Club 30 since it was established in 1930. My father opposed the change, resigned, and waived his member rights. He then became an active *Beitar* member and was elected as the movement's national commissioner. He was also active in *Maccabi* in Kalisz. Some of the club's boxers won the city championship. In these competitions, you could often hear the shouts "beat up the Jew!"

In the years before the war, despite continuing antisemitism, it seemed a new policy was exercised toward Jews. Amidst the worsening international atmosphere, in the shadow of the threat of Nazi Germany, Poland tried to give the impression that it acknowledges the rights of the Jewish minority by various gestures: on *Yom Kippur* eve, the radio played the *Kol Nidrei* prayer by a famous cantor.

Near 1938, upon completing its fall training, the Kalisz infantry regiment returned to town. Many of its heroes were Jews; for example, captain Zygmund Greenfeld was a WWI hero. His regiment marched into the city. The residents and the city mayor welcomed them with flowers. Greenfeld led the parade—a trivial detail, but one that filled the town's Jewish residents with pride. The Polish majority did not hide its criticism: our soldiers return to town welcomed by priests carrying the cross, yet, they are led by a Jew? The next day, Greenfeld returned to his work as chief accountant. I don't know whether he survived the Holocaust.

Those were, of course, single gestures, but perhaps only because they were such, they left a great mark on the city's Jews.

Meanwhile, the Polish parliament, the *Sejm*, discussed the prohibition of kosher slaughter, and at universities, Jewish students were forced to sit at the back of the lecture halls on designated separate benches nicknamed *"ghetto benches"* (as a protest, Jewish students kept standing throughout the whole lesson). The prime minister, General Składkowski, deemed it appropriate to condemn the antisemitic pogroms yet acknowledged the right to economically boycott the Jews.

In 1933, we left Kalisz for Warsaw. I joined a new Polish school and later a Jewish school. This created quite a turmoil for me. At first, we lived with my mother's brother. Their house on Twarda Street had a long and narrow yard, surrounded by apartment buildings, workshops, even tiny stands. It was dark, and sunlight barely came through. Even my uncle's large apartment was barely lit. The street was constantly noisy and busy. Commerce was conducted on the street in shops and in the alleys in strollers and in peddlers' baskets on the pavement. My uncle and aunt were friendly people but worked from day till night at their large and elegant store situated in a central junction. On my way from the apartment to the store, I had to cross a large square with a church on one side. From here, a new and different, calmer and cleaner Warsaw was discovered.

This city scared me. In Kalisz, everything was familiar; here, it was strange and different. Sometimes the streets only spoke Yiddish. I didn't understand what was said. After many years, when our uncles nor we lived there anymore, I discovered that some famous Jewish intellectuals lived there.

In our street was a public library called Universum. It was located at a medium-sized store, its walls filled with bookstands top to bottom. I never understood how one could find a specific book there. The owner told Mother, "Two-and-a-half zlotys for two books" for the two of us, "and two more for deposit." Then she looked at mother and said, "I won't take a deposit from you, but I demand the books be returned on time."

And, indeed, we tried to follow this rule. We "devoured" the books, exchanging them between us. We entered a world we hardly knew before. The library's owners' liberal-leftist political worldview, like that of many others in the Jewish intelligentsia, was evident from the book catalog. One could find the oeuvres of the European new wave: Anton Šiška's *How Petroleum Rules the World*, Karl Poláček's *Man in the Teeth of the Machine,* Upton Sinclair's *King Coal, Hunger* by Knut Hamsun, *The Fortress* by A. J. Cronin. The Russian communists were also represented, including Ilya Eherenburg's novels, Boris Pilnyak's *The Naked Year* and *The Volga Falls into the Caspian*, Belykh and Pantalayev's *Republic of ShKID*. Years later, I learned that both ended as victims in Stalin's purge. In order to get one of these books, you had to register and wait your turn. It often happened that we asked for a book that sounded interesting but were told it was too early for us and were offered something similar. We were often asked for our opinion following the returning of a book. Our ways in literature were paved by intelligent and clever people. I loved to read and used to take books at several libraries, including the high school. It was a rich library with everything a pupil could ask for, adults too. Some of its books were very old ones; looking into them was like stumbling into an antique warehouse. Not once was I scolded for not returning a book on time.

In 1937, I encountered another, quite different public library. It was for high school students, well-illuminated, and very modern and comfortable. It had an impressive collection of books and magazines. Two ladies helped around and managed the reading hall. They instantly recognized which reader was there to work and who, God forbid, came in for a meeting with a girlfriend. I usually came in to work. There, I could find material that I could not acquire elsewhere. On the history shelves, I could find books on subjects that were not dealt with in-depth in school. That's how I was introduced to the poet Norbid, who was added to the top list of Polish poets only after his death. I ardently read books by the pioneering writers' group Skamander, whose intellectual independence and contemplation were not always in line with those of the regime's, but they were greatly admired by youngsters and respected in left-wing circles. Leading this group was the Jewish Polish poet Julian Tuwim, whom I especially admired as Poland's poetry genius.

But the library was also grounds for social meetings and used as an introduction into adolescence. The last time I visited the library was in November 1939. The Jewish schools were no longer allowed to operate, and we were forced to wear a yellow ribbon. The library manager took a seat next to me and pleaded that I understand her. "The library serves only students; according to the new restrictions, you are no longer a student, and you are now wearing the yellow ribbon. We have strict orders..." For the first time, she addressed me as "sir." She was embarrassed. We agreed to meet after the war; it would all be over in no time. Several months after that, Polish schools were closed down too. I don't know the fate of this library. After the war, it became an academic institution. I haven't visited it until very recently.

In my new school, I went through everything a boy from a Zionist home, whose father spoke of a Jewish state on both sides of the Jordan River, should go through. The "baptism by fire" in the new school in Warsaw shocked me. Even mother's folk songs about *"viburnum in the woods,"* about a villager who died amid the fight between masters, even the visits to church with our maid before Christmas, seeing the stall with baby Jesus—none of that made it any easier.

Each school day opened with the students' praying and crossing themselves in front of the Virgin Mary—Poland's crown queen. I stood, bowing my head down, waiting for it to finish. At first, I felt like a miserable stranger in a strange world, but later I became accustomed to this ritual. My new friends were not hostile. They were not too sympathetic or sensitive, either; worse, they were very curious. It turned out I was the only Jewish boy in class. Sometime later, I discovered one more Jewish pupil, except he disguised his Judaism and did not participate in religion classes, claiming he was an evangelist. His sister, though, participated in the catechism classes with the priest, so the truth was eventually out. Until then, I was the only Jew, and in sports class, my classmates decided to find out what it looks like "down there." I resisted, kicked, and struggled. Later, at home, I broke down and cried so much that my head ached for hours. I declared I was going to walk back to Kalisz, but the next day I was back in school. I later met the guy I kicked in 1944 during a battle against the Germans. He didn't recognize me.

I was a good student, although I dedicated most of my time to the subjects that were of most interest to me, such as the humanities. In geography, history, and the Polish language, I was the best in my class. The teacher often sighed and muttered angrily to the class: "Aren't you ashamed that the best student in the Polish language is none other than one who doesn't speak Polish at home?" Only later did she ask me what language was spoken at home and was surprised to hear it was Polish. I was offended; I thought of it as pure antisemitism. Much time had to pass until I realized the difference between antisemitic hatred that was "ideological" and one that was a result of many negative perceptions that consolidated into a standard way of thinking. I was 11 years old, and I did not think I could ever analyze it in a non-emotional manner. I was commended for my achievements in grammar since I was the only one who correctly replied to all the supervisor's questions, and this elevated my position in class and even in the whole school. Some of my friends were even prepared to "forget" that I didn't pray with them every morning.

Especially then, I found myself thinking a great deal about Zionism and the establishment of a Jewish state. Father tried to answer my questions, but I still couldn't understand why Jews are divided into so many parties and why they were constantly arguing.

I began my high-school year in the same school my father graduated from 18 years ago, and my brother was already attending. I am in love with this school until this very day, although it is hard to describe my years there in an ideal way. I was stubborn and hard to control; at times, my behavior was even irritating.

The Merchants Association High School was established at the beginning of the 20th century by a rich and powerful organization. The tuition fee as well the academic standards were very high compared to other schools in the city. It was housed in a fancy building complex and included a cluster of schools quite different in designation. There were two high schools—a regular one and a half-boarding school—four "lyceums"—the last two senior years of high school, majoring in various subjects, one primary school, and a technical school of commerce. I attended the regular high school. Its teachers later became famous university instructors, academics, and writers. Some of them became politicians after the war, and one even became a minister.

Having been the sons of a graduate, we enjoyed a substantial discount on the tuition fee, but even then, the expense was almost half of my father's income. My mother's sisters paid the rest of the fee for my brother and me.

The high academic standard attracted many wealthy Jewish merchants and industrialists. They could afford the high pay and, therefore, Jews were about 40 percent of the school's students. Most of the Catholic students were sons of civil servants who also enjoyed discounts. There were also many non-Jewish kids of mostly wealthy families. The school policy was that all walks of life in it were to live together in harmony, according to codes introduced by the school through the years. No antisemitism was felt in the school, in stark contrast to what went on outside in most Polish schools. Many friendships were created among students of different descent. The very first Aryan papers arranged for my brother and me were prepared by a Polish school friend. We escaped the ghetto with these papers, and they assisted us in our toughest times.

As I mentioned before, I neglected the subjects I didn't like, which often led to a catastrophe. I once faced failing a subject, something that could easily have prevented me from acquiring the "small-matriculation" certificate.[3] I had to take that exam, and I passed it with distinction. It took my parents a long time to forgive me.

At that time, my mind was spinning with so many ideas and thoughts that I thought were originally my own. A young man is often assured that he is the source for all these novel ideas without realizing many have already thought alike generations before. I lived in a world of poetry and literature of the great romantics. It was a whole universe. I was overwhelmed with this beauty and esthetics. They became my own property. Had they actually served me as a refuge?

Unruly antisemitism raged outside. In the Polish parliament, Father Chechiak voiced his speeches in the "Elders of Zion" style. In the streets of Warsaw, near the university and other colleges, student thugs roamed with clubs in their hands and sword brooches on their lapels. They favored using razors and were called *"zyletkarze"* (*"Gilleters"*) accordingly.

When the Catholic students of my class attended religion classes, the Jewish and Protestant students attended lessons about the history of the Jewish people by Dr. Greenberg, who had also taught my father years before. He was very cautious not to touch topics of religious contention. Only years later did I learn that he was an atheist, yet kept this fact well hidden. The Catholic students returned from their lessons incited against descendants of those who killed "our Lord" Christ. They often needed hours, and even longer, to return and accustom themselves to the mixed class. And, still, no antisemitism was felt there. The street was different. The farther we got from school, the more we felt the aversion, sometimes hatred. It hurt us; it was hard to live in this atmosphere.

In the fourth form (sophomore year), we attended paramilitary classes. We dressed in military uniform and, in the evenings, sneaked into the streets to salute the officers. They were obliged to return a salute to us "soldiers." One evening, I was stopped by a captain. He pointed at my trousers, which were loosened around my ankle-cover, and said, "I could punish you for your sloppy appearance, but this time I won't do it. Step aside, arrange your trousers, and pay attention in future." It was all clear to us we were being childish, but still...

I was very successful in the shooting range. I was among the top three in my company. Our commander, who was also our gym teacher, an athlete who participated in the Olympics, announced that I would represent my school in the shooting competition in the fall of 1939. At home, they were quite surprised at the news. "Why you? Not your older brother?" He was the family's athletic talent; he was older and stronger than me. I was always a step behind. But just at that time, I got into the school's outstanding gymnastics team. The school competed for the Warsaw championship. I was very proud.

But neither gymnastics nor shooting really counted. Athletics was the top subject. Polish athletes were among Europe's best, and that influenced us young ones. The school had very fine sporting facilities, and competitions were held, but they preferred basketball and hockey in the winter. In order to practice athletics elsewhere, you had to belong to a club, but this was prohibited for students.

My brother and I were also fascinated by music. The radio played nonstop, even when we were doing our homework. Mom gave in to our pleas, and dad, who worked until the evening, didn't know about it. Warsaw's radio played many music programs, especially classical music, and dedicated a great deal of time to concerts, recitals, music competitions, and series about musicians and composers. As a matter of fact, music did hinder our concentration on homework, but we never fully admitted it. We learned many musical works by heart—entire parts of symphonies and concerts.

For years, I learned to play the violin, which turned into a great burden. I liked to play but was distracted by so many things. We longed to go to concerts and operas, but tickets were very expensive. You could pay 75 cents and hear the concert while standing at the back of the hall, but we often didn't even have that sum of money. But when my aunts came for a visit, we did go to the opera and theater. The first opera I saw was *La Traviata*. I was both fascinated and disappointed: that evening was supposed to be headed by an Italian prima donna, but she took ill and was replaced by Ada Sari, a Polish Jewish opera singer. She had an impressive voice but was far too obese to play *Violetta*.

We usually attended the theater with school. It was a celebration. These theaters were the best ones in those years, although they had a rather conservative style. Shakespeare was rarely played, but many French playwrights were often performed, such as Molière and Beaumarchais, as well as Polish national repertoire. Great masters of the Polish theater appeared, such as Solski, Zelevrovitch, and Ćwiklińska, alongside younger talents who were about to master our national stage.

In spring 1939, a new play was staged at the end of season: *The Rosemary Branch*, by a young writer. The play's protagonists were youths who, in the summer of 1914, were prepared to leave their peaceful life and taste the great turmoil of the upcoming war. This play caused unrest among many and urged a sense of the imminent unknown and the inevitable. Following a few months, when the war already broke out, I realized how lucky I was to have experienced these plays and concerts. At that time, I still believed everything would soon be back to normal, but I knew I would no longer be as young and optimistic as I once was.

I do not remember how I fell in love with Warsaw. It could not have been compared to any other city. When we took a class trip to Krakow, I realized even this historic city is unlike Warsaw. It turned out to be a province compared to Warsaw. At that time, much effort had been invested in improving the capital's appearance to that of a Western capital. It was clean, and many lawns were added as well as boulevards of trees and city squares. Special care was put into the appearance of the police force. They were recruited according to very strict standards, including a minimum height of 5'6", and high-school graduates. They could get dangerous, especially to unruly cab drivers. I was even almost fined for having dropped my ticket upon coming down from the streetcar.

It seems that in the years before the war, Warsaw housed events on a European scale. Poland strengthened its ties with the West. Visits of Western leaders became common and filled the local population's hearts with pride. Among those events were spontaneous visits by Jan Kiepura, world-famous tenor and champion of the Jewish people. He used to visit his homeland and perform to the common people. His radio performances were aired for free so that "less rich people can enjoy it too." In May 1939, crowds gathered in front of his Europejski Hotel suite balcony. He came out with his wife, also a famous singer, and for two hours, they sang for the frantic audience. Kiepura, in light of the German threat, expressed his patriotic feelings. The crowd cheered him for a long time. It was all broadcast on the radio. Mother said, "It seems like we are to part for a long time." How did she know?

I loved wandering around the city, discovering unknown streets, looking at pictures from films displayed outside the cinemas, astonished by the traffic, studying Warsaw. I visited the old city walls and the Barbican gates, which were restored at that time, Ujazdówski Park, newly replenished. We spent hours with girlfriends in the botanical garden. It's hard to put a finger on what I loved about Warsaw, but I saw my future in this city. I became a part of this city.

In summer 1939, for the first time, we did not go to school summer camp. My brother was about to attend a paramilitary course for a few weeks, and our parents thought my father would enjoy some fresh air. We rented a house in Jozefow new Otwock. Dad used to arrive almost every evening. There were many youngsters of all ages—company for everyone. We soon organized in groups, and couples were formed. We goofed around in the forests and dunes and bathed in the Swider River.

Meanwhile, each week brought new sensations from the political arena and suspicions as to the coming future. Our parents were uneasy. The young ones kept on hanging out, dancing, and having fun. But toward the end of August, as many families started getting back to Warsaw earlier than usual, we understood we were facing something, not within our reach. How dire it was, nobody yet knew.

On one of the last days of August, just before the school year that never opened, I met with the girl I befriended in Jozefow. We strolled along Marszałkowska Street in the summer twilight. The air was filled with tension and emergency. We were embarrassed, not because we were alone but because of the uncertainty around us. It was already clear that a war would break out, yet nobody knew what it would be like. It would probably be unlike the war described in Remarque's novel, *All Quiet on the Western Front*. I escorted the girl to her home on Zamenhof Street. We were about to meet again within a few days, but we did not meet until two years later. We spoke for about 15 minutes, each in a hurry to our own problems.

From right to left: my father, his mother, Aunt Stefa, his
brother Arthur, Aunt Stella and her Dutch husband,
Henryk van Oyen.

From right to left: my father's mother (Hanna), my
father, his father (Binem), his brother Arthur.

SEPTEMBER 1939

Already before September 1939, everyone knew war was inevitable. Did they know for sure or just talk about it?

Much has been said about Hitler's preparations for war. When the Sudetenland crisis took place in 1938, the Polish army took control of an area in Moravia, across the Olza River. On the one hand, the annexation was in line with the Polish patriotic ambitions and their territorial demands. On the other hand, Germany's greed for territorial expansion became a major concern. Polish students, such as we, went on school trips in the "freed territories." The youth got carried away with nationalistic slogans, influenced by media propaganda, but at the same time, no one really delved into the matter, neither at home nor in school. The media dealt extensively with the austerity measures taken by Nazi Germany: the restrictions the Nazis imposed on raw material and supplies, even on meals. The Reich military supposedly had to make do with lesser substitutes. All these stories did not contribute to a real understanding of what was in store.

On August 30, I returned home from town with my father. We noticed large posted announcements that were not seen two hours earlier. These were mobilization orders for reserve forces. Father was shocked. Apparently, at his age, he had to be recruited, but due to his medical situation, he was exempt. In this manner, I also learned that the Polish army lowered medical profiles of educated Jewish soldiers so that it wouldn't be compulsory to send them to an officers' course.

At home, my brother and I were told to prepare a small room as a gas shelter. Fear of poisonous gas was huge. Many remembered or heard of what happened in Ypres during WWI.[1] Within a few hours, we sealed the windows and prepared the door so that it could be sealed. Later, we had a hard time taking off the adhesive tape we put on the windows to prevent their shattering when bombs explode. Among all of us, my mother was the only one to rightly calculate what was looming, and for months she kept on accumulating food stocks for emergency times.

Early morning on September 1, we heard loud explosions. Only later did the radio officially announce the war had broken out. In the following days, the radio broadcast repeated warnings such as "look out! N6 or BD23 is coming."

We didn't know what these codes meant, but we quickly understood that the Germans are approaching, probably without any resistance. What happened to the Polish army we believed in so much? We were not only disappointed but also surprised and helpless.

We knew that the stories about the Germans building tanks made of carton boxes were propaganda fiction. Yet, we thought their tanks are made of substitutes since they don't have enough steel. Despite our patriotic fervor, no one thought the Polish cavaliers, with their spears, could stop the German tanks. Nevertheless, where were the new planes we heard so much about before the war? The German bombers attacked relentlessly. We knew nothing of the land battles that were taking place. We only heard about the battle on the banks of the Bzura River and of the bravery of the Westerplatte defenders in Danzig much later.[2]

The public awaited the Allies' response, but it was delayed. It wasn't until September 3 that the radio announced Britain and France would soon join the war. The anchor called the public to demonstrate in front of the Allies' embassies. I went with my father and brother to the plaza in front of the British Embassy with a large crowd. After an hour, the ambassador came out to the balcony, raising a glass of wine to salute the king and the Polish soldiers as well as the coming victory, as the crowd cheered. That very night, the ambassador left Poland together with all the embassy staff. So did the French that same day. The capital's residents still believed the Allies would keep their promises. Little did they know what dramatic changes were to take place in their lives. Meanwhile, stories kept coming in about how the Germans expanded their conquest, burning and exterminating anything in their way. Jews who managed to flee these areas told of brutal acts, especially by SS units.

Because of the bomber attacks, we mostly stayed at home. We kept in touch with family and friends only by phone. We couldn't learn anything from the radio. A few days later, newspaper publishing was interrupted except for sporadic spontaneous leaflets. Shops closed down as they were already mostly empty of merchandise.

Our relatives arrived from Kalisz. They managed to flee before the Germans invaded the city and were housed at our home and at my uncle's—my mother's brother. The radio kept on broadcasting warning codes such as MT8 or RS3, but we couldn't tell where the bombs would fall. Bombs were dropped mostly on the city's suburbs. On Thursday, there were rumors that the government was fleeing, and certain sources could tell just how many suitcases were taken by some minister's mistress. One of our neighbors, a civil servant, left at night on a truck from which crates full of documents were unpacked in order to make room for personal baggage.

On September 6, noontime, we heard Colonel Umiatowski's voice on the radio telling of fierce battles against the invaders, calling on all able men to leave the capital immediately southeastward in order to join the upcoming onslaught against the enemy. By evening, hordes of refugees filled the roads heading for Lublin / Lvov. Among them were my father, my brother, and me. Indeed, the colonel addressed only those who could bear arms, but news of German brutality caused many youngsters our age to leave as well. I was not happy about leaving Mother. This feeling would go on haunting me on critical occasions later in the war.

Our plan was mostly flawed. At home, we had two pairs of new bicycles, and instead of trying to get another pair for my dad, we decided to walk. We crossed the Wisla River and marched on the path we knew from the previous summer. Near Jozefow, the same thought crossed our mind—instead of slowly walking the road filled with refugees, we might rent the little house we had last summer, move there with Mom, and wait for the storm to calm down. But we didn't stop.

This march of thousands of refugees was a sign of the state's collapse. In these September days, we had to understand that our former lives were over. Only we had difficulty absorbing the change. We rejected it.

Different people, groups, or individuals prepared for it in different ways. Many had backpacks, but some carried suitcases or parcels or pushed baby carriages loaded with luggage. They moved on the roads and pavements, making military traffic difficult. That was the first night after Umiastowski's address. The next night brought even more refugees. Two days later, whispers were heard that the colonel was a German agent who intentionally caused this traffic jam in order to hinder the military movements. Many crazy stories spread about spies and terrorists walking among us. When I took out a flashlight to look at the map, a passer-by told me not to do so because someone might think I was signaling enemy planes. The night before, a man was almost lynched for using a flashlight. He could barely prove his innocence. Our father was in bad shape. He was only 39 years old, but his work did not let him care for himself physically. We were both active athletes, and we had to adjust our pace to that of our father's.

The roads were packed with people for whom the effort was above their capabilities. After two days, many barely kept on moving. We decided to rest for a while the next morning. It took us a long time to find a farmer who would allow us to sleep in his barn in exchange for a considerable payment.

For the first time, I witnessed the damage the war had caused. I already saw destroyed houses in Warsaw, but only in few places. In Garwolin, a town half-burned, only the houses' chimneys remained. They stood out from the rubble. The next day we passed through Żelechów. This town was completely burned down. Only a still forest of chimneys remained. Not even dog barks were heard. This scene was out of a nightmare. In those days, I learned that one could get used even to horror scenes when they appeared repeatedly.

The crowds on the roads were already exhausted. Some decided to wait in the villages to see how things develop. Some decided to go back, and some kept on walking persistently. We were in the second category.

We entered the city of Lublin with a person we didn't know. He claimed he knew Dad from university. Dad did not prove him wrong. Later we learned he worked there in the canteen. His mother lived in Lublin and he brought us to their house in the city suburb. In the yard stood an altar with a statue of the holy virgin around which some worshipers gathered. The landlady welcomed us as if she was waiting for us. "Glad you gentlemen are here," she said. "We will shortly begin the prayer." I remember being very thirsty, but she was busy and her son disappeared somewhere. As soon as the prayer began, whistles of falling bombs were heard, but the group of worshipers kept on praying and singing.

Our host returned and explained he was looking for a place for us to sleep. For that purpose, we had to cross the city to the other side. I was very thirsty. I approached the water pump in the yard, pumped some water, and drank it from my palms. The attack continued. After each series of bombings, there was a break, after which the planes returned and attacked again. We decided to leave immediately and not accept our host's invitation to stay the night. We were prepared to catch a nap under any tree on the road.

That night, we managed to get on a wagon that was part of a military sanitary unit convoy. The soldiers were looking for the division they belonged to, which was supposed to be around the Lublin area. After having received an advance payment from my father, the company sergeant allowed us to mount the wagon, but so that the captain will not see us. There was another officer there, a doctor, whom we later found out to be a Jew. He did not have enough time to change to military uniform and hung around in ballroom clothes. When the captain finally saw us, he was determined that we should disembark upon the first stop.

The convoy traveled fast. It was, in fact, the first military unit we've seen since the start of the war. The military coaches were equipped with various luggage, harnessed to horses confiscated from villages in northern Poland. The coach driver, the villager whose horses were confiscated, sat next to a soldier who was supposed to be the coachman had the horses been military ones. The villager said they were looking for their unit since the second day of the war. All we had on our minds was how far we could advance with them; perhaps the captain will forget about us?

We did not leave them on the first stop. When the captain discovered we were still on the coach, he was furious. He took out his pistol and threatened to shoot us as if we were spies. The havoc around us was such that he could have done it and gotten away with it. We left.

We were 80 kilometers south of Lublin and more than 250 kilometers from Warsaw.

Again we continued on foot. We were very tired. Our feet were full of wounds and blisters. We treated the pain with ointments Mother gave us before we left. We needed some rest. Father promised we would stop for 24 hours once we found a suitable location. Strangely, our walking became more paced with time, almost automatic.

In the train station canteen in the town of Zamość, Father met a high officer—a colonel or a lieutenant colonel who greeted him warmly. It turned out that he was Father's commander in the 1920 war.[3] He thought we chose the "right destination," although it could also happen to be "too close." He advised us to inquire about the train schedule to Lvov, which was supposed to leave within the next hour. It wasn't at all easy. Trains did not operate here; stations and railways had already been bombarded, wagons damaged. Father found some old wagons stationed within a distance from the station, waiting for an engine to carry them to Lvov and perhaps even farther. We boarded a wagon with doors on both sides, and the engine indeed arrived. Another person boarded it with us, looked at the doors, and said, "There's something good about it; in case of trouble, it's easy to escape through these doors." The conductor scribbled down our tickets since the ticket office didn't work anymore. Our companion asked Dad, "Why say Lvov? You should have told him 'only to Rawa Ruska.' He takes all the money into his pocket."

I was astonished: the state was crumbling down just before my eyes. Along hundreds of kilometers, we saw soldiers exhausted from seeking after their units, not knowing whether they still existed; some tried to pose as civilians. They feared for their families and did not know whether they were still alive. The news about the cruelty of the invaders was beyond imagination. I came across a soldier, fresh out of an officers' course, who wanted to swap berets with me: my green boat cap for his civilian cap. He had a uniform and arms but lacked a cap. I refused, to his disappointment.

Someone warned us not to open luggage in front of strangers: people had "big eyes." Who would stop them from taking something? The police practically didn't exist anymore. Many policemen marched eastwards, like us. How could we count on their help?

Our train moved along very slowly. At times it seemed like our driver hesitated or was afraid. Our companion thought he did not trust the condition of the railway. After about an hour's ride, we encountered an attack by German fighter planes. The train stopped immediately. People began jumping off and taking shelter in the field. So did our companion. My brother and I wanted to do the same, but Father stopped us. He claimed the situation outside was worse and that the wagon walls protected us from the shrapnel. The pilots also shot with machine guns. I understood that, but it was hard to hold on, kneeling down on the wagon floor with my head between my father's knees. Father sat in the corner, his face pale as lime. We counted the explosions and heard machine-gun shots. The attack lasted a long time, about half an hour, maybe more. We sat as prisoners in a cage. We knew it was a crime to shoot civilian trains. We were very scared, but when it was over, we all agreed the worst thing about it was being helpless. After the planes were gone, we found out we could not continue our journey. One bomb hit the train, and another hit the railway. Some passengers were injured, carried by an ambulance that appeared out of nowhere. Our companion said, "It will take them two hours to get to Lvov." The decision to remain in the wagon was right, but it was the first time we were a target of a bombardment.

The train returned to the origin station, Włodzimierz Wolynski, on the eastern bank of the Bog River. We decided that our way from there would not be longer. In addition, people said the Germans did not attack the other side of the Bog River. Only much later did we learn that the river was set as the border between the Reich and the Soviets (today, too, the river is the border between Poland and Ukraine). We did not enter the city; we bypassed it. There were too many junctions there between railways and roads that could have served as targets for air raids should the Germans decide to attack on the other side of the river. Upon leaving the train, we met a Jewish acquaintance of Father's from Krakow, who marched with us. He left a wife and a child in his town and missed them very much. He escaped hastily since the Germans were near the town.

We entered a large village that was home to the regional council. In front of the building stood several coachmen with their coaches, each harnessed with a couple of horses. Our new companion approached one of them and asked for a ride. The villager replied, "If we are to go, let's go right away." He lifted the covers from the makeshift seats and helped us load our bags. We understood he took us for the guests he was expecting. We did not say a word. Only after 15 minutes, we asked where we were headed. He replied, "If we are going to Horochów, then we should go through Lokacze and Swiniuchy."[4] For some reason, these names were engraved in my memory. I took a look at the map. Horochów was at an excellent location: a bit eastward but a short distance from Lvov.

Even two strong horses needed a whole day to travel 60 kilometers. Upon nearing Horochów, the coachman asked who do we intend to visit in town. We answered that we'd take care of that tomorrow, but first, we needed to find a place to sleep. The coachman preferred to return to his village. We tipped him well and parted. In the city square, there were several people who took an interest in us. The best place to stay, they said, was at Moshko's, the Jewish estate manager of Graf[5] Ledóchowski's family.[6] They would welcome us as well as any news from central Poland.

Moshko's house was spacious and housed several generations of the family. The tribe elder tried to find out who we were and where we were headed. The fact that my brother and I did not know any Yiddish was very surprising to them, and the conversation was conducted in Polish out of consideration for us. We were invited for a real dinner on a large table covered with a white tablecloth. We were able to take a bath, a pleasure we had long wished for. Being so tired, I almost fell asleep at the dining table, something that moved the grandmother, the host's wife. For the first time since we had left Warsaw, we slept in beds.

The next day, we started inquiring how to get to Lvov. Our hosts did not hide their skepticism. Moshko's elder son asked us who we are going to visit. When he heard we had no relatives there, he simply said, "Lvov is not Horochów, no one serves a cup of tea to a stranger there. You are going with two kids since both your sons are still kids. Think again if you have to go to Lvov." I felt he knew something he did not reveal. His words made a great impression on Father. But the man from Krakow would not compromise. He wanted to get to Lvov and urged us not to waste any time.

On that day, a lady arrived, the youngest of the Ledóchowskis, who had just turned 40. She rode a luxurious horse carriage on her own. As she arrived near the house, I was wandering in the yard, and she asked me to inform Moshko she was here. Moshko stepped out of the house, holding his hat in his hand, asking me to approach the carriage. He explained to the lady who his guests were, and the lady looked at me curiously. When she heard where we were headed, she said, "Yes, *'those from Warsaw to Lvov, and those from Volhyn to the Kingdom'* (a historical nickname for Poland's original territories, excluding Ukraine, Belarus, and Lithuania)." Then she turned to her manager, and said: "Well, then, Moshko says not to expect anything. Not today nor tomorrow?"

The old man replied, "Well, we hadn't gathered the harvest yet from the field. Who will pay us cash for that?"

The lady responded coldly, "Moshko knows where to find me until tomorrow."

The old man nodded and kissed the back of her hand, holding his hat, and said, "My lady, you know I will do anything to find something. The problem is time. We don't have enough time." And she left.

We took a walk with Moshko's son. Father asked him what people were whisperingly talking about among themselves, and he replied that they were expecting the Red Army to enter the town any day. The Soviets agreed upon it with the Germans already in August. That is why Lady Ledóchowski left so hastily. I was shocked once again. It was so obvious, yet none of us thought about it. Poland's entirety was such a stable idea in our heads that the possibility of it being divided again didn't cross our minds.

That night, our host woke us up. Soviet radio announced that it was time for historic justice. Tomorrow, Ukraine territories would return to Soviet Ukraine, and Belarus territories to Belarus. That was the night between September 16 and 17, 1939.

I demanded we reviewed our plans again. I didn't want a border separating us from Mother. When we departed, we still believed our separation would be brief; otherwise, we would not have left Mother alone. Now it looked like our farewell would be long—perhaps for years. This could not be decided without Mother. We had to go back and only then make plans for the war. I was quite eloquent, yet, I never made such a long and logical speech. The man from Krakow snapped at me. We were road companions, and he didn't want to stay alone. He asked what made me so sure of myself to speak of the family's destiny. I demanded that only the three of us should discuss it (my father, my brother, and me). This offended him, and he left the room. In the triple discussion, it was decided to go back to Warsaw immediately. We wanted to cross the Bog River as soon as possible so as not to bump into the Russians.

I don't have many recollections from the way back. Somehow, most details were forgotten. We were desperate for news, to know what was happening in Warsaw, but no one knew anything except for the fact that the defensive continued. We heard much talk about the German cruelty in the occupied territories.

In the villages we passed through, people were busy preparing victory gates and garlands, hanging signs in honor of the Red "liberating" Army. Only Father could read what they said. An activist with a red ribbon on his arm asked Father in Yiddish why we insisted on returning to Hitler, but he let us go when we answered we were returning to Mother.

After crossing the Bog River, we accompanied a man who worked for the district administration in western Poland before the war. He was with a 17-year-old guy. Both of them wanted to return after having fled east at the beginning of the month. We marched to Warsaw together. We were more emotionally exhausted than physically. In the town of Bychawa, we were offered a rental truck that would take us to Warsaw. The local teacher offered to sell us the gasoline at an exorbitant price—namely profiteering. Dad was hesitant. We were the only ones with some money since our companions were penniless. The teacher returned the next morning, claiming the price had increased during the night. When we asked him why, he turned to our new friend and said, "I'm not going to discuss this with a kike. For you, I'm prepared to lower the price, but I'm not going to speak to 'Beilis' here."[7] Our companion was embarrassed. The deal was off. The adults said all this was dubious. What would happen if it turned out it wasn't even gasoline?

We marched on and managed to advance, aided by some random passing wagons. On board one of them, we crossed the Wieprz River. The villagers said that on the other side of the river awaits a German soldier checking the travelers' identities. That was our first encounter with the German army. We had no choice. Father descended from the wagon, approached the soldier and, in fluent German, explained we were returning to Warsaw. I didn't hear the guard's answer, but he was courteous and wished us an easy journey. He didn't know whether we could enter Warsaw. He thought it was a matter of a day or two.

I looked at him, at his uniform and gear. None of it was made of paper. He was well equipped. The propaganda we were overfed with consisted of primitive lies. How could we "swallow" these stories? I stared at the uniform color; I've never seen such a color before. I later learned it was called "field-gray" (Feldgrau).

After having crossed the river, we advanced on the same road, marching east. We arrived again at Józefów. Here, we heard for the first time about the damage caused to our city—the dead and the injured. During the night before entering Warsaw, between October 1 and 2, I didn't sleep a wink; only a couple of days before, we heard about the fall of Warsaw. When we got on the Poniatowski Bridge, we couldn't restrain ourselves, and we began to run. We told our friends how to get home. Only a few days earlier, we couldn't walk with our hurting feet; now, we could run.

The remains of the destruction and fire were everywhere in the city streets, especially in the city center. The roads were cracked with holes, rubble spread everywhere, and crooked pipes stuck out at every corner. Our run home did not impress anyone; they were already accustomed to such scenes.

Our house remained intact! Mother stood near the gate among a group of neighbors, holding the dog's collar. She had a feeling we were nearby. Upon entering the house, she asked that we first take a shower; maybe eat something first?

Our traveling companions found the address and arrived as well. They envied us being at home. We found everyone to be well. Mom prepared a meal. I ate rice; that's all I can remember. Then we talked, and talked, and talked. There was no end to the stories. Mom was skinnier as well as pale, but happy that we were home with her. We all slept on the floor since there were not enough beds for everyone. We also had our family from Kalisz staying with us. Our friends left the next day. They intended to get to Kutno and proceed from there by train.[8]

At home, the stories continued. Mom wanted to know where we got to and why we came back. After hearing our stories, she began to tell hers. She told us what she went through during the air raids while the city was going up in flames, with no food or water.

In the next few days, I fell ill with a high fever. The doctor concluded it was fatigue.

Upon leaving the house for the first time, I went to school. I was shattered to see what had become of it: the familiar buildings burned and destroyed. Our high school, which only a month earlier was an elegant complex of buildings, the city's pride, was now completely in ruins. Where were the teaching halls? The well-equipped chemistry, biology, and physics laboratories, each with its own auditorium? Where were the elegant sports halls? I met G', the son of the main genitor. In June, before the war, he completed the matriculation exams in our school. Their apartment was in ruins, so they all had to squeeze into a tiny room, which luckily survived the hits. The only building that was only slightly hit was the primary school, and the army immediately confiscated it. In 1941, the German industrialist Többens[9] organized his notorious sweathouses, later known as "shops"(*szopas*), in this building.[10]

I stopped going out of the apartment. My world fell apart. I escaped into my books, but how long can you hide away from reality? I was 16. I had to participate in the struggle to find food since the food stocks Mother prepared were running out. Father managed several rental properties, a job he took over from his father. But now, he discovered to his dismay that none of the properties survived the fires.

In order to manage a rental property, you had to deposit a large sum of money with the property owner. My grandfather invested all his life savings in those properties, and now everything went down the drain. It was the livelihood of three families—our own, our grandmother's, and our father's sister's. The war inflicted many limitations and hardships. Our family lost everything right from the start.

One day, my mother took out some clothes, linen, and tablecloths from the closet. People said that in the nearby villages, you could exchange these items for food. So, my brother and I packed it all in two backpacks and rode our bicycles to the nearby village of Trojany, about 50 kilometers north of Warsaw. We had the name of one of the villagers. I was very weak after falling ill and asked to stop several times. My brother refused. He rightfully said that we had to get there in daylight, otherwise no one would want to see us. I gritted my teeth and we went on. We didn't find the owner since everyone was out in the field collecting potatoes. A woman at the house explained to us that since it was hard to find workers these days, everyone helped each other. "You will have to wait until they return," she said.

I was hungry and asked for a slice of bread. She looked at me in astonishment. "They will be back shortly and prepare supper. You will eat too." She was an employee and did not have the authority to slice the bread. The farmers returned at 8 p.m. They seemed content with their work and conversed cheerfully. After a brief talk, they decided, "We must eat, and then we'll take a look at what you have there." They sat down and started peeling and grating potatoes into "pyzy"—potato dumplings, cooked or fried in lard. There were about 20 of them. For me, it lasted forever. At 11 p.m., they finally laid a huge bowl on the dining table, filled with dumplings and fried lard. We were served a separate bowl. I tried to eat slowly so that they would not notice how hungry I was, but to no avail. After the meal, the trade began. They checked every item, felt and criticized everything. We did not respond; we didn't want to haggle. We only wanted to get pork loin, some potatoes, lard, eggs, butter, and whatever other food we can get. And we did.

We returned home as heroes. The ride was difficult due to all the food baggage we carried. At the last minute, my brother put a cabbage head on the bicycle handlebar, which caused people to stop us several times in

Warsaw. Fresh vegetables were quite a rare sight by then in the city. We arrived back with all the cargo, which made mom very happy and proud. I was so proud of myself for not having given up the ride in the middle. I gradually began to regain self-confidence.

We hardly noticed the Germans. They did not enter our street, and we seldom went out. One day in October, a German soldier stopped his motorbike in front of our house. I came out staring at it as if it fell from another planet. The biker, like his bike, was huge. The bike had tires as wide as that on a car, a huge gasoline tank, and additional tanks on both sides. Behind the seat was a big case. As the soldier opened it to take out some documents, I noticed it was divided into a few compartments designated for paper, gear, and food. Everything was neatly arranged. Already in the previous weeks, I took notice of the invading army, either in groups or singles, either riding or walking by foot. But this one was different. The bike was massive and heavy. Again I recalled the stories about carton-board tanks. The soldier turned to us and asked about the street name. Apparently, he took a wrong turn. People curiously stared at him with fear. I could not take my eyes off him. He was wearing a rubber cape with a hood. On his head was a helmet—a large round pot, cut at just above ear-level, different than the Polish or the French helmets the Polish army used. On the helmet was a pair of huge square glasses to protect against dust, rain, and wind. He wore very high leather boots. When he strode the pavement, we heard the clipping of his steel shanks. The bike and everything he wore, except for the boots, were in a uniform gray-green color. He beamed with power and competence, indulging in the glaring looks around him. I was both envious and astounded; I also felted anguish. What chances did the Polish cavaliers, with no firearms, have against this mass of steel?

Either knowingly or not, we were entering an era of occupation. No one yet knew what we were facing. Maybe for the better. Had we known what we were about to go through, I doubt if we would have had the necessary strength and commitment to survive the horror.

OCTOBER AND AFTERWARD

During the month of October, our house underwent many changes. Father looked for work. He tried to become a merchant, a common occupation in those days. Everybody traded everything. Goods swapped hands often. The joke went: "Candles with no fuse? No problem. These candles are not for lighting but only for trade." Funny? Only for a short time. The fewer scruples, the easier it was to climb upward, to become rich by speculation. The people's way downward was slow at first and then intensified quickly. The situation wasn't tragic until hunger came onto our doorstep. Father could not cope with the new situation; he couldn't become a speculator.[1] One day, he was caught in the street and forced to work all day in a military storage house. The work was accompanied by beatings, mocking, and humiliation. He returned home beaten and underwent a change. He didn't leave the house for a few days and then announced he would not stay here; he simply could not. He had to leave. This time, the flight to Lvov became real. My brother went along with him.

This farewell was supposed to be short. Father promised to arrange everything: to find an apartment and arrange the official documents to transfer my mother and me. In those days, the arrangement of a reunion of families separated due to the changing of the borders between Germany and the Soviet Union was still in place. The German travel agency Norddeutscher Lloyd on Krakowskie Przedmieście Street handled the transfers. We didn't verify whether this plan was truly feasible. Thousands of Jews fled eastward, mostly men. My brother and father had to steal across the border. The path went through a little village on the bank of the Bog River. They had to cross the icy river, something that was beyond Mother's strength. I stayed with her.

The family from Kalisz arrived once more. This time they were evicted by the Germans. They came to us almost penniless, having time to pack only a few suitcases, and settled with us again.

I was looking for work. At first, I gave private lessons. Schools did not operate anymore, and many parents feared their children would miss the current school year. In the spring of 1940, with the German attacks in Europe and Africa, it was evident that plans could only be made for the near future.

I became a teacher specializing in the final classes of primary school. My advantage was French, which very much determined my salary– 30 złoty a month for three hours of teaching three times a week. I had four students and sometimes even five. My work was stopped by the Judenrat, which was tasked with providing forced labor force for the German army. All men from the age of 16 were obliged to go, at first once in two weeks and later every week. Not everyone had to go; some were never summoned or only rarely. In order to get exempted from this work, one had to know someone at the Judenrat offices. Mom and I didn't know anyone. Our appeals were dismissed, and I had difficulty continuing teaching. In addition, many parents didn't have enough money to pay for private lessons.

I found a new occupation—substituting for Jews who preferred not to go to work for the Germans. They paid 6 złoty for a day's work—

worth a loaf of bread. The work was hard, sometimes a slave's work, depending on who was supervising the Jews that day. At first, I worked in the SS cavaliers' stables at the former Polish cavaliers' barracks in the southern part of the city. People were beaten there. I was also beaten once. Mom bandaged my wounds and wept.

At the end of December, Father returned and tried to convince Mom to leave for Lvov. He told her about the hardships on the way, stealing across the border on the frozen river. Mom was not healthy and feared she would not make it. She was afraid of the strange city, parting from her sisters, and wartime conditions. Many women remained behind as their husbands fled eastward. All believed they were parting only for a short time. Father then returned to Lvov, and Mom stayed with me in Warsaw.

Forced labor was discontinued with the establishment of the ghetto. The Germans preferred a permanent workforce instead of a daily-changing one. And, indeed, many were prepared to leave the ghetto daily for a bowl of soup and bread and to bring into the ghetto food bought outside.

I worked in various jobs, but we were sustained mostly due to selling items from our house. We didn't have much choice; it was the way to survive for a growing number of people. Nevertheless, I concluded I had to continue studying. Mom agreed. The war would end one day, and we would have to resume a normal life. I wanted very much to obtain my high school diploma in order to be prepared for the postwar era. When would this day come? When would the war end? The end was constantly postponed.

I initiated a group of five school friends and spoke to some of our school teachers. They, too, were interested in this project. They were jobless; yet, our modest payments were not their primary motive. Our "project" operated almost until spring 1942, also inside the sealed ghetto.[2]

By the summer of 1940, no one expected the war would end shortly. The Germans controlled all of Europe while constantly advancing in Africa. People would gather around the speakers placed at street junctions, nicknamed "barkers." Every few hours, announcements were aired by the German military: *"Achtung, Achtung! Das Oberkommando der Wehrmacht gibt bekannt!"*—"Attention, attention! The German Supreme Headquarters is announcing!" followed by a list of the day's successful conquests—a long list of new victories, a long and utterly depressing list.

The inhabitants were ordered to hand over all radio receivers to the authorities. There were still more painful orders. We were ordered to wear a yellow ribbon with a Star of David on our forearms. Many sewed the stripes from an expensive cloth, expressing their pride. The young ones wore them close to their palms so they could remove them quickly without being noticed. We didn't hand over our radio, bought in May, just before the war. We've long dreamed of such a radio. When the order came to hand it to the Germans, I took it down to the basement and broke it into pieces with an ax while sobbing.

We continued to live in Złota Street. Most of my friends lived in the vicinity, and we would meet often. We had a vibrant social life. This was a time when a young man begins his life outside school. We had surplus time, and we tried to use it enjoyably. We gathered to listen to music; someone brought a pack of records with Broadway music, which we did not yet know. We listened to it breathlessly, even those of us who didn't take any special interest in music. We felt almost like an anti-Nazi resistance. We heard Louis Armstrong, Ella Fitzgerald, and Benny Goodman for the first time. It was beautiful and different, strange to an unaccustomed ear, but left us longing for more. I imagined there was also another American music. Months later, Roman Kowalski played Gershwin's *Rhapsody in Blue*. It was beautiful and original, as if a new world had just opened before me.

We tried to discuss new problems, subjects that were not necessarily related to the situation. But, more than anything, it was important to keep in touch, to feel we were still part of the same bunch. There were also meetings with girls. The war hastened our coming of age. The young folks looked for entertainment, even dancing. A group of amateurs from Łódź was called *LZA*—an acronym of a presumptuous name, *Łódzki Zespół Zrtystyczny*. They were most talented, like their pianist, Roman Kowalski. The audience liked them. Mary Wittenberg sang American songs. She wasn't pretty, but always surrounded by handsome guys. She noted that in her diary, published after the war under her new name, Berg.[3]

During our first months of life in the ghetto, which was still open, we enjoyed some modest dancing parties and a few monologues from the Warsaw cabarets' repertoire before the war to resist depression. After a while, even that didn't work.

About mid-1940, a symphonic concert was announced in the former dance hall (*Palais de Dance*). The hall was adjusted for the new form of entertainment of about 60 players. My violin teacher, Zeidman, played in the fifth row. The concert was sold out. Ticket prices were ridiculously low, but still, many could not afford it. Mother agreed we had to go, although it was a significant expense.

The German orders forbade playing music composed by Jews. Despite that, the concert did include a violin concerto composed by Baruch (who I later learned was not Jewish) as well as work by Mendelssohn. In the ghetto, I heard several other concerts. For many, music concerts were the embodiment of a different world: clean, full of harmony, warless, no humiliation or fear of hunger. In practice, every concert was worth waiving a daily food ration. One of the concerts was played by my school friend, Henryk Reinberg. I think he played a violin concerto by Beethoven, although it was forbidden.[4] During the concert, a group of Germans entered the hall, one of whom was wearing an SS uniform. The conductor paused the playing, but one of the Germans signaled him to continue the concert. The entourage sat and listened closely until the end of the concert. Then they got up and quietly left the hall without a word.

The audience was fearful. What would the Germans do now that they've witnessed Jews playing a German composition? Nothing happened. The only thing that did happen was an ice-pick headache I got once the Germans entered. Since then, I keep getting this migraine attack each time I listen to the second half of the Beethoven concerto.

Warsaw was still an undivided city. The Jews could still move in all the city's parts, though they had to be on their guard. Some Jews continued to work at the same jobs they had before the war; some of them even had businesses. Businesses owned by Jews were appointed a new manager authorized as "trustee" (Treuhänder). Walking the streets became dangerous with time, and, in certain parts, thugs roamed the streets looking to attack Jews. It was easy to identify Jews because of the yellow ribbon they wore. Beating Jews, women included, and snatching purses became a regular phenomenon. The attacks became a regular scene, watched by passers-by as some sort of entertainment. Cops watched it from a distance without intervening. One woman, over 40 years old, especially stood out. Nicknamed by everyone as "the crazy woman," although many said she was totally normal, she excelled in attacking elderly men who could not defend themselves or run away. She became the nightmare of Marshalkowska and nearby streets. Later, she moved her attacks to Grzybowska Street, near the offices of the Jewish community. Adam Czerniakow, head of the Judenrat, mentioned her in his diaries. No one dared resist her. Anyone who responded was immediately attacked by a gang of men who "had to defend a 'helpless' woman." Then immediately, a cop appeared, arresting the "aggressor" (the Jew).

The Germans began paying visits to houses of rich Jews, taking an interest in their contents. Having arrived in Warsaw, the "master people" needed furniture for their new homes. They would pick a house in advance and turn up there accompanied by a soldier or two and a truck. They usually picked up a bunch of Jews in the street and entered the apartment. There, they pointed at the items they desired, and the Jewish workers would load everything onto the truck. Alas, the Jews owned beautiful furniture. I heard the story about a son of the master race who appeared in the apartment of a Jewish industrialist. He wore a black coat with a Nazi lapel pin. After having placed a soldier at the entrance door, he surveyed the apartment's contents and said, "In five minutes, everybody out! Everything stays here!" These were not isolated cases. They also underscored the ever-widening disparity between the Polish population and the Jews. Both populations were abused by the conquerors, but the abuse and injustice inflicted upon the Jews were far worse. And that was only the beginning; no one could have imagined what was still in store. People lamented the loss of property and furniture; once again, jokes circulated about touring Germany after the war under the slogan "locate your furniture."

All the authorities' operations had the intent of keeping the Jews under pressure. We began to fear the upcoming Jewish holidays since the conquerors systematically burdened them with ever-toughening decrees, laws, and abuse, carefully applying them to each holiday.

In the first months, special levies were introduced, one in gold and another in local currency. The Judenrat informed each resident the sum to be paid. Mother was not required to pay anything, unlike my uncles from Kalisz. My aunt and uncle said they left Kalisz almost naked, and therefore would not pay a penny. Should the community go on demanding they pay, they would leave the house and move to a refugee center. They exaggerated, of course, and the matter was settled for the time being.

Every few weeks, a new rumor suggested the ghetto was about to be closed. Optimists claimed it was impossible, unsound, and unfeasible. Where would they house the thousands who had already lost their properties, damaged by the bombings? And what about those constantly arriving from the nearby villages and towns, moving in with their relatives into already overcrowded domiciles? My father's sister from Sierpc arrived together with her husband and three children and moved in with my grandmother. Rumors about the closing of the ghetto kept repeating, each time supplemented with even more distressing details.

In the fall of 1940, it was evident to all that the ghetto would be sealed. The only remaining question was what its borders would be. A discussion began whether our street would remain outside the ghetto or be included in its boundaries. It was claimed it was dependent on the number of Jewish residents: streets with a Jewish majority will be included in the ghetto. In November, we already knew that our street would not be incorporated into the ghetto. We had to leave. Mom was devastated. She could only live in her apartment. She thought of leaving it as of being thrown to the street. But we were lucky after all. We found a Polish family on Sienna Street, just next to us. They, too, were ordered to leave their apartment and move to the Aryan side. They found our apartment to their liking, and we liked theirs. Both apartments were in proximity, which made things easier. Both ladies promised each other that as soon as "all this is over," each family would move back to its place. We moved in mid-November. The same wagon was used to move both families' properties. At the last minute, we left a wardrobe we could not disassemble. Mother was promised the wardrobe would be returned to her safe and complete.

We informed Father of our change of address. He wrote to us and sent parcels on a regular basis. To our surprise, the parcels always arrived, although many complained about mail theft. He even sent us money once. He paid someone in Lvov, and that person's brother was asked to send the money to Mother.

The travel agency NordDeutscher Lloyd was supposed to arrange our move to Lvov, since Dad pressured its officials and paid for each step of the procedure. They sent us questionnaires a few times, and Mom went to Krakowska Pzedmiasta Street to sign the papers. It was quite an operation. Walking around a German area with a Star of

David ribbon on her arm was facilitated by a letter from the German company, which was used as a permit. The letter exchange with the company continued until June 1941.

As time went by, the differences between my school friends and me were exacerbated. I was the only one in my group that got to the "complet" lessons after a whole day's work on a rickshaw.[5] That rickshaw was not even mine. I did not have the means to buy one. The neighbor who bought it did not intend to sweat carrying others, so I got half the revenue. At first, I sustained only half a day, even less. Yet, my appetite was immense. I could swallow a whole loaf of bread at once.

The streets of the "Jewish quarter," as the ghetto was officially called, were filled continuously, and it was increasingly overcrowded. Jewish refugees fled to the big city from the neighboring towns and villages, and even from the *Generalgouvernement*—"General Government" or General Governorate areas[6], just as they did during the Khmelnytsky pogroms, according to experts in Jewish history.[7] The refugees did not yet live on the streets, but the conditions of those who didn't have relatives with whom to stay were horrific. I once had the chance to witness one of the *"punkts,"* where the Jewish Judenrat prepared shelters for the newcomers. Even today, I cannot forget the horror I felt there. At that time, living conditions were still bearable. The community distributed help to the poor, soup for the hungry, and collected special levies from the rich to help the poor. But not all could be helped. There was a great deal of hunger and disease.

There was a typhoid outbreak in spring 1940. The Germans were terrified of this epidemic. They strictly shut down every infected location and kept away. Once a typhoid patient was encountered, they imposed hermetic closure over the house, and if additional patients were encountered, they extended the closure to a whole apartment block. Each location was considered plague-stricken, and a yellow plaque was hung in the entrance announcing, "Beware! Typhoid disease; Entry forbidden!" Breaches were harshly punished.

It was also forbidden to receive or deliver anything to the infected location. Such a house remained locked down a week after the disease had already disappeared. The stench of the disinfectants signaled the location from afar. The authorities did not care about the state of the ill or healthy in the shut-down house. Relatives or friends of the residents passed on food parcels while risking their lives. I witnessed how, near Grzybowski Square, a man shoved a package through a narrow opening in a gate on which the yellow sign was hung. At that same moment, a group of air force soldiers passed by. These young men filled Warsaw then. Apparently, they were sent to Warsaw at the beginning of their service so they could savor the taste of victory over the occupied land. They approached cheerful, loud, and confident in their dominating power. They saw the criminal pushing the package, and one of them jumped at him, trying to catch him. While running, he pulled out his dagger—they carried no other weapon since, in reality, no one could really threaten them. The "smuggler" managed to escape, but the package fell to the pavement: a few potatoes, slices of bread and cheese, and a little doll. The soldiers kicked it all up in the air and walked away, frustrated at not having caught the villain. Until that moment, I had yet to come across such abysmal hatred. It flashed into my mind what an incurable, contagious disease a whole generation of Nazis is plagued with. After the war, this whole generation would have to be annihilated.

In our everyday lives, we only concentrated on one thing—the daily struggle to survive and obtain means of sustenance. We did everything within our power to fight hunger. Mother repeatedly sold household items. We never owned any real jewelry, so all we could sell were clothes, linen, and tableware. In order to sell such things, one needed a buyer on the "other" side, the Aryan side. Many like us sold household items so long as entry into the ghetto was possible. An acquaintance would show up and take packages of clothes and linen. In return, he would bring food or pay with cash. But such deals rarely came along. Most of our friends had difficulty getting into the ghetto.

I came up with an idea to go out and sell things outside the ghetto or substitute them for food. Indeed, I did it several times, though it wasn't at all easy to leave the ghetto, yet it was easier than trading inside it. I definitely had trade talents, especially with the villagers. I was evidently not a professional tradesman, and some exploited this mercilessly while others rejected my offers. Twice I went to the village of Krasnystaw with one of my father's suits, tablecloths, pillowcases, and the like. They wanted to pay me with tobacco leaves, but I didn't know what to do with such a payment. I preferred food items such as butter, cheese, meat, and lard. But it turned out it was better to take the tobacco. Indeed, had I returned to the ghetto with such cargo, it would have been dangerous due to the serious penalties imposed on tobacco smugglers, including being locked up in a labor camp. But I would have doubled the profit selling it. Mom was delighted with my harvest. She thought it was a great success. I think that for the first time in a long time, she wasn't hungry. She long claimed she lost her appetite, and it never crossed my mind to find out the truth. I had an insatiable appetite.

I did not tell anyone at home that upon arrival at the Warsaw train station a group of boys picked on me and threatened to call the cops. I took a watch off my wrist and gave it to them, and they went away. The watch was not worth much, but I could not calm down for quite a while. For the first time, I felt what it was like to be blackmailed. And there was another aspect. In the first months of the war, we discussed among our friends which one of us, according to his facial features, could move around among Aryans without causing suspicion. Only a few of us were designated as "safe." Most of us clearly had a "Jewish" appearance. I was designated "in between." I convinced myself and others, most of all my mom, that my proficiency with the Polish language and the local customs would grant me full immunity. I had also started planning an escape from the ghetto, an idea I had been thinking of for some time. When the young blackmailers harassed me in the train station, doubts crept into my heart regarding my chances of success. I felt that if I surrendered,

I would never be able to think again about any attempt to escape and save Mom or myself. Meanwhile, with every day that passed, it became clearer that the ghetto was not established so that the Jews could go on living.

I told Mother that I got the butter in return for my watch. She thought I acted correctly. It would be difficult to get a new watch, but we'd manage. She was encouraged. The food items I procured could not have been obtained inside the ghetto.

I once went to Ostrowiec. The trip was long, and the load I carried was big and drew attention. I felt uncomfortable being examined by other passengers. I still managed to arrive in the village undisturbed. Yet, the operation was unsuccessful. The villagers were accustomed to other traders. The Jews in Ostrowiec were familiar with the villagers' needs and provided them all. After ten days, I came back frustrated. Mom looked at the situation differently. She asked if I got enough to eat and whether I got a bit of fresh air. Isn't that important?

Our street was different than most streets in the ghetto. Prior to its inclusion in the ghetto, both Poles and Jews lived there side by side. Most houses were beautiful and predominantly modern, providing a sense of living "on the outside." The place soon turned into a boulevard where one could stroll and meet friends. It slightly relieved the feeling of being enclosed. Some entrepreneurs opened an elegant café named *Stuka*, which means "art." Ladies who had no financial cares would sit there, and Mother ridiculed them, saying they were deceiving themselves as if nothing was happening around them.

On the floor just above the café, the Judenrat had opened professional courses. It had to be approved by the Germans, and the program presented to them was of graphics and technical drafting. The initial purpose was to prepare the youth for art and polytechnic studies. The opening presentation by a famous Jewish architect was attended even by guests from outside the ghetto. It was most unusual in the ghetto. The presentation was about "the influence of French architecture on Polish architecture." The lecturer's final note was that throughout the generations, the conquerors of Paris used to feast in the hall of crystal mirrors in the Versailles Palace. They saw their own reflection in the mirrors but were unaware that many invaders before them saw themselves in those same mirrors and later vanished, but the same shiny mirrors are still there after all.

I registered for the drafting course, which seemed the most practical. I craved learning and continued studying for my matriculation exams. I kept on driving rickshaws to pay part of the tuition. Within a few months, I had to give up the course because it was too expensive.

Shortly after having left the course, I drove the course manager, Mr. Poznański, in my rickshaw. I heard he used to be a member of the board of the Warsaw city committee. He felt uneasy when he noticed that the driver was his student until recently. I calmed him down, saying that I'm just as good a driver as anyone else, and suggested that he recommend renovation of our roads to the city board. He replied politely, saying it would be the duty of young citizens like me to make the required changes.

Through my rickshaw occupation, I got a chance to discover Warsaw's northern neighborhoods, which used to be known as the "Jewish quarter." I had learned the features of every street—which streets go uphill or downhill. All this was important for me to sit and study in the evening after eight or 10 hours of work, meet a friend, or read a book.

I understood quite quickly that if a resident of that part of the ghetto addressed me, I'd better not respond in Polish. Most of the residents of the northern part of the ghetto were Orthodox Jews. They believed that all our troubles, including Hitler, were a result of Jewish assimilation. I only knew a few words in Yiddish because I refrained from speaking it as much as I could. Questions regarding price or destination were answered half-heartedly, in single words. I did not always manage but never even considered learning Yiddish.

Rickshaws were the central means of transportation in the ghetto. In time, in order to attract passengers, owners equipped them with padded, colorful soft seats until the passenger seat resembled an armchair. My rickshaw had a tough wooden seat, which was not very comfortable. Clients began to distance themselves, but luckily not for long since soon there were rumors of lice infesting the soft seats. I was relieved. No more preference for soft seats.

The passengers were very different from one another. Some went on their businesses; some wanted to take a trip. Once, I drove a very heavy and tall man in my rickshaw accompanied by two young women. He wanted to go from Ciepła Street to Moronowski Square—thereby intersecting the whole ghetto. He himself occupied both seats, so he put the girls on his lap. I did not object. Competition was hard. The passenger did not determine the price in advance. Money probably was no issue for him, or he wanted to impress the girls. This trio was heavy, very heavy. I was already experienced and could withstand hours of strain, but this ride was especially tough, and I breathed heavily. My client couldn't care less. He turned to me angrily a few times, demanding I hurry up since strolling was not his intent. I did not answer, only kept thinking how I would respond should he decide to descend before reaching the destination. I was prepared to argue should he refuse to pay. One of the girls understood what went on because she turned to the man, telling him she just remembered she had to get off to go somewhere on the way. He rudely told her to sit quietly. She quietly looked at me as if telling me: You see, I tried, but to no avail.

I brought them to their destination. The man paid for two passengers. I did not argue. The girl who tried to descend earlier secretly shoved a coin into my pocket, but I refused to take it. She looked at me anxiously, did not say a word so the man would not hear her, and asked me with a glance not to give her trouble. She, too, was anxious for her livelihood, and my ego could have ruined everything for her.

Soon I started looking for another job. From time to time, I took some breaks from work. I am embarrassed even remembering them; each break involved losing the day's wages. But work was very exhausting, and I had to get some rest every once in a while. I wanted to meet my friends so much, or have some time to read, but was often too tired to think about it. Mom understood my condition but tried to convince me we had no choice. Only my work was there to sustain us.

The situation in the ghetto was worsening. The only food left was that which was smuggled from outside the ghetto. Large-scale smuggling was left to people who had connections with the authorities, mainly the police. The lockdown on the ghetto became gradually harsher until it became hermetic, and with each stepping up of the lockdown, food prices soared. People bought less food and ate less. The Germans provided the ghetto with a "nutrition system," meaning food supplied in exchange for vouchers distributed to the residents. But the amount of food provided this way was minuscule. The monthly ration was barely enough for two to three days. Fat and sugar were not distributed at all. A few grams of the lowest quality meat were provided once every few months.

Among the products distributed was flour, which was delivered to a master local bakery in charge of distributing bread to the residents. It belonged to a Jew named Bleiman, who was famous before the war for his matzos. He baked the bread for the ghetto residents and soon became a millionaire, like Kohn and Heller, the owners of the horse carriages that replaced the trams.[8] The ties of these two with the Gestapo offices in charge of running the ghetto were well-known. Bleiman's bread became darker with every passing month, and its water content grew gradually. Its taste became sourer with time, and people said it was due to the talc that was added to the flour to make the bread cheaper. Bleiman and his German associates continued to grow richer as the people of the ghetto were eating talc.

My cousin from Kalisz, the beautiful Nina Kutnowski, worked as a waitress in a café on Leshno Street. She told me that when Bleiman's son arrived at the café, the girls cast lots on who was going to serve his table. Young Bleiman would tip generously.

My hard rickshaw work was not profitable enough for our existence; sometimes, it wasn't even enough for the dry bread. Some days I waited for hours for a customer. Sometimes a customer asked to wait for another in order to split the pay. What could I do? I stood and waited. At times, I felt rebellious. I felt this occupation was destroying me, that I had to find something else to do. But then came a more successful day. Mother was happy, and I was ashamed of the trouble I had caused her.

Mother was a young woman, and in our eyes, she was very beautiful. No one believed she was the mother of such grown-up sons. When the war broke out, she was 36 years old. Before my brother left for Lvov, she went to the market with him to buy him boots. Here, too, the war forced many goods to transfer from shops to markets. When he insisted on closing a deal at one of the stalls, the seller shouted at him: "Young man, how come you listen to your wife? Who wears the pants at home?" The whole family laughed at the story. Mom was proud of her eldest son and of herself. Shortly afterward, she remained without a husband, with no work, totally dependent on my job. The fact that her condition was similar to that of many women in those days was of no comfort.

In the spring of 1941, the Germans decided our lives were far too good. They announced they were removing one side of Sienna Street out of the ghetto boundaries, the side on which we lived. The exact timing was not published, but soon they began to build a wooden fence in the middle of our street. They put up wooden poles and nailed boards to it. Only part of the fence was completed, and many parts were left open, which gave many, as always, a reason to believe "not all is lost." It was already June 1941, and it was unclear what kept them from finishing the fence.

On June 22, we were all notified of the German offensive against the Soviet Union. It took us all by surprise, and some were pleased. The majority said that a war against the USSR could not develop as it did in Western Europe. The Soviets are different. Even Napoleon learned his lesson. This time, the Nazis would be defeated, and this would also have implications on our situation.

As a first response to the news, the youth began to tear down the fence on Sienna Street. I can still hear the sound of the wooden boards being broken. It was the sound of a rebellion, of victory in battle, of tearing down the Bastille. It took time until the neighborhood's elders stopped the outbreak. Broken wooden boards were scattered across the street, many disappeared. The neighborhood's elders didn't know how to settle the affair. The German response came later: they fined the street with a huge sum in gold.

We waited a few days for initial news from the front line. So far, no official news had been published. We had no alternative sources of information. We presumed the Germans were reluctant to publish news due to their lack of success. The "barkers" on the street corners were silent; no military marches were broadcast. After a week, the speakers returned to play. The Germans were already inside Belarus and the Ukraine. The list of occupied cities, number of prisoners of war, of destroyed Soviet tanks—it all struck us out of the blue. The Germans being successful at the first stage would have been a realistic scenario since they had already had some experience at the western front together with surprising momentum. But such news after a week of an offensive was way beyond any imagination. The German victories dragged the ghetto into complete depression.

Weeks went by. The Nazis continued to advance. It seemed that no power in the world could stop them. Many families like ours, whose sons remained beyond the Bog River, tried guessing what their fate would be once the Germans entered. When would they be back?

That kept us, for the time being, from thinking about the exclusion of our street from the ghetto.

In the middle of August, my brother returned. He left Lvov a month after the Germans occupied the city. The invasion caught them like a sudden disaster. For the past year and a half, he lived a quiet life, completed his matriculation exams, and began studies at the university. My father supported him. Studying, playing tennis, skiing on the hills near the city—all that sounded unbelievable, incomparable to our lives here. He returned alone, since my father went away in mid-June to a sanatorium in Georgia for a few weeks. He was supposed to be treated there for a stomach condition from which he had suffered for years. A week after he left, the war broke out. When the Germans entered, my brother decided to leave. The house maid where he rented a room got him a baptism certificate, which helped him set westward and cross the still-existing border.

He arrived in Warsaw and jumped over the ghetto wall. Mother was endlessly happy. Our father's absence remained unexplained. Mother did not condemn nor complain. I could not forgive nor understand my father for leaving for Georgia. Undoubtedly, this affected our relations years after the war. After a few days of rest, my brother decided to work on a rickshaw like mine. I was desperate since I thought of his return as of our chance to leave the ghetto together. I tried to explain to him that he didn't understand the gravity of the situation. I still did not have any proof, but I felt the ghetto was destined to be exterminated. If famine and disease did not exterminate us all, the Germans would do it in another way—indeed, they excel in nothing but systemic killing. I felt I was beginning to convince my brother. We still did not see things the same way, but I felt he was beginning to hesitate, to look at things differently.

In the ghetto, the number of suicide cases grew, yet many, namely young people, thought about escape as the only chance to save their lives. Insecurity and uncertainty forced people to try and predict what the future holds. Our neighbor, Mrs. Roma, a civilized woman, could also read the palm of your hand and predict the future. I refused, which surprised everyone. I told them I did not need a fortune-teller since I already knew I would survive.

"I don't know about you guys, but I will live, I will go through this," I said. I believed it. Today, when I recall this, I am filled with shame. My words must have sounded cruel.

I was preparing to leave the ghetto. I learned Catholic prayers. I kept reiterating to anyone who was prepared to listen that we must plan our escape. My brother grew more tolerant of my ideas. My mother and uncles tried to address the idea. Mom claimed, in a practical sense, that her face would hinder any chance of her surviving on the Aryan side. My uncles said they were too old for this kind of adventure. Furthermore, finding a hideout required large sums of money they no longer had. Yet, both my mother and my uncles were convinced that both my brother and I must try. This helped me convince my brother. He, too, began thinking of a solution.

THE GHETTO, 1941-1942

The idea of somehow fleeing from the ghetto became an obsession, and not just mine. My uncles were all in agreement that we all would benefit should some of us manage to make it outside the ghetto walls. My mother was full of doubts yet expressed general consent.

Already in 1940, after having entered the ghetto, I moved into the house of a Polish agronomist by the name of Stashinski, who lived in the village Iwiczna, about 20 kilometers from Warsaw. My aunts helped him some years before, when he had difficult times, so a friendship grew between the families. He visited us in the ghetto several times, and at one time, it was decided that I would move in with him. He even thought he could find me a job and attain Aryan identity documents. Both he and his wife were very friendly, although his wife could not hide her concern. They could not find me a job, and it was evident that they were beginning to doubt the task they had undertaken. I tried to help them and make myself useful around the house. Mr. Stashinski was away a lot for work, and his wife did not want me to stay out of the house much. I had a feeling I betrayed my mother. I missed her and my friends and family. After a few weeks, I announced I was going back to the ghetto.

They were relieved. I came back like a hero. Mother was happy; my aunt, who planned the operation, was disappointed. Afterward, I only left the ghetto a few times and for short periods of time.

In the fall of 1941, we had to leave our apartment in Sienna Street after our side of the street had been annexed to Aryan Warsaw. Instead of the wooden fence built earlier, a wall was raised in the middle of the street. Its top was adorned with pieces of broken glass. Mom found a room on Leshno Street, across the street from the "Office to Combat Usury and Profiteering." That was the infamous "Unit 13"—a semi-overt Gestapo unit so nicknamed for its location on street number 13.[1] Before the war, I visited this house to see my friend Wittek Horenstein. By the time we moved there, he was in a camp for foreign subjects under Ukrainian nationality. When he came across Ukrainian nationality papers, he could not foresee the war between Germany and the USSR. Our new shelter was spacious but hideous looking and very costly too. We didn't have much time for searching around, and mom had to take whatever was available. We moved some essential furniture, suitcases and many packages. The new room was supposed to give us a sense of security, but it failed to do so. We moved our belongings using a two-wheel cart. Our previous move was aided by a horse-cart, but we knew our next move would be aided only by our backs. Each move involved giving up some of our belongings. This time, we had to leave behind the kitchenware. There was no room for them at the new house. The traditional kitchen oven was replaced by a small cast-iron stove with a pipe that ran out of the window. It was called a "goat;" I don't know why. This stove was designed for both heating and cooking.

The winter was very hard. But before it began, we had already left for another location. Mother found a nice room in Novolipie Street with a nice elderly couple, the Rosa family. Their apartment had three rooms. One room housed them; the second room was rented by a widower and his grown-up daughter. She was good looking, not much older than us, but she treated us like kids, which made my brother very angry. Our uncles, who had lived with us up until then, moved to an apartment across the street from us. Another aunt from Kalisz arrived after some months. The Germans held up her husband in the factory he was managing. She joined us too. It was very crowded but much nicer than on Leshno Street.

The latest changes in our lives left their mark. Each move out of an apartment was dispiriting and accompanied by a feeling that things were deteriorating. It wasn't only our own feeling. Most people's lives worsened significantly. Food prices soared, and people felt desperate and gloomy. Everybody knew the ghetto's territory would be reduced and anticipated the looming catastrophe. Our everyday life was dedicated solely to obtaining food.

On the top of the closet, one of the few furniture pieces we brought with us, were two magnificent violin cases of the highest quality. The more expensive one was mine. I got it from my uncle in Holland. He was a violinist and always said I had to learn to play. I hadn't held this violin in my hands since 1939. Mrs. Rosa pleaded with me to play, but when I tried, I was convinced it was a mistake. My fingers betrayed me. I never touched a violin again. On Sienna Street, our neighbors played concertos on their record player. Here, there was no need for violins. In order to listen to concerts, it was necessary for one not to be hungry.

I wanted to leave the rickshaw work and looked for other means of earning money. I met Shmulek Weingort, a friend of my brother's, from Kalisz. He stood out from among his many brothers and sisters in his dream to go to university. His family was traditional and modest. They had been living in Warsaw for two years after they were deported from their town, which was annexed to the German Reich. Shmulek was also looking for work and told me about people who grind wheat or rye in a manual grinder and sell the flour.

He heard that wheat was better than rye since its grains were easier to grind, and you could also make finely sifted flour, which was in high demand in the ghetto market. The problem was to find a space in which to work. Shmulek said he knew a man from Kalisz who owns a basement where we could work. This person had worked in grinding flour before and could guide us—provided, of course, that we make him a partner and buy the grinder from him.

The grinder cost a few złoty. Near the ghetto walls, we bought five kilos of wheat from smugglers. It took us almost three days to grind this quantity of wheat, then clean and sift it. Turning the grinder's handle caused a great deal of pain in my hands. Only the two of us worked in grinding. Our third partner was old and ill and physically weak. Yet, he did not save us the counseling and instructions. The basement, like in most houses, was a dump, dark, and stuffy. One lamp illuminated the space, and the owner was afraid of changing it in case the neighbors notice us.

In order to clearly see the results of our work, we used a carbide lamp.[2] That lamp stunk so bad, we had to take turns going out to breathe some fresh air.

Our working day continued until the curfew hour. Our "instructor" ate turnip soup a few times a day. The turnip dishes were one stage before the last one in the ghetto food-ladder. The last stage was not eating at all. In order to avoid thinking about the soup's taste, he told us stories of his years in Kalisz. Shmulek and I had not eaten anything all day. In the evening, we ate with mom, but I suspected Shmulek did not eat every day. We did not talk about food. It was the rule.

We learned the art of grinding within a couple of days. Cleaning the grains from the skin was even harder than grinding. We sifted the ground material for hours. The skins gathered on the sieve, and we had to clean it gently. But we couldn't overdo it—cleaning it completely meant we lost much material, but leaving the skins meant the flour was going to be dark. It was a monotonous, physically exhausting job. At the end of the first grind, we got 3 kilos of flour and one kilo of finely sifted flour. Both were not completely white, but we were very proud of ourselves. We started looking for customers in the shops, which apparently were hard to find. They all claimed that for the same price, they could buy a nicer and cleaner smuggled produce, so we had to sell for a lower price than we expected. After having paid the fees for the basement and the grinder, we were left with a few pennies.

The next time, we bought a larger quantity of wheat. We intended to produce more finely sifted flour since its price was higher than that of regular flour and was in higher demand. We almost made it but were required to pay more for the basement. Our partner argued that his neighbors claimed their share since we put them in danger because our "work is illegal." Again we looked for customers, but very few were prepared to trade with us. Until one day, in a tiny and dark store on Pawia Street, with almost empty shelves, a woman came out and hugged me and started sobbing. It was my aunt, my father's sister. She said she hired the store in order to support her family. Our relations were not close. Her eldest son and I didn't like each other, and relations between the adults were also tense. She asked about Mom and Dad and could not stop sobbing. She thought I was meant for a better life, certainly better than those of her children. Now she realized what the war has done to all of us. I tried to comfort her. I said we did not give up and that everything would be alright. But it didn't help, and she continued crying. She told me how her three children suffered, how her husband had a breakdown. We already heard some details from our grandmother and tried to keep in touch. But at that moment, I felt terrible. There was no doubt her life was much worse than ours.

My aunt bought almost all the flour from me. She didn't have enough money to buy it all. She gently tried to explain to us why we would not succeed in our work and that we had to stop it. Our business was too small to gain a real profit. She also said we were too honest and that we offered clean flour while others mixed it with various

67

supplements. We already had a tough time competing with the smuggling "sharks" of the ghetto, as it were.

This was my last meeting with Aunt Sala. I later discovered that all the family—my aunt, her husband, their three children, and their grandmother—were all taken in one of the first transports. The eldest of their two daughters, 15-year-old Genia,[3] was released from the prison on Gęsia Street, where she was detained after being caught smuggling.[4] She was released when it was ordered to evacuate the place upon exterminating the ghetto. She made it home just in time to be taken with everyone to the Umschlagplatz—the gathering point of the ghetto's Jews on Stawki Street near the railway station, where Jews were assembled before deportation to the death camps.

The third round of grinding was planned to be the last one. Indeed, we were prepared to stop already after the second round, but we couldn't find someone to buy our grinder. We broke up the partnership with the older man and only continued to pay him for the use of the basement. On this last grinding, the produce was surprisingly of good quality. It appeared much better than the last one. Again I carried the flour and some finely sifted flour and started looking for customers. The completion was immense. The big suppliers had regular customers, and tiny fish like us had to look hard for buyers among the food stores and on the street. We decided to try our luck in the market. There was no real market in the ghetto, but at the end of Ciepła Street, on a lot near a ruined house, a sort of bazaar was arranged. I went there, and Shmulek stayed in order to finish cleaning the finely sifted flour.

I stood there with my merchandise with a sign saying: "flour, finely sifted flour." I managed to sell a bit in two hours. Suddenly, a couple approached me. The woman smiled and asked whether the finely sifted flour is made of pure wheat. The man didn't take interest and only pressed her to hurry up. But she tasted the flour and said she would buy everything. Her partner objected, but she convinced him

68

with a whisper that this time it was indeed good merchandise. He was convinced, and they didn't even haggle much on the price. They offered to pay me with a note of 500 złoty and even agreed not to take the change, since I didn't have any. They paid and quickly disappeared. Well, I thought, they were in a hurry. I returned to the basement, told my partner with pride about my sale, and showed him the banknote. My partner looked at the banknote, sat down on the clay floor, sighing: "My god! Haven't you ever seen a 500 złoty note? They gave you a banknote from before the war. These banknotes had been replaced already in 1939!" I was devastated. We lost everything, all we had, including a many days' hard toil. I ran back to the market. Shmulek tried to convince me it was no use since the swindlers were long gone. He was obviously right. I found no one. More than hurting for the loss, it was awful to cause such damage to a friend. I was already 18 but yet so childish! I could not believe these swindlers could hurt someone as poor as me. On the other hand, who else would they hurt? They can't deceive rich people like that; they certainly knew what a 500 złoty banknote looked like. Shmulek did not mention the subject ever again. We remained friends, but the grief over the damage I caused him continued to torment me for a long time.

In spring 1941, we were still living on Sienna Street. That's when I met Stephan Weinberg. I met him through two of my high school friends, Yurek Lehman and Rishek Edelberg. Stephan, a handsome blonde of 30 years, was the house gatekeeper in house No. 32, just across the street from our house. Being a gatekeeper in the ghetto, especially on a street with many luxurious houses, guaranteed a good income. Those with ties in the community's offices, which are the ones to approve such a job, did everything they could to get it. Mary Wittenberg-Berg wrote in her book that her father, who was a rich art and antique dealer from Łódź, managed to attain such a post in

Warsaw after much effort and lobbying. Stephan probably had such advocates in the community offices.

My friends told me secretly that they were connected to an underground organization and suggested that I join. I agreed without hesitation. A more mature person would have asked what it was all about. What was the organization's political affiliation? But they were as young as I was. I gathered from their stories that they hadn't asked questions. It was more important to belong, to act, to do something. Speaking to Stephan, I learned that they got his permission to speak to me about it. Apparently, he knew quite a lot about me, like my father being an activist in a revisionist Zionist organization.

Also participating in the first meeting of our group was a guy named Kazik Lis, who arrived from outside the ghetto. One look at that blond guy with an upturned nose, and you would have never guessed he was a Jew. Our group, he said, was designated to operate outside the ghetto, which made us very content. Stephan also disclosed the group's political affiliation; they were Polish socialists associated with the Barykada Wolnośći (barricades of freedom) newspaper. We were supposed to be the militant arm of this organization. He said that in the present situation, the organizers also recruited members from different political groups. He himself used to be a member of the Communist Party until it was dissolved. We chose our underground aliases—mine was "Rickshaw"—and we agreed on means of communication. We went on to meet during the days up to the curfew hours or at night. I was bothered by the fact that these meetings clashed with my work and studies. I didn't want all my efforts at studying to amount to nothing. Nevertheless, I continued to meet with the cell group. We met twice in a basement. We first learned to assemble and disassemble a pistol. In the next meeting, our instructor, a reserve officer, explained how a machine gun operates. He showed us drawings on pieces of paper. He was a young man whom we found hard to describe. We wondered whether that was part of the conspiracy. We already knew about pistols, since we learned to operate them in the premilitary organization in school, but we did not learn much about machine guns in our nightly meetings. However, it was there that I heard there for the first time about domestic manufacturing of hand grenades made out of paper-thin tin boxes. The boxes contained powder for metal polishing, named Sidol, which is why these homemade grenades were called Sidolka.[5] The grenades contained an explosive material called "plastic" that wasn't in military use before the war. They were lightweight, exploded easily, and caused a strong blast, but in fact, did not cause much damage to the Germans in the 1944 uprising.

We wondered how this organization would operate. We obviously did not have any practical qualifications. Nevertheless, we were very content with the fact that we belonged, that we were trying to do something. Occasionally, we would receive the underground newspaper printed on very thin paper, passed along from hand to hand. Apparently, some copies had been copied on regular paper in the ghetto. It was small, but granted a feeling of power we so missed in those times; it symbolized our endurance. However, its content was quite disappointing: many subjects were described only briefly, even telegraphically. We could understand why, but our own fate— the plight of the Jews and the ghettos—was almost never discussed. Some tried to explain that because it was an underground paper, it had to limit its content only to areas of majority interest. This Jewish tendency to compromise, so well-known from the prewar era, was now accepted only by a few. Other underground papers, not only ours, hardly discussed the Jewish problem. The ghetto was already facing extermination—not by crematoriums but as a result of hunger and disease. The Jewish public completely and painfully comprehended it should not expect any help from the world outside the ghetto.

In winter 1941, Yurek told me that Stephan had been arrested. They took him at night, probably with other resistance activists, to the Pawiak—the prison on Pawia Street.[6] Yurek advised me not to sleep at home for a while. Stephan knew details on all of us, and that made us feel insecure. Still, I stayed at home. I told my mother and brother what has happened, and we all agreed I had nowhere to hide. We had to look for a shelter that could hold all of us because once the Germans did not find who they were looking for, they would arrest the whole family. It was tense for a few weeks. No one knew what had happened to Stephan, but we minimized our communication. The fact that I was already living in the northern part of the ghetto and they remained in the southern part, on Sienna Street, made it difficult to keep in touch. After some time, Stephan's two sisters came to see me. They collected donations to send their brother packages and also spoke of redemption of the captive.[7] I donated twice at the expense of my daily bread. By the time the sisters came for the third time, I was informed by Rishek that Stephan had already been executed two months earlier. The sisters knew it but continued to collect donations because they were starving. My heart was with Stephan. In my eyes, he was a brave man who sacrificed his life. I was sorry for his sisters; we were sorry for us all.

Even in the wealthy Sienna Street, one could already feel the signs of the ghetto's deteriorating condition. The sight of numerous people who had nothing left but to ask for help from passersby became a daily routine. Many didn't even know how to beg for alms. They tried to do it humbly, shyly stretching out their hats. Not far from our house stood a singer. He wasn't young, wearing a suit that knew better days. He sang Italian songs and was evidently a professional singer. Now this voice was a little hoarse, tired, and when at times he had to take a lower octave, he smiled apologetically. When a passerby put a few pennies in his hat, he thanked him, nodding his head. With time, his voice was ruined by the cold and rain, and he stopped singing, just stood there, and asked for help with a glance. I once passed him by on another street. He tried to sing but couldn't—his voice sounded exhausted, and the clothes he wore were worn out. I met him once again on Leshno Street. He sat against the wall, not asking for anything. Nobody gave anything. Mother, who every few days brought him some bread, found him dead after a few days. He had already been stripped of some of his clothes.

Smuggling was one of the central activities in the ghetto's history. Most of the ghetto's food supply came from "big smugglers." Their actions shocked many. There was a story about a dairy barn organized on the third floor of a residential building. The entrepreneurs decided it was easier to transfer a cow into the ghetto than to take pains at smuggling fresh milk into it. I also heard how the cow was carried up the stairs all the way to the third floor. Later on, they had two cows in there—a prospering business.

The smuggling depended on the German gendarmes at the ghetto's gates. There were also two policemen there: a Pole and a Jew. The watch (*Die Wache*) was, in fact, the authority that filtered and directed the ghetto's supply. Without it, the ghetto would have ceased to exist. Should the gendarme decide to block the entrance or exit of a vehicle, there was not a power in the world that could make him change his mind. Most of the gendarmes quickly learned the power in their hands that could offer them an opportunity to improve their lives as well as those of their superiors. When the trio standing at the gate agreed on a smuggling operation, it was carried out under the nickname phrase, "the breakfront is playing" (as in music "*Szafa Gra*").[8] The initiator was always the Jewish policeman. When the "breakfront" was "playing," trucks and carts full of merchandise passed through the ghetto's gates.

Sometimes, the gendarme at the gate became bored and looked to amuse himself. One of them was called "Frankenstein" because he was especially brutal. When he picked himself a victim, he would take the gun off his shoulder and begin shooting without thinking twice. At times, he settled for one victim; other times, he was only satisfied with more. Among his victims were men, women, and children. At times, it was even the Jewish policeman standing at the gate next to him. People warned each other: "Don't go there, 'Frankenstein' is in ambush."

The "official" food in the ghetto was distributed in exchange for food stamps given by the Judenrat. They were nicknamed "bons." In street language, possessing a "bon" meant to sustain, stay alive, and the word "bon" became part of the ghetto dictionary and folklore. The Judenrat offices regularly checked who was entitled to food stamps and who wasn't alive, and therefore there was no need to print stamps for them.[9] When someone died, it was said "he surrendered a bon." While arguing, people used to scream at each other "return the bon!" meaning "drop dead!"

At first, two trams operated in the ghetto. On the platform stood a Polish policeman intended to prevent Poles from straying within the ghetto boundaries. Nonetheless, people did jump off the trams while they were driving because they had business to take care of in the ghetto. The policeman was forgiving yet reacted fiercely to those asking to board the tram. One such passenger told the policeman decisively, "Sir, can't you see who's of our own?" It sufficed. But within a few months, it became harder since there was only one transportation line left inside the ghetto. Instead of a tram line number, it carried a Star of David sign. A few months later, that line was gone too, because of two Jews from Łódź, Kohn, and Heller. They both had exceptionally good ties with the SS men in charge of the ghetto transportation system. A new means of transportation was introduced into the ghetto—a "tram" with no electricity—operated by a pair of horses. It only moved along Leshno Street.

The streets gradually became more crowded along with the narrowing of the ghetto's area. Every few months, the Germans transferred a fragment or whole streets to Aryan Warsaw. The ghetto's inhabitants were forced to move into already extremely crowded quarters. Walking the streets required a "slalom" technique, a zigzagging ski-type course. It got even more complicated when a

German appeared out of the blue. The "sons of the Aryan race" demanded that the Jews descend to the road upon walking past a German; some demanded that they take their hats off. I once refused to take off my cap and was slapped in the face. Since then, I never wore a head-covering again, not even in winter. The masses "poured" onto the road to walk and avoid contact with others out of fear they would contract typhoid through lice. Mom used to check us first thing when we got home for fear we carried something on our clothes.

In order to get from the "small" ghetto in the south to the "large" one in the north, one had to overcome the masses on Żelazna Street, exclusively connecting the two parts together. After having excluded Żelazna Street from the ghetto boundaries, the Germans built a wooden footbridge above the junction. It was an impressive construct, carrying masses of pedestrians. It connected both parts of Żelazna Street over the Aryan Chłodna Street. The mobile gates alternately closed transportation on both directions; a few minutes were allocated for Jewish carriages and rickshaws on Żelazna to go through, then the same amount of time allocated for the few vehicles in Chłodna; an equal amount of time to both—"order must be kept" ("*Ordnung soll sein!*"). The order was determined by the gendarme while the gates were moved by the Jewish police officers.

In order to streamline traffic in the most crucial part of the Warsaw Ghetto in early in 1942, the Germans built a wooden footbridge for the pedestrians over Aryan Chłodna Street. For vehicular traffic, especially for the ghetto's rickshaws, they installed a special mechanical gate at the intersection of Chłodna and Żelazna.

Special mechanical gate at the intersection of
Chłodna and Żelazna.

Despite the high death rate, the ghetto's population did not diminish, and it did not become less cramped. The residents of the various villages and towns where the Jewish ghettos had been liquidated kept arriving continuously. Jews also kept coming in from neighboring countries such as Slovakia and even from distant places like the Balkans. The community tried to arrange shelter for them. They were miserable, estranged, and even outcasts. Many didn't know the language and could not communicate with the locals. "The points" was the name of the place where these newcomers were assembled. They looked like scenes from Dante's *Inferno*. These people were left with nothing and immediately rendered paupers. The Judenrat collected donations through special agents who were passing from door to door. A neighbor who worked in such a fundraising effort told Mom that he gets 5 percent of the money collected, so it appeared to be a tempting job. I was introduced to the job by a girl already in the business. In order to collect a worthwhile wage, one had to be assigned the "good streets," but we didn't have any. There was also another problem: upon calling a wealthy family's apartment, the head of the family, who was dressed in traditional Jewish clothes, was outraged that the collector did not know any Yiddish. Only after I left, he gave my partner five złoty and said that had it not been for me, he would have given more. She took my commission and brought it home to my mother. I wasn't home since I had immediately returned to my work as a rickshaw driver. Once again, I realized I had to look for salvation elsewhere, far from here.

One scene that gradually became more and more common in the streets was the *"khappers,"*[10] a Yiddish word that means "to snatch"—a "snatcher." These snatchers were so desperately hungry that they were prepared to get fiercely beaten as long as they succeeded in grabbing a package of some food and managing to take a bite of it to somehow satisfy their hunger. They would jump on their victim like predators. A person holding a food package did not expect such an onslaught. The khapper would stick his teeth into the package, biting the food as well as the material it was wrapped in. He tried to bite as much as he could, leaving the swallowing to a later time—that is, until after he endured a beating by the victim and the crowd trying to salvage whatever they could from the food in his hands. I once carried breakfast for my brother, who used to leave early for work, when he managed to find work. It was usually my mother who carried food for him, but this time she asked me to do it for fear of the khappers. I set out for him just before going to work on my rickshaw. I held two slices of bread wrapped in thick paper and a bit of carrot jam in a separate pack. The jam had to be spread just before eating so that the bread would not get soggy since the jam was very watery. I didn't think anyone would dare to attack me. All of a sudden, I sobered up: the parcel was almost completely devoured together with the paper. This khapper was already taking beatings from passersby while protecting his head with his hands so that he could swallow the food as fast as possible. The stench from his body was so bad that I refused to take what remained from the parcel.

Many street beggars, among them small children, filled the sidewalks, leaning against house walls, standing or sitting. Some were swollen from hunger. This swelling appeared first around the eye sockets, then spread and intensified until leaving only small cracks for the pupils. The hands and feet also swelled; the face and body appeared greenish-brown. It mostly struck young children. People who passed them by on the street knew they could not be saved. Most of them turned their heads to avoid seeing these children. This heartbreaking, painful, and embarrassing sight haunted me for a long time. But eventually, one becomes numb.

The image of the *"Muselmann"* appeared in the ghetto long before it appeared in the concentration camps. It was a person—skin and bone —who could not take a step or move a limb.[11] They were so skinny that they turned into walking skeletons. At first, they could still walk around; later, they could not move at all, only sit down until dropping motionless. Every morning, Pinkert's burial service's two-wheeled hearses picked up the previous night's corpses. Pinkert was the ghetto's only legitimate undertaker. Before the war, he had an honorable burial society. In the ghetto, it was only operated through the Judenrat offices. The service workers dragged the naked skeletons from the pavement. They had already been stripped of their clothes by paupers. The workers threw them on the hearses, piling them up until they carried them to the Jewish cemetery on Okopowa Street. In 1942, they were hurled into mass graves—a common grave for the unidentified—and only rarely were the dead buried in a full ceremony. Most families settled for a separate grave with a name sign on it. In order to get to the cemetery, one needed a transit permit, arranged by Pinkert.

Near the end of 1941, my friends and I deliberated on how to graduate from our high school studies. We could see that soon we wouldn't be able to study at all. For two years, we had made a huge effort to keep some sort of a normal study routine. Meanwhile, our lives had changed beyond recognition, and we tried to adapt to new circumstances. Out of the five group members who started out in 1939, only two remained. Others were replaced, some by those who came from other schools. The teachers had also changed. Ever since the closing of the ghetto, not many teachers were prepared to come. Some teachers found themselves substitutes in the ghetto. Occasionally they would coordinate the study schedule and meet us in the court of justice building on Leshno Street since it was possible to enter it from both sides. They shared the dismal wages we paid them. We couldn't afford any more than that. Our teachers and we thought we could easily fill in our gaps in academic knowledge after the war. I must say, with pride, that throughout my extensive and diverse academic years, I never needed any completions of any kind.

We decided to take the matriculation exams without delay, mostly in writing. On exam day, a messenger on behalf of the teachers arrived with all the exam papers. He was a biologist and had an assistant from within the ghetto, a young physician, Isio (I think was his name) Tunkenbaum, appointed by Professor Zinkowski (who was appointed the Warsaw polytechnic dean after the war). Tunkenbaum was a whiz kid and Zinkowski's favorite student. According to the old professor's order, he taught us physics and mathematics. I don't know why—perhaps I was working too hard to be a student, or perhaps he was an excellent teacher—but for the first time in my life, I truly enjoyed studying mathematics. I was the only one from my group who was present at the graduation ceremony to receive his matriculation certificate. A special committee, gathered especially for this purpose, issued the certificates. Among other signatures was that of our high school's principal, Pawel Ordynski.

Again, I became a wheat grinder for a short while. My brother knew a person with "free money" who was in the grinding business until he became ill with lung disease. He offered to find a location with electricity for my brother to operate the grinder. He had a grinder that could grind 15 kilos of wheat in one night. He was prepared to buy the grain for 70 percent of the profit. My brother found a suitable basement on Żelazna Street, not far from the ghetto gate. We agreed that since we had experience in grinding, I would help him at work. On the first night, we ground 15 kilos of rye—unbelievable!

The air in the basement was stifling, full of thick dust, and both of us were covered with a thick layer of flour, which was hard to shake off before going out to the street. Other than that, we had no reason to complain. It was no longer the hard manual work that caused our hands to swell. The flour was quite fair; the grain coats were heavier this time, making the separation easier. We were very optimistic. The next day, I was supposed to work alone because my brother went to buy grain. In the morning, there was noise in the corridor. I did not open the door. I waited for a sign from my brother. When the agreed knock on the door was heard, I opened it. My brother walked in with two men. One of them had a policeman's cap; the other wore only a police badge. They could have probably entered earlier but had been waiting for my brother. They demanded that we pay them a monthly sum, and in exchange, they would "let the business go on." We were shocked. We had yet to face such outright blackmail. My brother tried to resist and asked what they would do if we did not pay. They replied that he was naïve. "You could not do anything without us. First, we will shut off the electricity. We will send over porters who hang around the guards. If you don't pay them yourself, you will be properly bashed." My brother replied that he must talk with our partner first. Clearly, we could not bear such expenses. That same day, we liquidated the "business." We carefully managed to transfer the flour; at least we succeeded in that.

Apart from Emanuel Ringelblum, Janush Korczak, some poets, and ideologists, there were also people in the ghetto of a different kind. These circumstances exposed some tendencies in people that otherwise would not have been known. Before the war, my parents knew a nice and civilized man, Mr. Fierst, who was the Jewish youth hostel manager. In the ghetto, we discovered he was a Gestapo agent. At first, Mother said she would never believe this, and then she cried all night.

When I think about that period, I am overwhelmed with painful memories. The injustice caused by people who experienced the same

80

tragedy was even more painful to comprehend. Conditions in the ghetto were unprecedented. It was hell. Hundreds of thousands of people lived in it, stripped of any rights and any means of subsistence. They did anything in their power to survive, although they stood no chance. It took a long time before they had realized it. Until then, they lived and tried to ensure the lives of their loved ones, for whom they were prepared to do anything. Nevertheless, the majority did not allow themselves to digress from moral principles and dignity.

What can one say today, many decades later, about a person giving away a slice of bread to a hungry man while he himself is all swollen and agonized by hunger? Is it fortitude or transcending to some other moral high ground?

There were some tens of thousands of "Korczaks" in the ghetto. They all marched alongside their children to death. Only a handful decided to save their own skin and desert their loved ones.

Contrary to the truth, it was widely held that the ghetto inhabitants marched to death without resisting or rebelling. How can one explain that these people had been shattered, crushed, and shredded into dust years before, so they would internalize and get used to the thought that they had no salvation, no way out, no future? Even so, they did not succeed in turning them into immoral, conscienceless people! Only a few digressed into inhumanity. The great majority remained honest, dignified, pristine, and heroic. These people knew very well no one in the world wished to help them. They knew that those in their surroundings, both near and far, would not do any deed nor gesture to aid them. Has any other nation prevailed in crossing such an abyss in a more honorable manner? Many monuments have been raised in honor of the ghetto insurgents; yet, no monument has been established for heroes like my mother, who did not break in the face of the ghetto's horror. She remained honest, humane, and righteous until her last moments. The silent stones of Treblinka are the only memorial to her.

Our window overlooked Milna Street. Just across from the street stretched the wall which separated the ghetto from the evangelical church on Leshno Street. In order to enable the entrance into the church from the Aryan side, a long and narrow corridor had been created, which penetrated the ghetto like a knife. Despite this effort, the church was almost completely isolated from the Christian side and was barely active. It was usually quiet and empty, and only rarely did events take place there with little audience. The quiet atmosphere that prevailed there always filled us with longing and envy. We observed the peaceful sight, yearning for the vacations we spent in the countryside not so long ago.

Since Milna was a dead-end street, our surrounding was very peaceful. Yet, in the evenings, just before curfew hour, beggars of all kinds began their "shows" there. Most of them were familiar with the surroundings and knew which window to approach. A considerable part consisted of young people who brought along children with them. The pledge was almost ceremonial: "Jews, show mercy" ("*Juden, hat rachmunes, hat Mitleit*"). They felt obliged to explain that they were not professional beggars. They were, until recently, from wealthy families with houses and livelihoods, and could never have imagined they would stoop to begging. They always supported the poor. Now they had no other choice—they must beg in order to provide their children with at least a slice of bread. They trusted that those who heard their pledge would not let them die. Of course, all that was chanted in Yiddish. Mother did not always understand what was said, but she would open the window and throw down a slice of bread wrapped in paper. She would turn to us and say, "That was some bread that I didn't eat. I couldn't have. Yours for the morning is waiting."

We lived on the first floor. Quite often, as if by chance, the bread fell into the hands of a girl, who was walking her sister—a little toddler with a face pale as paper. We asked Mother why she was giving her the bread. She told us that the girl once "confessed" to her that she hailed from a town not far from where our mother lived with her parents before they moved to Warsaw during WWI. At the end of spring 1942, the girl began to appear alone. When she was asked what had happened to her sister, she burst into tears. She said she was exhausted too, that she felt the end was near.

That spring, disturbing rumors began circulating about the extermination taking place at the hands of the Germans in the "labor" camps. I had already heard about a systematic execution of men from my brother's high school friend Tadek Zilberg. When I saw him, I hardly recognized him. He had been taken from the street for "just a few hours" of work and was sent with others to a camp 60 kilometer north of the city. The camp commander was a sadistic SS man. Prisoners were starved and tortured systematically. Within a few weeks, he lost about 10 kilograms. His mother, a wealthy widow whose only son was her whole world, bribed, with considerable effort, the German labor office manager (*Arbeitsamt*), who was in charge of the camp. Tadek returned home and did not leave bed for weeks. I met him when he was still weak. He had peeled skin and unhealed wounds instead of fingernails. He had been terrorized. When he was about to leave the camp, the commander told him he'd be out to get him. I asked him what precisely they were doing there. He smiled sadly and said they were, in fact, doing nothing. They kept digging holes and filling them over and over again. After the war, it became known that special SS units were trained in camps in various techniques that were later implemented in the death camps. In the ghetto, it was common knowledge that there were several such camps in the Warsaw area, from which most prisoners never returned. New prisoners, who were detained in the street, were constantly sent over in place of those who perished.

It was mandatory to keep everything dark at night. The windows were open only after the lights went out. The lack of traffic in the street created an illusion of peace and quiet. On one of the nights in May, a car's noise woke us up. At that hour, it could only be the police or the Gestapo. After a few moments, we heard the cries of people being beaten. We then heard some gunshots, followed by cries of women and children. Mother stood behind the curtain, did not let us come near the window, whispering to us what she was seeing. At one moment, the cries grew, and something heavy was heard falling from the apartment to the street. And everything was quiet again. We heard the details the next morning. The Gestapo executed underground activists, two of whom were detained near us. One was shot on the site, and the other, a disabled man in a wheelchair, was thrown through the window onto the street.

In mid-July 1942, about 700 Jews, who were citizens of other countries, were taken out of the ghetto, as cited by Mary Berg. As they marched through the ghetto streets, one may have mistakenly thought there were more. They were heading through Leshno and Kremlizka streets to the Pawiak prison. Their faces were solemn and concerned over the fact that they left their friends and relatives in the ghetto. They had tags with symbols of their countries attached to their clothes. The column marched the street while people stood agitated on the sidewalks. All understood that deporting foreign subjects was an omen of crucial times to come for the ghetto. Some of them could tell that they were being sent back to their countries. Some said that they were to be exchanged with German prisoners held in various Allied countries, while others said the Germans demanded ransom in exchange for the Jews.

A week went by. Despite all the ongoing thoughts, analyses, and the many omens, the liquidation of the ghetto came to all like a thunderbolt out of the blue.

END AND BEGINNING

Until 1943, except for the Lvov period, my brother was part of all my life experiences. As children, we were inseparable, always together. I was just over a year younger than him and always a step behind. At school, I was one year his junior. In those days, it was significant. Arthur was an excellent student and got a scholarship for the senior years of high school. By contrast, I was hardheaded, at times wild, and the teachers, to put it mildly, didn't like my conduct. My brother also excelled in sports, and my parents were very proud of him. Occasionally, he was asked to check if I did my homework, and this sometimes resulted in fights, which diminished with time. The truth was that we loved each other, even a lot.

Upon returning from Lvov in 1941, Arthur went through a difficult crisis. The shift from relative freedom, a steady routine, and a full stomach to the ghetto reality of persecution and hunger had left a grave mark on his soul. He kept reminiscing about the Lvov life. I didn't understand all his stories, though I wanted to hear them. How was it there? Who were the Soviets? How did they behave, look, or speak? In September 1939, I didn't have time to meet them. In Warsaw, there were some funny stories about them: about guns carried on a string instead of straps, about boots without leather, about tanks for 64 people—four inside and 60 pushing it along. These jokes made us very sad: how will such an incompetent army cope with the German might? In the face of the Allies' defeat at all fronts, it looked like our salvation would only come from the east. Only my brother could tell me the truth about it. He did not get into politics. The Red Army, in those days, was beaten and retreating all along the frontiers. My brother described his everyday life, which consisted of studying and training in sports every day. There was a great deal of propaganda on every possible channel—a lot of simple, catchy, and captivating melodies with simple themes intended for anybody's ears. These songs raised yearning and sorrow. This was the first time I heard *Katyushka by the river,* as well as about Stalin, *our leader and pride in battle.* Even for the inexperienced ear, it was an obvious personality cult, only to be followed by an immediate exegesis: it's only a symbol. I didn't try to criticize it; I just listened. The songs transferred us to another world, far from oppression, humiliation, and starvation.

My brother needed some time to recuperate and return to a routine. Once he did, he wanted to get back to work and take part in winning the family's bread. He thought the simplest way to do it would be to take my rickshaw work, but I refused. As far as I was concerned, it was just another way to perpetuate our stay in the ghetto, putting up with our fading away, collaborating with everything that surrounds us, including lack of hope. I hoped that once he was here, we would begin to look for a way out. He did not agree with this idea, and we entered into long discussions. Finally, he prepared to check out our chances on Warsaw's Aryan side. He met a school friend who was in the freight carts union. Warsaw, who remained with no automated transportation, solved the problem with horse carts. Its owners were organized in a union under the municipality's auspice, thus protecting their safety and freedom of movement. Arthur's friend got us two such certificates. I didn't get the chance to put it into use, but just the mere fact it was in my pocket was important and encouraging.

The idea to leave the ghetto remained a dream and illusion for a long time. My brother was very skeptical about it, and our mother was our greatest difficulty. Her Semitic beauty made it almost impossible to find her a hiding place outside the ghetto. We weren't even concerned with financial difficulties. We could only assume we would both work and obtain the means to pay for mother's refuge expenses. We avoided discussions on whether this plan was feasible— the idea of leaving Mother behind alone in the ghetto didn't cross our minds.

Work was very hard to get in the ghetto, and the hunt for it continued endlessly. My brother was busy with everything that involved investing money. He also occasionally worked on the rickshaw, and for several months was employed in a tiny workshop that manufactured socks. The work was carried out in a one-room and kitchen apartment, where the "manufacturer's" family resided with its three children. They manufactured the socks with three old machines and supplied the products to a German who lived near Warsaw. In spring 1942, Arthur found a profitable job that allowed me to return to my studies. I met my wheat-grinding partner, who told me of various accounting and stenography courses opening up. We both registered and, for a few months, these courses allowed us to divert attention from the surrounding events. After a few weeks, I could write a whole lesson in shorthand, type rapidly in a typewriter, and deal with basic accounting.

But one day in July 1942, everything changed abruptly. On my way out from the course, my brother caught up with me and remarked angrily: "While you're fiddling around here, they are beginning to liquidate the ghetto." He was familiar with the details: the next day, they would start deporting the "unproductive" residents, those who do not possess working certificates approved by the Germans. The Jewish police were required to transfer 6,000 people every day from

87

the ghetto to the Umschlagplatz. No one knew where they were taken.

Two announcements were posted on the street walls. One of them was about how the unproductive population would be transferred to the east, where they would live and work—without indicating exactly where they would be sent. The announcement called upon such people to turn up voluntarily. Whoever volunteered to go would receive four kilograms of bread and one kilogram of jam. The second announcement reported the sudden death of the head of the Judenrat, Adam Czerniaków. After a few hours, the details were disclosed: Czerniaków committed suicide after refusing to sign the deportation announcements.

Residents who did not work in an "approved" working place were the majority of the ghetto population. The Germans almost entirely banned any private production and confiscated any such machinery and raw material. Only small workshops operated inside the ghetto, some of which were officially unapproved. The only approved places were the "shops"—the large-scale workshops owned by Germans, such as Többens and Schultz. They both established tailor and shoemaking workshops for the German army. Immediately after the two announcements were publicized, the ghetto residents began to desperately look for work in those shops. A certificate of work in a shop (*Ausweis*) granted its owner and his immediate relatives the privilege to remain in the ghetto.

Long before the war, Mother completed a course in sewing. Her skills were crucial since the shops expanded rapidly and lacked professional manpower. The whole family contributed to the purchase of a new sewing machine for Mother because a worker could only be accepted to the shop if she possessed her own machinery. Mom's machine was very old but still working. It was supposed to grant not only her right to live but also my uncle as ironing assistant and my aunt as his wife. I was too old to present myself as the worker's son. My brother still had the certificate confirming he manufactured socks for the Germans.

Textile manufacturing shop in the Warsaw Ghetto

I began to desperately look for work to obtain a shop certificate. For three days, I stood in front of the door of the office recruiting workers for a shop that was due to open soon. At last, it was my turn. I paid a fair amount of money for registration and got the certificate I yearned for. My brother showed the paper to a policeman he knew, and the latter declared with much assurance that this shop no longer existed. I ran back to the office. The courtyard of the office building, which only the other day was filled with hundreds of queuing candidates, was now empty. Only a few fraud victims, such as myself, were hanging out there. One of them told us that his friend got such a certificate, presented it to the Germans only to be taken immediately to Umschlagplatz. No one knew where to find the organizers of the fraudulent campaign, and really, what good would that do?

Every day brought another curfew on another residential quarter, which was nicknamed "water boilers" (*kotły*), perhaps because everything inside them was boiling. The SS would surround a building or a whole block, getting all residents to come down to the courtyard and systematically search each apartment. Residents who had no proper papers were immediately designated for the next transport. They somehow never entered our apartment, but more than once, we anxiously stood in the courtyard waiting for the search in the neighboring building to end and for them to get to us. Aunt Basia, the newcomer from Kalisz, had no papers. That is why each time a "water boiler" was announced, she laid in the bed, hiding underneath numerous blankets, until the danger had passed. She cried, the poor woman, and said she preferred a bullet instead of suffocation. I didn't have any other choice but to go downstairs and wait. Mother asked for a paper from the shop confirming that I was about to be hired there as a regular worker. She got such a paper with no official stamp, which rendered it worthless with the Germans.

The ghetto streets were empty during the day. People worked or were in hiding from day to night. One day, I saw the face of ghetto beauty Hanka Javerbaum peeking into a store. She was the girlfriend of my friend Bobby Guttmann, but they separated due to the circumstances. She approached me. "Please help. Maybe you know some policeman who will marry me? If I don't find someone, they will take me to die straight away." I looked at her. Her hair was a mess, and she looked miserable and tattered. How could I help her? I myself barely managed to get away from the police and SS ambushes. I didn't tell her that, two days earlier, I had given Bobby a baptism certificate my brother had brought from Lvov. Bobby intended to escape but didn't know where to. He was born and lived in Berlin until his family was deported to Poland. Now he wanted to go back west. Years later, I learned he made it. He continued to use the name I gave him.

In order to meet the daily target of 6,000 Jews rounded up at the Umschlagplatz, they first emptied the deportee shelters, the "points" originally organized for the refugees from the various countries. Already, at the very beginning, most of them became paupers. Many of them readily joined the transports in the hope of getting the promised four kilos of bread, which seemed made of clay, and a kilo of watery carrot jam—the Germans still kept their promise, but very soon they stopped.

The "water boilers," the escapes, and the constant hiding became our daily routine. Whoever held some kind of certificate believed he would be saved. We stopped believing in the magic of paper when it was discovered that the Germans had kidnapped a shop worker's wife and put her on transport. It even happened to the relative of a cop. The cops themselves were protected—they did the dirtiest part of the job.

Within a couple of days, word was out in the ghetto that there is no work in the east and that the whole story was a bald-faced lie. The transport's destination was also discovered: Treblinka. The ghetto had new tragic heroes—those who managed to escape from the transports and returned. They described the traveling conditions to "the new life." Illusions were forever crushed. From now on, all discussed whether the Germans would settle for deporting 60,000 people from the ghetto—the original number discussed—and allow the others to stay. Meanwhile, families were shattered by the selection, which separated relatives—in the Umschlagplatz, a husband was looking for his wife, a son for his father. They were often found already behind the wagon's locked door, and nothing could be done.

I went to sleep and dreamed that when the morning came, this nightmare would be over. I woke up the next day, and the nightmare was still there, a reality.

Into the second week of the liquidation, I was staying with Mother in Shultz's shop on Leshno Street. The order came at noon. Everyone had to get out so the SS men could check on who was allowed to be in the protected compound. People exited the building and stood along its wall. On the pavement across the street, near a small table, stood the SS men, the Jewish cops, and a column of trucks awaiting the "passengers." People approached the table from both sides of the street in order to identify themselves. Even Mr. Shultz himself appeared and agreed with the soldiers that his workers should be checked at the shop entrance according to a list prepared by one of his employees. I was not on that list and had to take a stand before the SS man. Mother was pale as death, standing petrified against the wall. I said to myself: *Let the chips fall where they may, you only die once.* I believed the good star above would not desert me, although it didn't quite pamper me in the ghetto so far. I approached the table.

Near the young SS Scharführer (sergeant) stood a Jewish policeman. It was... Yurek! He was my cousin Irka's newlywed husband. Some years ago, we stayed with them after returning to Warsaw. The couple had just married in the ghetto but did not invite my brother and me to the very modest wedding—two portions saved. The young husband knew who we were; he noticed us from afar. When I approached the table, the German was already quite bored. He asked how old I was. I replied. At that moment, Yurek told him decisively, "Fritz, this is my cousin, you know what to do with him." The long days they spent together on the job of emptying apartments from people and property must have created some cordiality. Fritz knew what to do with me. He raised his hand to the left, which meant I was to go back to Shultz's people. Mother held my hand, completely shaking, and couldn't say a word. We returned home. I was no less upset. Not far from our apartment, a truck was still standing, ready to take me away. Other trucks, loaded with people, were already underway.

My great-aunt always knew how to take the initiative in crucial moments. She declared that such miracles do not happen every day and that I don't stand a chance here, perhaps for the better. They would exterminate all of us here sooner or later. She said that I must leave the ghetto the next morning because it was the only way. I was skeptical, although I agreed we did not stand a chance. Therefore, I proposed we shut the windows and switch the gas open on the cooking stove at night. She slapped my face fiercely and strictly commanded, "You must survive, to take out your brother and anyone else you can take—and, remember: You must avenge!"

I was given a few dozen złoty, my mother's tiny golden watch, and my parents' golden wedding rings, the out-of-fashion kind. Inside were still inscribed their initials and their wedding date: October 30, 1921. I would have given anything just to get them back!

The plan was simple. A Jewish cop would transfer me to the Jewish cemetery, and one of Pinkert's employees would take me to the guy who waited every morning on the other side of the wall. In exchange for 20 złoty, he would drive me to the East Warsaw train station. From there, I would continue to the town of Węgrów. This place was connected to my aunt, who joined us in February 1942, when she was forced to leave Kalisz, which was already "Jew-free" (*Judenfrei*). A young woman—Yashka Maliniak, the daughter of a Polish policeman—had transferred her to us.[1] Her father had been forced to hide since September 1939 because as it turned out he had arrested a German subject after the German invasion. The unlucky policeman, before escaping into the General Governorate territory, went into hiding in my uncle's apartment in the factory he then managed in Kalisz. He later managed to cross the border into the General Governorate and became a policeman once again and a detective in the Węgrów police force. His daughter went to him and smuggled my aunt across the border.[2]

Yashka was a brave, energetic, and kindhearted girl. She visited us in the ghetto several times. My senior aunt, the "tribe-chief," asked her once whether we could rely on them should conditions in the ghetto become impossible. She explained that she meant the two boys and the aunt Yashka had already saved once. Yashka replied that she thought it was possible and promised to talk about it with her father. On her next visit, we got a positive answer, but there was a reservation—on the condition that circumstances remain the same. We preferred not to delve into interpretations. She fancied some of my mother's and aunt's garments, so in return for dresses, shirts, and handbags, she brought us food, which was of crucial importance. The refuge issue was not discussed again.

I said farewell to Mother. I held her in a strong hug. I can't remember what she said and what I said. It was difficult for me to think straight.

So many thoughts ran in my head. My senior aunt said again, "You must survive! Avenge!" My uncle wept.[3]

I jumped over the cemetery wall. A fair-haired guy about my age stood on the other side and said, "Well, now we go to the tram, then to the train station. The trams near the ghetto are now occasionally checked, so we'll get on a bit further away." It was July 30 or 31, 1942. We walked for a long time; I don't remember which way. I don't recall how we got to the Hala Morowska food market. It was very early, and the streets were almost entirely empty. All peace and quiet. The stores on the other side of the street were closed—because of the early hours? Or was it Sunday? One store carried a sign: *"Obst und Gemüse"* (fruit and vegetables). Signs in German? On a Polish store? Are those the (new) rules? We got on the tram and arrived at the train station. My companion said he was going to the ticket office and returned with a ticket. I gave him 20 złoty. He wished me a safe journey and disappeared. I don't recall the train journey. The way from Łochów to Węgrów is about 30 kilometer. I got there at night time. I asked where Maliniak lived; they showed me. I knocked on the door and went in. Yashka welcomed me with no questions as if we had just parted yesterday. The next day, her father returned home. He spoke little. I asked at once what could be done for my brother and my aunt, whom he had known from Kalisz. He replied briefly, "Stay, watch, listen. There's not much we can talk about now." He was right, but I felt terrible.

After seven days, a postcard came by mail. It was from my senior aunt. Without stating any details, just one name, she reported briefly, "Basia is very ill and has to see a doctor immediately. We request an urgent appointment at the doctor's and that she'd be escorted to it." It was evident that my aunt was in clear danger and must be taken out from the ghetto and transferred to a safe place. The postcard did not mention other family members, so I deduced the shop was still active and sponsored my relatives. I decided not to let go of Maliniak and to keep on asking for help. I hoped that he kept in mind the days of hiding in Kalisz and would be therefore prepared to help us.

People around me were friendly. Since her mother was still held up in Kalisz, Yashka became the master of the house. Apart from her, there was her brother Yuzek, quite a go-getter, a few years my junior. They both tried to be nice, even cordial. They didn't cook during the days their father was out of the house. At times, we went to a neighboring field and collected small potatoes. Yuzek would go into an oil store owned by a Jew, say it was for Maliniak, and get a golden oil bottle. We grated the potatoes and fried fritters. Yashka and Yuzek had friends: a girl from the Wilna area, who was older than Yashka; her close friend, Leshek; their cousin, handsome Yanek; the affable Stashek; and another guy with a hunch.[4] For some reason, the latter won my almost full trust. All the others had engagements and activities, their entertainments. They were cheerful and enamored, which kept them busy. Whatever took place outside, their world was of lesser importance, if not of no importance at all. The fact that they were barely attentive to the plight of their country simply astonished me. The news about the Jews, the liquidation of the ghettos, the transports, the death camps—all occasionally surfaced in their conversations, and even then, only as bagatelle. They spoke with indifference of what was happening almost on their doorstep. They talked with other people as if these issues did not concern me, despite my presence. I found it hard to cope with these conversations. I often feared I would burst with tears or shout; nevertheless, I remained silent, only asking myself where I got the strength for it. I was concerned with the fact that everyone in the group knew about me. But they treated me as a friend. The days passed by cheerfully. How could I ruin the atmosphere? At night, I remained alone with my thoughts, keeping me awake.

Near Węgrów were the Treblinka camp and the train station. All transports from Warsaw went through Łochów. News of what was going on in Warsaw and Treblinka reached Węgrów too. For the people there, I was Maliniak's other cousin, and no one found it necessary to soften or censor in my presence about the stories about the Jews' extermination. I listened to everything and thought I'd go crazy.

I repeatedly asked if I could bring my aunt. So, as not to sound cheeky, I said in one of the conversations that as soon as I found a job, I'd be gone, and that probably wouldn't take long. He looked at me as if content with the idea that I wouldn't stay forever. He noted that soon his wife and two daughters would be arriving, and then it would indeed become quite crowded. However, he promised to think about how to bring "Mrs. Basia." The next day, he asked whether "Mrs. Basia" could pay if she'd be required to stay with someone else. I replied that she had some jewelry and property of good value near Kalisz. I didn't tell them about my aunt's big, most expensive diamond. I gave the valuables I brought with me to Yashka the next day. I later saw my mother's watch on her friend's wrist, the one from Wilna.

Yashka knew about the diamond, probably from my aunt herself. She simply went to Warsaw, entered the ghetto, and took my aunt out— that simple—with a lot of spunk and courage. Already, on the Aryan side, they had been approached by two men who presented themselves as cops. They threatened my aunt that if she didn't give them all she had, they would take them both to the Gestapo. My aunt unpicked the seam in her dress and gave them the 3.5-karat diamond. When they recounted that story in Węgrów, I could not help feeling that the whole event was planned in advance. My aunt had a kerchief over her head that covered all her dark hair. Her nose was straight, her lips were not plump, and the Polish she spoke was impeccable. What could suddenly arouse suspicion in the middle of the street that she was Jewish? I did not say a word. What good would that do? Before leaving Warsaw, they both visited a friend of my mother's. She bought my aunt's property from her. They drafted a handwritten sales agreement in front of a witness. The buyer paid a pitiable sum

96

of money in comparison to the property's real value. The sum served as my aunt's "maintenance expenses" with her hosts for a few months.

My aunt didn't know any details about life in the shops, what mother and my uncle do there, nor about Arthur's condition. During the past few weeks, she had been locked up in the apartment the whole day, lying in her bed, preparing to get covered at any moment. Nonetheless, she did know that Arthur's document was not to be relied on and that he had to be taken out of the ghetto urgently.

I decided to call Mom. In our house in Nowolipie Street lived David Kline, who was an official in the *Transferstelle* (the institution that handled the transport of goods from and into the ghetto). He owned a telephone, and I knew that they would call mom if I phoned her. I announced to Yashka what I intend to do. She said I'd better not tell this to her father. I went to the post office, gave the telephone number, and entered the phone booth. I heard a woman's voice was heard in the receiver. I asked her to call Mrs. Hanka from the first floor, and said it was urgent. I waited while on the other end of the phone they kept pacifying me every few minutes that everything was fine and she would be there any minute. They probably felt it was an emergency. And suddenly—mom's voice. As if she was standing right next to me, as if I could reach out and hug and kiss her, and be with her at once. She kept calm, although I could hear that her voice was trembling. She addressed me without disclosing she was speaking to her son. I addressed her with her name. I looked outside the booth window. The office worker was busy with her papers; she had no earphones on. Mom began by saying she wouldn't be able to talk for long. She said that everything was working out, more or less, but there was a serious "problem" with Arthur. His "illness" required "treatment" that was nowhere to be found on location. She could not refrain from asking how things were coming along with me. I replied that there were no problems and added that the aunt was safe and healthy. I didn't mention the diamond issue; they had enough problems in the ghetto as it was. Mom pressed a few times to finish our conversation, but I kept asking something new each time. Finally, she said she had to go. I asked once again, "And how are you doing?" She replied, "How I'm doing is completely unimportant." I couldn't help it and cried "Mommy!" but there was no reply.

I had to calm down. I approached the office worker to pay for the call —only a few pennies, since the Germans made the mail service affordable, almost free. She remarked, "Sir, you have called the Jewish living quarter." I pretended to be surprised. "Really? What do you know..." She explained, "Yes, sir. All the numbers in the Jewish quarter begin with the digit 7." I went on pretending to be astonished. "That's the first time I heard of this." I composedly put the change in my pocket, kindly parted from her, and went out unhurriedly to the street. I could not calm down for a long time, and not because of the post-office lady. I couldn't care what happened. I feared I would never again hear my mom's voice.

My landlord silently dismissed all my questions and hints regarding my brother. By now, he was already recounting everyday details about the ghettos, where they march columns of Jews to Treblinka, and where they are transported from by trains. He also knew where the fugitives from the trains were caught and what was done with them. He even mentioned the price demanded for a bottle of water by the boys standing at the points where the trains to Treblinka stop.

One day, Maliniak announced that he had organized a visit for me at his friend's house. They were supposed to find me a job. He emphasized that I should make an effort to make it succeed. I thanked him and promised I would do everything to make it happen. He replied, "Well, well..." It was not quite an expression of great faith that this effort would be a success.

It was mid-September. One night, I heard knocks on my window. Yuzek, who slept with me in the same room, also woke up. I asked who was there and I heard my brother's voice answering! I let him in, telling him I feared I had nothing to offer him to eat. He said he was not hungry, and he spoke no more than a few words. Our landlord asked from his room what was going on. He did not conceal his unhappiness about another newcomer. Yuzek said we must want to talk, so he would go and sleep in Leshek's room.

Finally, Arthur started talking; it didn't come easily. Mother had been robbed at the shop. They took her sewing machine and gave it to someone else. There were changes in the shop; it was reorganized with fewer workers. According to rumors, the Germans canceled some of their orders. People saw it as a sign that the ghetto would be liquidated. One day, all ghetto residents were rounded up into Muranowski Square with the aim of making another "selection," this time a "comprehensive one." Clearly, they had all been taken to the Umschlagplatz.[5] Many searched for hiding places. My brother had gone looking for a way out and found a breach in the wall. When he went back for Mother, she was no longer there. He jumped over the wall, just under the Ukrainian's nose—one of the guards who surrounded the ghetto. He had fled and made it to Węgrów. Now he was lying beside me.

I did not ask any more questions. We lay down with our eyes open till the morning.

An assembly point (the Umschlagplatz) in the Warsaw Ghetto for Jews rounded up for deportation. Warsaw, Poland, 1942–43. https://encyclopedia.ushmm.org/content/en/photo/assembly-point-in-the-warsaw-ghetto?parent=en%2F5199

KSAWERÓW

Maliniak's wife and two daughters arrived, and at once, the house became very crowded. The lady dominated the house while my aunt assisted, her chores increasing gradually—that is despite the fact she regularly paid for her "sustenance" from the day she arrived.

One of the lady's two adult daughters was Christina, a bit younger than Yashka, who immediately caught Stashek's enthusiastic interest. The third daughter was a little girl, so different from the other family members that I doubted she was their biological offspring.

But I had other problems. Maliniak sent me to the flour mill near Łochów, whose owner was a friend of his and was supposed to find me a job. I got an old bicycle with no license number. When I asked what I should do in case they checked my bike license, the landlord looked at me as if saying, "If these are your questions, how would you cope with serious problems?"

Clearly, the three of us couldn't all sit in the same place, even if it was a policeman's house. Presented as Maliniak's cousins, we said we also hail from the Kalisz area. It wasn't easy to check these details—a border separated the German Reich from the General Governorate.

Our weak spot was the documents—Maliniak looked at our coachman papers scornfully.

I hung around the mill and the yard for three days. If not for Maliniak, they would have thrown me out earlier. Wagons loaded with wheat sacks came in every day. Bunches of villagers stood smoking and conversing near the mill—a great opportunity to meet some friends, hear some news and drink vodka. I had nothing to do there. On Tuesday at supper, the mill owner asked me if I thought I could find a job that suited my capabilities. I had no answer. He went on to say, "If you were a village boy, I would have let you carry sacks. But you're a city boy, a school graduate. There's talk about the central wheat-grinding activity for the Germans being moved here. There'll be a lot of office work to be done. When it does, I'll notify Mr. Maliniak." We parted.

The next day, I was on my way in the early morning. Instead of turning to Węgrów, I headed north, to Małkinia. I wished to delay my return as much as possible. I rode along the railroad tracks. It was all empty and quiet, so I could think peacefully. What would I do? How would I solve our problems before they threw us out? I had no answers.

A cargo train stood on a side track between the towns of Ostrówek and Sadowne. Ukrainian guards walked around it, shouting at the kids who tried to approach the train with bottles in their hands. Only then did I notice the hands stretching out of the wagon's narrow windows sealed with barb wire—hands begging for water. The kids tried to confuse the guards and hand the water to the pleaders in exchange for something. I heard calls: "Jews, throw a watch!" I was frozen in place. I could not move. One of the Ukrainians suddenly lowered his gun, pointing it at one of the "smugglers." The latter dropped the bottle while escaping. I picked up the bottle from the grass. The engine's whistle was heard, the train moved, and the guards jumped aboard. I stood petrified with the bottle in my hand. I picked up the bicycle and headed to Węgrów. I didn't have the energy to think—hardly had any energy at all. I recalled my brother's smile as we parted, a sad smile of helplessness. I only wished to find a deserted spot in the woods and fall asleep. Not to think.

I arrived in Węgrówearly at noon. There were carts loaded with baskets standing on the road. Among them strolled women with bundles on their backs and baskets in their hands. The coachmen stood in a small bunch, vigilantly discussing something. "What happened?" I asked one of them. "Well, the Germans are taking all the Jews out of the village. They were taken to the stadium, and now they're looking for the escapees. They surrounded the town and didn't let anyone in. There won't be a market today." I was breathless. It was to be expected, and still, I didn't expect it to happen so soon. My first thought was that my brother and aunt were in a safe place. They would not look there. But what about me? As if the farmer heard my question, he said, "Well, if you reside here, you can enter. They let the locals in." *That's all I need now*, I thought to myself, *to hand myself into their hands*. I told him I didn't have the proper bicycle papers and they could take it from me. He wondered: "Who owns bicycle papers?" He talked no more, and neither did I. I turned away. I needed to distance myself to a quiet place and think over what I needed to do.

I recalled Yulek, who used to visit Maliniak's house. He lived in the vicinity. Before the war, he worked in Warsaw as a waiter assistant, which earned him some credit in the village. At the onset of the war, he returned home but dreamed about city life. He didn't want to be a farmer. I didn't know how he became acquainted with the Maliniaks. He used to come by, bringing eggs and butter with him. The young folks befriended him, and he knew Arthur and me as Yashka and Yuzek's cousins. I couldn't tell him that the restaurant where he worked in Ziviecz was near our street. Yulek once said that his father pressured him to stay in the village and help with farm work, but he refused. He found another occupation: digging water wells. The salary was fair, and meals were included. Since Mrs. Maliniak arrived, his visits became more frequent. They always had orders for dairy products and eggs. He once remarked that I could always drop by his house if I was around. We could go out in the evenings to meet girls. "There are some eligible and educated girls there." I didn't know his last name and in which village he lived. He once said that on the way to Węgrówhe, he stopped in Karolew. I remembered that name. I decided to find Yulek on some pretext and stay there and see how things developed. I rode to Karolew. In the woods, I bumped into an old woman carrying dry tree sprays. She knew about whom I was asking. "Yes, there's one who digs wells. Must be from Ksawerów. When you get to Czerwonka, they will give you more details." I rode to Czerwonka. Already before arriving at the village, I learned about Yulek: he stayed with his father. Father Suchetzki would have preferred that his eldest son works for him, but the youngster didn't like fieldwork. He dug wells. Apparently, he was not home on weekdays.

There was no one at the Suchetzki house. I went around the yard and saw a girl next to a grazing cow. I asked how I could find Yulek and got a strange reply. It seemed the girl had some brain damage, and I couldn't understand her, though I did gather that the father and brother were plowing in the field. Yulek was nearby, in a house near a willow tree. I rode for about a mile and found the house near the willow, but it was empty. Suddenly, I saw a shovel lift in the air. I turned around and saw Yulek in a shoulder-deep pit. He was amazed to see me. I told him the Germans forbad anyone from coming into Węgrów until the operations were completed.

That's why I thought I'd check up on him. I didn't realize his amazement was mostly at the fact that I managed to find him without actually knowing where he lived. People in the village know everything about each other and readily notified guests. I proposed to Yulek that I'd help him in his work. "No way! Why should you get dirty?" Someone was supposed to help him dig but didn't show up, so he dug alone and is almost done. The landlady would be back shortly to prepare supper. He intended to introduce me to his father and brothers. We could go out later. I didn't really feel like it but did not refuse. I felt Yulek would gladly introduce me to his family and neighbors.

The Suchetzki family house was just an ordinary farmer's house. It was surrounded by an area of 7 morgen fields.[1] Zosia, the youngest daughter, ran the house after their mother passed away. The father looked like a tolerant man who mostly listened and spoke little. He listened to the youngsters converse with a warm smile. Both Zosia and her brother Czesiek were younger than Yulek and helped their father with the fieldwork. They were handsome and cheerful and happily received the new guest. The next older sister was Hela, the mentally disabled girl. She lovingly looked at her older sister and followed her orders. There was an ambiance of mutual understanding in the house.

Yulek introduced me as a friend, a relative of the Maliniaks from Poznań. He added that I would be staying with them "for a while." They accepted it doubtlessly. If I'm already there, why not stay for a few days. The father agreed silently, and Zosia said, "There's plenty of room for guests and enough food, only we don't eat like where you come from. You'll have to do with that." She said it with a mischievous smile and open admiration. She certainly was a pretty girl.

Things kept happening until I could hardly keep up with the pace. I was cautious not to talk too much, but I had to answer a few questions posed by the landlord. I half-heartedly said that my brother and I were deported in 1940 from our city after refusing to identify as Germans. In the Węgrówthere area, there were villager families who were expelled for the same reason from the western Polish regions, which were annexed to the Reich. Locals here disliked the foreigners and mocked their language and manners. Zosia remarked, "You are not like them. One can instantly see you're a city boy." My host did not ask which city it was that I came from.

I was welcomed as a guest. In the evening I met their cousin. Later on, we became close friends. That evening there was no time left for long conversations. Yulek insisted on going out to the next village in order for me to meet a "female friend." I had no choice; I rode after him.

The visit was unsuccessful and didn't last long. The girls were busy with another guest from another town. I thought it was useless to sit there expecting to gain their attention, so we left. Yulek was disappointed. While riding back, he remarked that I didn't have to be so modest. "You came from a place farther away, and you are educated. Their friend was not worth the fuss. They should have gotten rid of him." He mentioned something else. In the next village, they were about to drain a big meadow and were looking for workers to do the job. It's a matter of a few thousand złotys, but he himself will not be eligible for this job. "You could present yourself as an engineer who is familiar with the subject and get the job. I will do the actual work, and we could split the pay." I had to explain to him that the youngest engineer had to be at least 23-24 years of age, and I don't look that old. They would ask to see credentials. Just the very thought of it gave me shivers—what would I show them? Such a job requires approval from the district agriculture office, and they would be checking all the necessary papers. My reasoning worked. Yulek was convinced, though with much disappointment.

A few days went by. How could I get any news about Węgrów? I tried to get some details. Allegedly, Węgrów was emptied—the ghetto was devoid of its inhabitants. The houses were looted; any high-value property was taken by the Germans. The Ukrainians and the local cops took what was left. Whatever wasn't looted was thrown and scattered in the streets. Rumor had it that the Jews concealed a great deal of gold and jewelry inside the houses' walls. Now they were about to take apart every wall and stove in search of the treasures.

I proposed that Yulek and I go to Węgrów. He didn't feel like it. He preferred to stay and go to church on Sunday on the pretext that we would meet "some guys and girls in the church gallery." I tried to object, claiming I had no proper clothes for such an event since I took no spare clothes with me. Yulek insisted. "You look elegant enough." His father intervened by saying, "It's not proper to be seen in church with casual dress. Youths today do not deem it important to dress properly for church. They don't know you here. And if you're thinking of staying here for some time, even for a short while, you'd better go back to Węgrów and get some proper clothes. When you get back, you'll make it just in time for mass and also for what Yulek has in mind—drinking vodka with the guys in the inn after mass." This long speech surprised me coming from the father since it implied that I was welcomed to stay for a while longer.

I rode my bike to Węgrów. I did not come across any Germans on my way, nor Ukrainians. Of the ghetto, there were only piles of filth and neglect left, mostly from the dismantled walls and diggings. It could be seen at a distance.

My aunt said nothing. She was tired from the kitchen and laundry work. My brother whispered to me that he wished to help her in her work but feared it might be interpreted as a protest—many eyes inspected us, some of them unsympathetic ones. He was broken. They watched behind the wall how the Jews had been drawn out of their homes and how they shot whoever tried to escape on the way to the stadium. The Germans also announced that for any one person who escaped, they would kill ten. Nevertheless, many managed to hide. There was talk that every cop's house had "a few Jews of its own"—all of them rich ones who could pay for the shelter. It was clear for my brother that our presence stands in Maliniak's way to become easily rich. I told him what I went through and what the chances of finding shelter in the village are. I tried to encourage him and said, "Soon, we will find shelter outside Węgrów." I told the landlady we had found a place to stay for both my brother and myself, but I had a problem—I needed clothes. I left home while it was summer, and now it was already fall. I also asked to keep the bike. I would pay for everything when I started working. She was quite content and said I need not pay anything. "We will look into Yuzek's clothes if anything fits you. Don't even mention the bike. Of course, we want to help you." She remarked that three people crammed together are indeed too much. "Now everyone around has big eyes. We will be in touch should you need anything, don't hesitate to turn to us."

Yuzek told me privately that there was talk in the village that his father was keeping a sanatorium for Jews. He thought that every one of them was doing the same while taking large sums of money from the escapees. What would be their fate? People keep talking, and the German police are everywhere. Sooner or later, they would take action. Yuzek indicated he only said what he heard from his father and others. This was very important. I understood that I had to urge arrangements for Arthur. Obviously, I had to do something for both him and my aunt simultaneously. Despite the feeling of urgency, I could not openly initiate something. How, then, should I operate?

In Ksawerów, I was welcomed heartily as a desired guest. This was a relief after the cold atmosphere in Węgrów. My hosts boasted of my presence in front of the villagers. I knew I couldn't let them down. I tried to behave as naturally and humbly as possible since such behavior wins greater appreciation. I offered again to help Yulek in his work. He refused. "But I have to do something," I claimed. "And what did you do in Węgrów?" he replied. I explained that in Węgrów I was a guest. We are not so close. Maliniak looked for a job for me and sent me to the flour mill, where I was to handle paper supplies. But nothing came out of this, and now Maliniak was offended by my departure and no longer wanted to help me get a job. I tried not to lie about too many details. Yulek recalled that in one of the district's villages, there was a guy whose job was to supervise the mandatory wheat supply for the Germans. It was called "contingents." Yulek suggested we go to him. They would actually hold a party in that village, so we might as well talk to the district guy about some work for me.

I had serious doubts over whether working for the local German administration was not a too cheeky idea, but I could not turn down this opportunity. That being said, the fact is that in these offices, most of the workers were Poles. So we set off.

Our destination was a village mostly populated by former Polish gentry families, who had become impoverished throughout the generations, and now live like simple peasants. However, they had preserved the tradition by which they must distance themselves from other unadorned folks. They tried to marry among themselves much as possible. Their family coats of arms, inherited by their forefathers, were hung in a specially designated place in their homes. This region inhabited quite a few such "noble villages." The man we were going to meet was Mikhail Kosieradzki, whose name was derived from the Kosierady village. He was about 23 years old, tall, and skinny. In our conversation, he proudly noted that he had graduated from school before the war. For a son of a farmer from the Podlasie sand-dunes area, this was quite an achievement. He further noted that he meant to study in university, but the war disrupted his plans. He found himself working in the district agriculture department in Sokołów. His department supervised the mandatory supplies for the Germans. This involved rushing those who were behind in paying their dues and required travel from one village to another. Failure to comply with the German injunctions incurred fines and even heavier penalties. Yulek talked about me as if he had known me for years. He added: "It's a pity to waste such a guy in fieldwork." Mikhail asked how many years I had studied and how well I spoke German. I replied, "Some knowledge in German is very common where I come from." Our host nodded his head with understanding. Then he started to think aloud. "Getting work at the district offices is no easy task. It is better that they see you in advance to make getting the job easier." Therefore, Mikhail offered me an informal job as his assistant during his trips between villages. There was a lot of paperwork involved, but the main thing was to be present out there since both the supervisors' presence was crucial. He said he would try to obtain a temporary assistant's certificate, although it would not be a formal one. If I consented to this proposal, I could start working as soon as Monday. I replied I needed a day or two to think it over since I had another proposal, but his was more appealing. We determined that should I decide to work with him, I should report on Monday morning. It was Saturday. That evening, we went to a ball, and I met some new people, one of whom was Mikhail's cousin. I found it hard to believe I could still hang out, even have a good time.

Yulek thought my reply to Mikhail was proper. "Don't let him think you jump at the first offer. He obviously thinks of upgrading his own status—the official that has an assistant." I also suspected that was the purpose of his offer, but in my case, it didn't really matter. The most important thing was that I not sit idle. My hosts did not let me work in the field. They claimed it was beneath their dignity to make a guest work. How long could I go on this way? With Mikhail, I could move from one place to another. That was crucial. The full board included in the job's benefits was another advantage. The appearance of a district administrative official would grant position and safety, at least for some time. I would see how things worked out. I hoped that if I sustained several weeks in this work, I could bring Arthur to Ksawerów with me.

The first week, Mikhail did not quite meet my expectations. My boss wasn't very talkative. However, when you spend days and nights together, you get to know each other even without words. I could drink vodka better than him. He had some stomach problem, so I "officially" drank for both of us with the village chief. In the villages, as everywhere, one wins appreciation and honor when one can drink. I remembered when I should stop drinking and start eating so that I would not get drunk. I also quickly mastered the paperwork to Mikhail's satisfaction. He himself was not too happy with his work and tried to convince me that someone had to do it. "Government officials work not only for the Germans but also for the citizens." I had no quarrel with this approach. As far as I was concerned, it was a political issue with which I didn't argue.

On the second day of our visit, a farmer's wife knocked on our door. My boss came on strong with her family since they hadn't delivered the required crop quota. Their farm was, in fact, one of the wealthier ones in the village. Mikhail threatened to fine them. I came out to speak to her, and she requested that we annul the fine, and her husband would deliver the first part of their debt that week. In return, "the master," that is me, would receive 100 złoty and "resolve everything with supervisor Mikhail." I answered that I had to find out if there was still a possibility to annul the fine. I went inside and told Mikhail about the offer. His reaction was clear cut: "Tell her such a sum more suits the church donations plate. She should think it over." I returned to the lady. I already knew what was expected of me and the procedure's details. Finally, I received 250 złoty and was told that on the day of our departure, there would be two geese waiting for us, clean and salted. The intensive work week yielded satisfactory results. I understood why Mikhail never raised the subject of salary.

In Ksawerów, it was already common knowledge that Suchetzki's guest was dealing with contingents—that is, working in the district office. I knew some people from the village but preferred to keep my distance. Some guys used to visit us, but it was clear that only Zosia was of interest to them. They looked at me with curiosity and envy that was hard to hide. One evening, a woman turned up at our door. She was from the village and said her request to annul the fine imposed by the district was repealed, but her husband died recently, and she was not familiar with what to do. She asked if I could help her. I told her I was new in the office, but I thought she had to write a convincing appeal. I read all the papers and notes and drafted an orderly and reasoned request. The woman offered to reward me for my effort, but I kindly refused. "I don't take money from a neighbor for writing letters." The woman was content, and so were the house residents. Czeshik, who until now kept his distance, determined agreeably: "This is a guest deserving of our hospitality, will help folks without reward." He was proud of me. My appeal helped, and they promised to waive the fine. My reputation became widespread in the village and its surroundings, and as a result, many other help-seekers appeared on our doorstep.

On Sunday, I went to church—not at nine o'clock with Yulek, but at seven with his father. The old man said decisively, "Yanek is a newcomer. He has to get acquainted with the community, its elders, the priest. Those who go at nine o'clock are guys who only wish to stay briefly and slip away to the pub for a drink. The farm owners, the serious folk, go at seven. This time, Yanek will come with me; he can later do as he wishes." It was clear that he wanted to introduce me to his friends, neighbors, and the priest and win a cordial welcome. And so it was. I also got to meet the priest. He glanced at me curiously, asked a few questions, and hardly listened to my answers. Apparently, he had already heard of me since he remarked something about the contingents, which were very high that year. The visit to the church was successful, and Father Suchetzki was very content.

The next week, Mikhail decided to go out working only on Tuesday, so I had another free day at my disposal. I remarked that I had to see my brother, and Zoshia said simply, "Tell him to come to us for a while. When you return on Saturday, you can both meet here." She spoke in the presence of her father and brother, so I knew they did not object. I thanked her and did not bring up the subject again. On Saturday, I went with Yulek to Węgrów. What I found there didn't seem to look that bad. And, still, my brother whispered in my ear we had to get away from there as soon as possible. The Maliniaks openly remarked that their house was too crowded, and it was becoming

112

inconvenient. Arthur said they wanted to hide a local Jew in their house. He was in temporary hiding at the moment but had to be transferred from there to them until he found a permanent hiding place. This protégé was very rich, and that could explain it. My aunt sufficed in saying that should Arthur move to another place, her situation would become easier. I found her tired and tattered. I was exasperated since I was helpless. I felt like a boat lost in a stormy sea.

The three of us returned to Ksawerów on two pairs of bikes. My brother sat in front of my bicycle, trying to appear calm, yet, his nerves were on edge. He completely lacked self-confidence. I stayed with him in Ksawerów for two more days and then left for work on Tuesday. I tried to encourage him, to boost his self-confidence, but to no avail. We received a warm welcome at the house, and very swiftly, everyone turned to their daily chores. On Monday, they went to their work and did not agree that he would help them. They said the work season in the field was over anyway, so there was practically no need for helping hands. When we parted, my brother looked like a lost child.

In those days, it began to appear to me that Yulek envied me for my work travels. He complained that when I return, I'm too tired to hang out with him. He was right. I willingly stayed home. I brought something from each trip—a goose, a duck, some honey. Everyone praised my haul, but undoubtedly, I had to pay more attention to Yulek. "Perhaps we should go to a ball?" I suggested. In response, he proposed that we hold a house party. A harmonica player would have to be invited at a cost of 120 złoty. I told him we could spend that sum. We decided he would call the harmonica player, and I would bring liquor from town. I already knew vodka was served on such occasions. The party was open to all: for people from the neighboring villages as well, only they had to bring their own refreshments—each place and its customs.

When I returned the following week, I found my brother in deep despair. He was sitting alone in the granary and immediately said he had come to the conclusion that we had no chance to make it together. In the village, he was already suspected to be a Jew; the boys in the village told him this to his face. He decided to leave. If he didn't, we would both die. The granary was dark. My brother sat on the beam above me. I kneeled down and embraced his feet. I tried to explain, to persuade him to do something together with me. Of course, we had to react harshly to any insult. I still didn't know how, but I would think of something. We must keep cool and quiet. If we did not succeed, we would both flee together. But why give up now? We were both emotional. I asked him to describe what the two guys that called him a Jew looked like. He described them to me and knew their names. I was relieved. These two "didn't count" in the village.

My father's photo on his coachman work certificate,
1941

My father's photo during his work in the Sokołów
District administration

We held the party on Saturday night. All furniture was taken out of the living room, and only benches were left along the walls. Valuables were also removed in case of theft. The player arrived carrying a huge harmonica with "120 bases." He was already somewhat drunk. I mentioned it to Yulek. "He's always like that," he responded, "otherwise, he will not play well." And, indeed, he played and drank all night, although he wasn't any drunker than all the other guests. Alternately, I drank well and made it evidently clear that I was drunk. The vodka had its effect, although I was in control of my deeds and words. People knew that the party organizers were Yulek and me, so I gained the position of host. They also knew that I worked for the district office, work considered to be extraordinary here.

In a matter of two hours, it became mayhem. The majority of the guests came to blows with each other under the influence of vodka. I went out since I meant to confront the two who attacked my brother in the first place. I was lucky to find that one of them was already involved in the fight. His friend was there too. As the host, I had the privilege to respond to the riot. I approached, shoving the rioters aside aggressively in order to get to the center of the fight. I faced the guy who was my target. "What is this row about? You can rage all you like at your place, not at a decent party. But can't you behave like a man? Remember what you shouted at my brother? Have you any idea what one replies when someone calls you a Jew?! If you don't, I will sure teach you right now!" I neared him, shoving away those who tried to separate us; I broke a peg from the fence and hit the guy forcefully. He was a head taller than me, weighed some ten kilos more, and could have made meatballs out of me. But, for some months, I had been eating well and was no longer the skinny boy from the ghetto. I knew perfectly what the game was about, and the alcohol had its effect too. I raised my hand again, and the guy began to run away, followed by his friend. I chased them, striking a few more blows.

Upon my return, I was welcomed by laughing faces. I was their entertainment for the night. There is no such thing as a party without any blows, but when a guy from the city hits a guy from the village, much bigger and stronger than himself, in front of the whole village—this was unprecedented. "You sure gave him what he deserved," they praised me. Among the cheerers was Czeshik; the whole affair was to his liking. Once again, I scored points in my favor. We went back in, and he and his cronies were offered good vodka, not just homemade liquor.

The party was a success. It was the talk of the town. One boy about my age, Yurek Malinek, approached me. He wanted to get to know me since he, too, worked in the district office. It turned out he was in charge of one of the sanitary teams who wandered from one village to another, disinfecting against lice. They would disinfect everything in the house with a sulfur stove. I explained to my "colleague" that I had just begun working. I would be formally employed within a few weeks. That didn't change his attitude toward me. The agriculture department was one of the important ones in the German district committee (*Kreisleitung*), with no comparison to the sanitary department. Yet, I was most fascinated with the sanitary department

116

where he had worked. I inquired about what the work there was like. He replied in detail. They work in teams of three to four people; the head of the team must complete a professional course. He himself was about to be sent to such a course. Most of the workers came from the nearby villages. I asked whether they were looking for new recruits. He was surprised. "You're not thinking of changing your job for a wandering job like ours, are you?" I made it clear that I was looking for a job for my brother. We had family in this area, and we wished to settle down here. One has to settle somewhere, and ever since we had been expelled from the Reich, we kept wandering from one place to another. The story seemed convincing. Yurek was of the opinion that a job could be arranged for a guy such as Arthur. They were currently assembling new working teams, and they must be looking for an educated guy. Although Yurek himself was satisfied with his job, he asked what would happen should Arthur dislike the "stinking" work. The job was safe, and you could organize your life with no special effort.

That same evening, Yurek spoke with my brother. They appeared to get along quite well. When I got back from my travels a week later, my brother was already a formal employee of the sanitation department of the Sokołów-Węgrów district. He received a certificate with a photo as well as approval to carry out mandatory disinfections. He was told he would soon be sent to a head-of-team course. I inquired about his meeting with the official who interviewed him. "Nothing special," he replied. He had to explain why he had worked as a coachman, and he resolved it by saying he had to make a living once we had been deported from the city. "Obviously," he was later employed in various jobs, and the certificate remained. It made sense to the disinfection supervisor. The rest was surprisingly easy. Arthur was worried about the course: where and when it would take place, but he was already reassured and grew more self-confident. Having gathered practical experience with Yurek for a week, he began to travel as an independent head of the team. The villages he visited provided him with meals and accommodation. Every farmer was grateful that the "director" agreed not to throw his best Sunday outfit into the sulfur stove. The gratitude was expressed as customary. The team members returned after a week with cash in their pockets. Some, like Arthur, even stayed in the village for the weekend if it happened to be a long distance from home.

The district Mikhail and I were in charge of included several communities (or regional councils), whose center was situated in the town of Kosów Lacki. I soon became familiar with the favorable accommodation possibilities, cheap meals, and where cheap provisions, such as soap or shoe paste, could be found. We tried to sleep where we worked; it was usually convenient and free. We often sat at the local pub, meeting with the agronomist with whom we coordinated our work plan. Sometimes, a local resident invited "the gentlemen from the district" for a drink. The pub owner knew us and treated us as distinguished gentlemen. These small benefits made our lives easier and enabled me to assimilate better into my surroundings.

Despite what appeared to be a "normal" life, I could not forget that all that time, I was a mere 5 to 10 kilometer away from the Treblinka concentration camp. Most of the transports passed through Łochów and Węgrów. The route passing through Sokołów was often less in use. From the neighboring towns, the columns of Jews were led by foot. By now, those operations were all over. The ghetto in Węgrów was one of the last to be liquidated. In the villages we visited, the extermination of the Jews was not discussed. The silence seemed like collusion. It was astounding, as if nothing was happening. I assumed the subject was discussed privately at home, among themselves. Nevertheless, everywhere we called upon, life carried on as if no one knew that a stone's throw from them, there was a genocide going on. Only in the villages of Wólka Okrąglik and Guty, which are situated about one and a half kilometers from Treblinka, did they incidentally mention the neighboring camp. The village chief warned that the wind carried a stench from the crematoriums.

In the village of Guty, Mikhail asked one woman how she would catch up with her dues of grain supply. She replied that since her husband died, she did not work in the field. The village chief confirmed that she was widowed at an early age and earned her living as a prostitute for the Ukrainian guards in the nearby camp. They visited her regularly and paid generously for her services. Someone mentioned how Ivan pulled out a handful of banknotes from his boot. Mikhail inquired whether the village was somehow connected to the camp, whether they provided the Germans with any services. They replied that the camp was entirely secluded; the Germans did not allow anyone to come near the fences and didn't let anyone in since they were in need of nothing and had a sufficient workforce on the site. Just recently, there had been some prisoners who managed to escape, but by nighttime, they were all captured. That same day, they found a woman stark naked, and in the morning, the Germans took her too. I listened to these stories, struggling not to make any movement that might reveal my feelings. Was I numb? I tried to explain to myself that right now, I needed to think of how to assist my brother and possibly my aunt too. Helping my aunt became a bigger problem by the day.

I prayed devoutly. In the church, it was an easier task because no one looked at you there. I knew how to overcome my feelings and think level-headedly, unlike at the beginning when I arrived in Węgrów, and I often feared I could not take it anymore.

I visited Węgrów occasionally in order to see my aunt. It was important that she knew she was in our thoughts and that we loved her and feared for her fate. But these visits left no room for optimism. My aunt did not complain but occasionally remarked that she did not believe she would survive, and she was getting used to the idea. In one of my visits, Maliniak told me he had recently been in Warsaw and met a friend from Kalisz who was a cop. The friend told him he was in the ghetto and bumped into Yuzek Kempner, my uncle. The latter told him he remained alone since just the other day they took

119

his wife and sister- in law—my mother. My uncle added that he knew he only had a few days left. Maliniak was in Warsaw at the end of October. What he heard confirmed our assumptions. That was the last news we ever heard of our mother and the rest of the family.

Mikhail muttered once that he was having difficulties arranging my job officially. I had nothing to say; somehow, I felt perhaps it was for the better, avoiding discussions and inquiries about me. I felt calm hanging around the environment into which I had already assimilated by virtue of my behavior and personality. We often sat the three of us—Mikhail, the local agronomist, and me. The agronomist was an educated and friendly young man, yet, I realized a few times he was examining me. I decided to react. I began treating him less friendly, and when we raised a glass—nothing happened there without liquor—I said bitterly that had my father seen what I was doing, he would have banished me. Both my friends were astonished. "Gentlemen," I said firmly, "my father is a reserve officer who is now in a prison camp while I'm trying to collect contingents for the Germans." They began to justify themselves and explain that almost everyone had someone in a prison camp. Should the Germans decide, they can make us work for them. From that moment on, they treated me with greater respect, but I was concerned. I hated giving away details about myself. The less they knew, the better.

More than two months had gone by, and Mikhail admitted he could not obtain a certificate of approval for my work. He thought he should let me know. It was not yet a formal notice about the end of my work but definitely a foreword for our separation in due course. The winter was near, and there was no work for two. I told him there was no need to worry; I was not worried either. I would manage. Since then, I only visited him upon being invited.

Yulek decided he had dug enough wells and would like to join the disinfection teams too. His father mocked him, saying he did not like to work hard, but he was glad he was walking in Arthur's footsteps. Arthur quite quickly secured his position, and his superiors were content with his work. He took care of his team members and distributed the "incomes" fairly. Some workers even asked to be on his team, especially some women.

In the fall of 1942, the Germans determined that all General Governorate residents had to obtain new certificates. Each resident had to apply personally to the census bureau under German supervision. At first, the residents did not take the new certificate (*Kennkarte*) seriously, and when they were commanded to present it, they said they still hadn't got it.[2] But, as time went by, more and more people possessed this document, which made Arthur and me very concerned. In order to obtain this document, one had to present either a birth or baptism certificate, which we did not possess. As long as I accompanied Mikhail, I had less need for it, but my brother often had to identify himself. We didn't know how to solve the problem.

Miss Jadwiga from the village of Czerwonka, a serious and pleasant girl, worked at the local district office. She was introduced to my brother at a friend's meeting near the church after mass. She patronized most boys in the village, yet liked my brother, who often visited her at her house. She once asked him why he was so depressed, and he told her that he had sent a letter home to the Reich, asking for his birth certificate, but to no avail. That was why he could not obtain the new Kennkarte in Sokołów. Her response was unexpected: "Why in Sokołów? At my office, we issue similar certificates to all the residents. It is my job. As a Ksawerów resident, you are entitled to issue a certificate here."

"And what about the birth certificate?" he asked.

"You are so punctual, just like all these Poznań people," she replied. "So many people don't have birth certificates! You write down a protocol, and two witnesses sign it. Many people around here are misplaced and refugees! You'd have to bring two photos... and one for me." After a week, my brother had a real German identity card—a great achievement in itself. Miss Jadwiga got the photo she desired.

Our stay in Ksawerów was extended. A brief visit became a long stay. No one could tell how and when we became part of the Suchetzki household. We tried to limit our presence in the house as much as we could so as not to exploit the hearty welcome, but it was not always possible. Luckily enough, we both found jobs quickly and so could be absent for long periods of time. I returned home on Sundays, and my brother appeared after longer periods. We soon gained the family's confidence, especially that of the father, but also that of Zosia and Czesik. We also won Yulek's confidence, only his counted less than could be expected from an elder son. I would never know what they really thought of us, yet, I felt they cordially related to us as if we were close family members. At times, this hearty relation even surprised me. They knew we had nothing and that they could not expect any material advantages—none whatsoever. Did they guess anything? Even today, I find this question hard to answer. At times it appeared they didn't want to know. They respected our privacy and did not ask questions, but that was the common custom in the village. Neighbors in the village had known each other for many years and knew much about each family. We knew the village was inspecting us; however, we were both such authentic Poles that even had a doubt been raised, the immediate response would be that we were different since we were city boys. We often had doubts as to whether it was fair to put the family at risk, but we didn't have a choice. The house and its address were crucial to our survival.

We dedicated much thought to self-criticism, which consisted not only of what to say but also how to say it. That mostly meant refraining from using words and phrases that are considered too sophisticated, which was typical for Jews, as well as too much gesturing, face mimicking, and expression of feelings—all characteristics by which Jews could be identified. Our prayers had also been examined. Most youths in the village were not too pious, a fact that quite astonished us. Our kneeling while praying morning and evening was only admired by Hela, the mentally disabled sister. Zosia and Czesik did not express their opinion; perhaps they were a little surprised. Yulek ridiculed our piety. We agreed among us that we should gradually moderate our piety. At that time, we would pray silently. We analyzed our behavior. We were aware that our profile more resembled Jewish features than did our faces. Accordingly, we made an effort to face the person we were talking to. We also tried, as much as was possible, not to appear together; while separate, we exhibited less resemblance to Jews.

An entire study had been dedicated to hairstyle, hair straightening, and haircuts.

We examined ourselves closely every day, every hour, every meeting or conversation. At the same time, we were directors and actors in our own show. During encounters with people, we constantly contemplated what we could and could not say, how to say it, and how to express something in different situations. We later discussed how this or that person looked at us, how he behaved, of whom we should be skeptical or worse, who should we suspect. Such analysis took place every day and, with time, became second nature. It was a burdening nature, an exhausting and discouraging one.

At the same time, we had decided on a means of behavior: the surer you were of yourself, the more convincing you were to your surroundings. Anytime you could, try to be self-assured, strong, emanating calm and invulnerability. We developed a knack for improvisation. Sometimes, we had to add or augment some detail in our life stories. Occasionally, we were asked about our parents or our home. We coordinated the tiniest details among us.

Toward the end of November, I mostly stayed home. Mikhail's travels had practically ended. Once or twice, he had asked me to accompany him to a village that did not meet the quotas properly, and for which he was reprimanded. Once, he asked that we go to another district town by train in order to meet some girl, and for that purpose, he needed the pretext of traveling on the job. I was to be the cover for his travel. I was very angry but eventually, put up with my role. After all, it's better than staying at home and thinking about which subject should be discussed or not.

In that period, I grew closer to Yulek's father. He was no great chatterbox but liked his conversations with me. He did not try to squeeze any details I didn't mention, and yet, I felt his sympathy. Moreover, he once said he valued the fact that I did not condescend. Most city people unjustifiably consider themselves better than the villagers. They thought that a farmer who could barely read and write didn't understand anything. Nothing was further from the truth! He thought I was different despite being more knowledgeable than Mikhail, and I would have done a better job than him if only given a chance. Perhaps it was better I didn't. People in the village had long memories. "After the war, you will return to your city, but Mikhail will forever be remembered as forcing farmers to deliver crops to the Germans. The fact that he hailed from a noble family would not make the situation any easier for him."

In one of our conversations, he said, "When you are back in your hometown, remember to take care of the old man. I will no longer be able to work in the field. Perhaps you'd be able to find me a job as a house porter with your friends or family." I was astounded. I had never mentioned that we had a house. I once mentioned my aunt lived in a house of her own; indeed, one cannot put a lock on one's mouth.

Unfortunately, father Suchetzki did not live to see me fulfill his wish. He passed away before I could do anything for him, and I could never take comfort in the thought that I did.

Winter was getting near, and we had nothing to do at home. I played a little Garmoshka-like accordion, which I took from the Maliniaks, every day for many hours. They, themselves, preferred an elegant gramophone with a pile of records, mostly of ballroom dance music. I thought it best not to ask them where they got it from.

It was then that I heard Peter Kreuder's music for the first time and the easy listening German music of that era. The stores in the General Governorate were filled with that type of German music, and the records were cheap. I later learned that this music was supposed to constitute a substitute for Hungarian and Viennese operettas, whose composers were mainly Jewish. I must admit I liked Kreuder's music a lot and looked for his records after the war, only to find out that not everything that is nostalgic is necessarily of true value too.

I played the common songs, folk music I remembered from home, and of course, the upcoming Christmas tunes. I needed to practice alone out in the granary so as not to bother the others until I could master the art of playing the accordion. With each passing day, I was more alone. I was homesick again, not only missing my family but my school friends too. I decided to engrave their names and faces in my memory. I remembered each class and its students, my friends from the ghetto lessons, even some of the girls. How could it be that so many good and young people, better than myself, have vanished? I could not imagine that I would never see or talk to them ever again.

Yet here, life went on as if no one had heard massacres of people who, until recently, had lived together with them under the same roof. I kept resonating Maliniak's words about what he heard in Warsaw of my family. Is it ordinary that I have not yet committed suicide? And still, I couldn't let go of the dream that someone would survive. Who from among my friends had the chance to escape, assimilate into the Aryan environment? These tantalizing thoughts kept creeping back into my mind despite the daily news about the discovery of Jews and their extermination.

One of the few people that I had become friends with was Olek, the Suchetzkis' cousin. He was just a little older than me. We conversed openly and easily, and I could feel his honesty. He liked to hear stories of my years in high school, a subject I could elaborate on without a problem. He was interested to know my opinion about the war, how it would unfold and when it would end. Once or twice, he remarked that his friends were also preparing themselves. There was no doubt as to what he meant. One evening, I bluntly asked him to speak in my favor so that I could also be accepted. He replied hesitantly, saying this could take time and that I have to be very patient. And indeed, the reply took long. After some weeks, he whispered he had tough problems since he talked about this delicate subject with a stranger. I could gather that there was some organization in the village whose members were local, all of whom knew each other and were not open to a stranger like me. What should I do?

Being unemployed, and the lack of confidence that came with it, prompted me to run away from home at times. I could not take the eyes glaring at me, no matter how friendly these eyes were. I went to Sokołów a few times and, because it was very cold, I wore a sheep's wool slipover I borrowed from Zosia, on top of which I wore a coat I bought after several weeks' work with Mikhail. It was leather-like and appeared similar to coats worn by the Germans. Black leather coats were the Germans' almost-formal attire by which they could be spotted from afar. I was also told I looked like a German; I didn't mean to look like one but didn't regret it.

Every few weeks, I had to pay a visit to the barbershop in Sokołów. Each visit there was a bitter experience. My hair was my weak point. It tended to get curly—an evident Semite characteristic. I worked hard to straighten it, stubbornly wetting it and "ironing" it. It was eventually successful since my hair became less unruly and straighter, but I loathed the visits to the barber. Already on my first visit, he told me my hair was beautiful and not at all like that of others. "The girls must like your curls, if only they weren't so tough." The barber, like many in his profession, liked to talk. He talked incessantly and liked to ask questions. I had to give away some details about myself, one of which was that I work at the district office. I tried not to disclose any more.

At the newspaper store, I once saw a German newspaper. I thought I should read, at least at a glance, what is happening in the global frontier. "It's in German!" the shop owner warned me. I replied a bit scornfully that "I'll manage." I knew that in a small town as this, every such little event attracted attention, yet the curiosity to know what the Germans wrote about themselves could not be overcome. In the village, they never spoke of the war. What of the situation in the frontline? Come on, it's at the other end of the world! But when I brought the paper home, it appeared I could read it easily. Indeed, in my conversations with Mikhail, I admitted I knew some German, but demonstrating too much knowledge in German could create suspicion that I was Jewish. In fact, I didn't quite understand some of the articles and columns. I had to read them over and over again in order to understand: The Germans continued the siege on Stalingrad, still victorious, yet, no longer insisted they were about to raid Moscow from the south. First, they cut off the Russians from coal and iron supplies, and now they were to cut off their fuel supplies. They wrote about pilots who, after having intercepted huge amounts of enemy planes, were themselves intercepted. The heroes were granted decorations with outstanding names: Knights' Cross of the Iron Cross, Knights' Cross of the Iron Cross with Oak Leaves, Golden Oak Leaves with Swords and Diamonds. The paper also had lists of Nazi submarines that had been ambushing the Allies' shipping convoys for weeks and successfully sinking them. Indeed, they also suffered losses. A novelty: up until a year previously, the Germans had never mentioned any loss or failure. The most important item was that about the halting of the offensive on the Stalingrad frontier. Did that mean a real change? Did this change, providing it exists, have real implications for us? It seemed not.

Indeed, all that happened on the other side of the world. The police and the Gestapo were right here, near us.

I dared to go to the district office to look for work. I met the agronomist, who heard they were looking for a worker in one of the departments and gave me the name of one of the officials. I met an elderly man who posed questions and asked me to fill out forms with my personal details and await a reply. Throughout the conversation, he made sure I understood there was not much of a chance to get the job. When I asked whether they needed a worker in any of the other departments, he recalled they were about to begin building a wall surrounding all the warehouses storing the "abandoned property." He gave me the name of the person in charge and warned me he was German or "half-German." He was not always pleasant, but he was in need of workers. I went to see the man in charge of the wall construction, who ordered me to wait tomorrow morning on the site where the works will be launched. I showed up there the next morning. He wrote down my personal details as well as those of two other local guys. They, too, were interested in the job and stared at me with suspicion. They were more familiar with the work than I was. I assumed the abandoned property was that of the Jews after they had been deported to the death camps. What I didn't know was that Jews were sorting and packing it. They had been left alive for that purpose. I did not at all know there were still Jews in Sokołów. I could not think of any pretext that would absolve me from this new problem and enable me to escape.

The construction work progressed slowly. Once every hour or two, someone appeared and shouted that the wall would disrupt his family's normal lives. The work was discontinued every once in a while, and the supervisor would disappear for hours. When he returned, the wall outline would change. It is reasonable to assume he took bribes for each change. The Jews employed in sorting and packaging were held in a separate building—in effect, with no guarding. There were about 15 young men and women. The guys from Sokołów took great interest in those girls. The Jewish workers looked at me with amazement. How could someone who is clearly a Jew get this job? All I could do was keep silent and not get near them. My job did not involve any connection with them, but it was a hazardous situation. One could not isolate oneself. One 16-year-old boy dragged his leg wrapped in dirty bandages. I asked him what happened. He replied that he tried to escape from one of the transports and was shot. The bullet remained in his leg. He had just arrived in Sokołów and did know where he was. I told him I would bring a doctor who would take the bullet out of his leg. He begged me not to do so and explained he did not belong to the local group, that he was only hiding here, and a doctor could expose him. If no one took an interest in him, perhaps he would organize his escape. Of course, this confession made it clear he recognized me too.

In the morning, the supervisor asked to talk to me privately. He explained that the whole thing was in big shambles, took up too much of his time, and it was only a supplementary job. He intended to appoint me as *Vorarbeiter* (chief worker) so that I would supervise the works. He later disappeared for the rest of the day. My work colleagues said they spent a cheerful evening with the Jewish girls from the warehouse. According to them, one of the girls insisted that I was Jewish. She was sure about it. They said it smilingly—smiles that could have been interpreted in various ways. I shrugged as if I wasn't impressed. The supervisor showed up in the afternoon. Without further introduction, he announced the wall construction had been halted. He moved to another job, and we were all dismissed. We were to turn to the office to get our salaries. Surely there was not much money in it, but I decided to redeem it. Had the guys talked about me, then my appearance in the office would contradict their stories. After that, I refrained from visiting Sokołów again.

A few days before Christmas, a new problem arose: the village chief published a new decree that each village must send a fixed number of young men to work in Germany. At first, we didn't think it had anything to do with us, since we weren't really local residents, but the decree became the topic of debate among all the village's residents. There were some young men who didn't think of a transfer to Germany as a problem because they wanted to leave home and see the world. But their enthusiasm diminished once they've heard of the work conditions in the German factories, about the hunger and treatment. They could be sent to work in one of the villages. They already knew the work, and intentional starving of the workers was unthinkable. Yet, who guaranteed they would be sent to a village? For some days, I kept thinking that perhaps going there would be the best solution for me. But as I learned about the obligatory medical checks needed in advance, I waived the idea. The whole thing died down; the talk about it was over for the time being, yet I felt that not for long.

Leshek was the Maliniaks' cousin. He had been living with them when I arrived in Węgrów. He was a little younger than Yuzek, and we developed a special relationship. Like us, he was away from home, so we were in the same boat. He once discretely remarked that it wasn't enough just to be a cousin, even a close one. I was surprised since his mother was Mrs. Maliniak's sister. And then, just before Christmas, came the sensational news: Leshek signed a disclaimer claiming he belonged to the German people[3]. His father was indeed of German origin, although all his life, he was known to be a devoted Pole. Toward the end of 1942, it was not difficult to obtain privileges as a German subject, even when not bearing a "pure" German name. We were astounded. The youths that dropped by Maliniak's house were ardent Polish patriots, and Leshek was no different. We wondered what the implications of Leshek's move would be for us. He knew everything about us and about our aunt. We heard he had left his uncle's house after a bitter row and then roamed around the village, often drunk. He once bumped into my brother and began to tell him why he chose a new way. He emphasized time, and again we had nothing to fear. Besides, he was going to join the military soon, but first, he had to resolve financial matters, on which he did not elaborate, and we preferred not to inquire. Since then, we avoided Węgrów. It emerged that he had some quarrel with his uncles regarding incomes they had from hiding several rich Jews. Leshek considered himself an eligible partner, thereby claiming his part and even threatening. After a few months, he was no longer alive; he was lured into the woods, ambushed, and killed. We had only learned of these details much later. We worried that, being a German subject, the Germans would set out looking for him and might hear about us. Both of us were not staying at the same location and could not even meet in order to assess the situation properly. My brother roamed around the distant villages and was content that he was not under the villagers' constant scrutiny.

In January 1943, I went with Zosia to the market in Sokołów. It has been weeks since the wall episode around the Jewish property, and I considered the situation to be safer. We boarded one of the neighbor's wagons and waited for him to take us back in the afternoon. Zosia bought some groceries and arranged the packages and bundles in the wagon. I did not spend any money since there was hardly any left from my travels with Mikhail, which by now had come to an end. Once we were ready to move, a man approached us, wearing a dark gray-black coat. Under the coat, he wore a uniform of the same color. I already knew that certain German services wore uniforms. Every postman wore a cap resembling that of a navy admiral. That man's uniform resembled that of the train police (*Bahnschutz*). He turned to Zosia directly and asked if he could join the ride for a few kilometers since he was going in that direction. He had a heavy northwestern Polish accent. He was all smiles and undoubtedly had been acquainted with Zosia beforehand.

Zosia turned to the wagon owner and asked him to take her "friend." She also introduced me to him as "one from Poznań." During the ride, he turned to me several times, although it was evident only Zosia really interested him. I asked him which uniform he was wearing, and he replied it was one of *Obchod* (patrol), although I thought he was wrong since it was impossible for a German service to carry a Polish name. The details he delivered were no less interesting: he recently served as a sentry at the German army warehouses in Łochów (again Łochów!). According to him, Obchod Company replaced the military soldiers who guarded there. At a distance from there were the ammunition warehouses, but the sentries there were Ukrainians. He left because he wished to be near his family. I could not understand how a "company" could fill the duties of guarding a military facility. He replied with impatience, "Of course it's a company, not the army. At first, they only took Volksdeutsche and Ukrainians because the guarding was conducted with handguns. Now they were recruited into the army, so they had no other choice but to take Poles to do the job."

I continued inquiring and asked,"But they surely don't take just anyone. What are the job requirements and conditions?"

He replied, "Listen, my friend. What requirements? What conditions? If a person wants a job, they hire him, give him a uniform, a job certificate, one meal per shift. That's it. Over there, where we're going now, they give you two meals because it's a military facility."

I was still not yet satisfied with the information I got. "And no one inquires whether you're healthy or sick?"

By now, he'd already had enough of me. He looked at me with boredom. "What health checks? What company does this?"

I was shocked. After some time, I asked him to whom I should turn in order to get hired. The horse dragged the wagon laggardly. The man was engaged in a so-called romantic conversation with Zosia. He flattered her excessively and buttered her up in a coarse manner. Zosia tried not to burst out laughing. Nevertheless, the suitor spared a moment to inform me that the base in Łochów was supervised by the

Warsaw office. The guard administrator was an elderly guy from Poznań whose name was Zalewsky. He was a decent man, took care of his people, and didn't get in their way to make a "side income" in their free time. If I was interested, I must meet with him. I would not be the only school graduate. There were a few there. After a few kilometers, the man sadly parted from Zosia, wished me luck, and disembarked from the wagon. Zosia kept laughing for a long time. She had met him in a ball a year earlier, and that same evening he asked her to marry him. She kept declining his offer, disfavoring his ignorance and older age.

I couldn't help but constantly think about this idea. Perhaps this was my chance to finally get away from here. The place has become "hairy;" many menacing events had piled up with no solution in sight. The thought of moving to Łochów—to the flour mill and the nearby Ukrainians—was objectionable.

And all of a sudden, the issue of work in Germany popped up again. The village chief arrived in order to determine who would go. He made quick and simple calculations: there were four young men on the farm, and although he could demand even two, he would settle for just one since he was a family friend. The father was supposed to determine who would go in three weeks' time. When he left the house, there was sheer silence. The patriarch withdrew to his room, claiming his head ached, and he had to think quietly. In actuality, there were only three of us in the house. Arthur had not returned for over a month. Yulek was staying mostly at home, saying he had inhaled gas and had to recuperate. Zosia laughed because he had hardly worked in the past months.

In the evening, the father called upon all of us. He began saying that he wanted no quarrels, not with the village chief nor with the village. He could insist there was, in fact, just one young man in the house since Yulek worked with the disinfectants team and the two others are guests who work outside the village. However, that was not the right way. He had to decide who would go. Arthur was out of the question; he was far away. Who could burden him with village commitments? As far as I was concerned, this trip was not for me: working in the field or a factory would kill me. He would have sent Yulek, but he was lazy, and the Germans were quick to get rid of people like him. So there was only Czeshik left. Here, his voice broke, and he had to stop for a moment. Czeshik was his beloved son, his right hand in field work. This decision must have taken a real toll from him. I sat there dumbfounded. I could sense the reasons that were not mentioned. He feared that if he sent me, I would escape and the whole farm would be castigated. Maybe they would even have taken a girl instead. Perhaps he suspected something else? That he would have been blamed for housing a Jew? It seemed everything went through the old man's head. I didn't say a word. Yulek sat with his head between his hands.

The only one to react was Czeshik. He straightened up on his seat and said, "If Father tells me to go, I'll go; I won't make a scene. He'll need someone to help him in the field come spring." Not a word against us; no finger-pointing or blaming. Only later I understood they would have taken one young man out of the house anyway, but my mind was made up. I would leave this house, this village, this area. Leave.

The warehouse base of the Reich army in Łochów was situated outside the town. The supervisor was away, gone to Warsaw, and would be back only in a few days. The guys who welcomed me were desperate for company. They explained that since I was already here, I might as well meet Mr. Zawalski. There was plenty of room for all, and the food would suffice too. Indeed, the warehouses held a stockpile of mattresses, beds, and blankets—all straight from the factory. The guards joked that the equipment had been lying here for years, unattended and on the verge of rotting. Near the dining table, they added scornfully that the famous "German order" is today an empty slogan. I felt I was being treated as one of the boys, a fellow countryman, holding similar opinions as well as fate. I explained I got the address from a friend of Zosia's. They smiled leniently. "Oh, that one from the little village." They came from large towns and thought of themselves as part of the intelligentsia. They complained that the war had forced them to become servants of the Germans. I also got some clarifications. The company's precise name was "*Obhut,*" which means "supervision." The company was originally from Breslau and had dealt with guarding warehouses, commercial centers, and building sites before the war. Now it had changed its activity and was mainly engaged in guarding military sites outside the Reich. They began hiring Poles after most Germans and Ukrainians had been drafted into the army. The guards on the site went on patrol using weapons and ammunition that were strictly counted. People came to work here in order to get a uniform and a certificate exempting them from being sent to forced labor in Germany. Both the uniform and the certificate help them to move around rather freely. The pay was not high, but on most bases, meals were offered for free. It was like that in Łochów, too, until the army had left. Now, mostly dry alimentation was supplied. And above all, they were quite content with the fact that someone new had arrived in this forgotten "hole" in order to keep them company.

I listened to every word being said. Many strange ideas kept going through my mind. I could solve several pending problems, such as documentation, payment, and provisions. They would look at me with new examining eyes, yet, was there any other alternative? It would be this way everywhere I went. At least I could start here. This was just the beginning. If I ever got the job...

In the evening, one of the locals brought in a big sack from the village. In one of the farms, a cow had been slaughtered, illegally, of course. The man, being a professional butcher, helped the slaughter, and in return, got the intestines. He invited anyone who'd like to help clean it and later eat it. I helped scrub it till late at night and also on the next day. The cleaning became a ritual. The guys boasted that they were committed to very strict hygienic rules, unlike here, in central Poland. I was commended for my thoroughness, and the group work helped advance social contacts. I was a stranger no longer. Still, I kept my distance.

The next evening, three Ukrainians, whose camp was situated a few kilometers away, came for a visit. They brought *"bimber"*—homemade vodka—and their visit seemed like a meeting of brothers in arms. I sat in the corner and listened to them with fascination. In my wildest dreams, I could not believe I would be sitting with Ukrainians drinking vodka. Their language was mixed: a bit of Polish, a bit of German, a few words in Ukrainian, and a lot of hand gestures. The subject of discussion was the education they got in their home countries. They probably used to often talk about every possible subject, mostly about what bothered them and what they were missing. To hear the Poles praising their school system was of no surprise, but to hear the Ukrainians praising the soviet education system was a total surprise. After a few shot glasses, one of them remarked that he missed home very much. Asked why he shouldn't take a short vacation and visit home, he replied that he was not allowed, and besides, how could he travel with this uniform, not having "those of the SS units? The Ukrainians were considered as Wehrmacht units—the ordinary army." The conversation turned quiet at once. I sat in the corner in the dark. I could hardly believe I was really there, seeing, listening.

The guests left; those who didn't go out for patrol went to sleep. I lay awake and couldn't sleep. How far can I get with this self-confidence and audacity? My Poznań colleagues drew a clear line between themselves and their Ukrainian friends: they emphasized they belong to Poland. But the situation was not a simple one. They went out patrolling with German arms. How could I fit in? How would I be treated? How would I treat them? Although I was not yet in, the darkness was a blessing since they could see me, and I could not see them.

In the morning, I met Mr. Zalewski. He was nearing 50, tall, and a bit chubby. His mustache covered his cheeks. He looked like the owner of a medium-sized country estate—that's how I pictured him. His blue eyes examined me with sympathy. "Already at the train station, I was told a guest is waiting for me," he said. I expressed my surprise. "Yes," he continued, "one of the boys came out to help me with the uniform packages." He constantly inspected me. "You really want to be a *Wachmann* (guard)?" he asked. "Your looks are more of a schoolteacher, but if you're interested, in wartime, we do things we never thought we'd do. I, too, didn't expect to be in charge of boys who all have a good reason to run away from their families and surroundings." What could I answer him? That I, too, am looking for a place to hide? He asked what city I came from. I could not lie. He knew the Poznań area very well. I said my family was originally from Kalisz; at least I knew that city. I added that during my school years, I lived with my aunt, though I did not say where. "Ah, from Kalisz," he said. "I knew one from Kalisz," and mentioned a name that sounded Jewish. "I don't know, never heard that name," I replied. "Oh, of course," he continued, "that's because you're too young. He was a grain trader, a very decent man." Luckily, we thus completed our survey of Kalisz. "Now, let's get to business. Over here, I don't have anything available for you. It's not necessarily a bad thing," he said. "This company doesn't suit you anyway."

Yet, he can give me a letter for Mr. Brzozowski, the office manager in Warsaw, a good friend of his. Higher-ranked jobs in the company employed only Germans. "If you can wait," he said, "in about two weeks, I will be in Warsaw again. We can go see him together. Do you have where to stay in Warsaw?" I replied that if necessary, I could stay with some friends." "Perfect," he concluded. He determined a date on which I had to meet him in a small pub on Tamka Street. "We'll have dinner together and set a meeting for the

137

next morning in the office." If something happened in the meantime, he would leave me a message in that pub. In any case, he would notify Brzozowski that he's bringing him a new sentry so that he could prepare. This was a comforting conversation.

I did not return that night to Ksawerów. I was in no hurry to get back. The boys announced I couldn't leave before I tasted the intestine chunks. It was almost ready. I stayed willingly. Zalewski disappeared, went to sleep after one of his visits to Warsaw. Business went there as usual. It was no coincidence he mentioned that his boys prefer to get away from people. Perhaps the Germans were looking for them? Maybe there were simpler reasons? They made sure their work carried on smoothly. I found no reason to think about it any further, having already come to my decision after the event with the Ukrainians. A job in Warsaw was of prime importance right then. The meeting in the pub would cost me a little money. I would have to "rob" my brother.

The thought of going to Warsaw excited me. I could not imagine how I would feel. I wasn't afraid. I already knew that if I was fearful, I would deem myself to be annihilated. It worked. I was not fearful because I acknowledged fear was dangerous. It was strange but true. And still, hanging around Warsaw again, I decided not to think about it until I was there.

IN WARSAW AGAIN

Again I was in Warsaw. It was unbelievable. I don't remember how it happened. I had many journeys at that time, and I remember them all very well, but the one from Ksawerów to Warsaw, I can remember nothing about it: the train, the station, or where I went from there.

I met with Zalewski in the little pub on Tamka Street, as planned. It was already dark. There was a curfew from 8 p.m., but in February, dusk starts early. No one looked at me in the pub—perhaps thanks to Zalewski's uniform and his girlfriend. There was nothing militant about my table mate. He looked handsome but chubby, more like a friendly dad rather than functionary in the German army, and I felt he actually meant it to look that way. We ate something and, of course, had a few drinks of vodka. Then he wanted to pay, and naturally, I didn't agree. We decided to meet the next morning, and he said he had prepared everything. He commented that Brzozowski might ask me if I have something in common with the Germans. I naively asked him whether he was not allowed to employ Germans. He laughed and said, "Well, you might as well put it this way."

On my first night in Warsaw, I slept at Loda's, one of my mother's closest friends. She used to stay with us for weeks, sometimes months. For many years, she and her husband parted and rejoined numerous times until finally he left her and went away. Despite her close relations with my mother, she was never bold enough to visit my mother in the ghetto. She was very pious and was glad to see me kneel down and pray. But above all, she desperately feared the Germans. Nevertheless, full of fear, she let me spend the first night at her house.

The Obhut offices were on Bracka Street. Later they moved to the elegant quarters in Ujazdów Avenue, designated for Germans only. Brzozowski, a middle-aged man, welcomed us at an early morning hour. He examined me carefully, asking only the necessary questions. He was the one to accept the new conscripts and refer them each to the job that suits their qualifications. I knew he was a captain in the Polish army; the German management knew it too. After having learned that I possessed the "small matriculation" certificate (after ten school years), he resolved, "That means you've had paramilitary training; a gun doesn't frighten you."

He asked further questions, but I felt he was mostly interested in the manner in which I responded to his questions, less in their content. I felt he was inspecting me and not necessarily my Aryan background. I tried to answer as thriftily as I could. I am a son of a Polish family in the intelligentsia; my mother remained ill in the Reich. He asked whether I could find someone to testify that I was telling the truth. I calmly replied I could name some friends' names if necessary. The whole interview lasted for 15 minutes. Brzozowski concluded, "We are in need of people at the airport, but first I will send you to RWD, near the airport, not far. We will later think what to do next." He added, "Take this form to the warehouse." He handed me a signed paper. "They will give you a full uniform because you will be serving in a military unit zone, not just an ordinary suburb. You'd have to be very determined to get what you deserve because this guy behaves as

140

if these items are at the expense of his own kids. Then you will transfer to the airport at Okęcie with this application." And he handed me another form. "Go to the certificate office. And finally, go with the certificate to RWD to Melshecek. He's in charge of the guard. He's Ukrainian, a quiet person, you'll see."

After two hours, I came out wearing a uniform. Shoes were not included, and a matching belt and cap were out of stock too. I got a beret in which I looked really bad. I gathered that I could not return to the quartermaster empty-handed, so I told him I would return with some lard. His eyes shined all of a sudden, and he promised to replace my coat with a better one. I later learned that he was a German from Łódź who was keen on lard. All the items I received were made of substitute material; the original high-quality materials were dedicated to the military. The uniform I was wearing did not fit my body, so I had to fix it with the local tailor.

Throughout this event in the Obhut office, I didn't have a minute to reflect on what was happening. It was hard to grasp how such a nerve-wracking episode had gone by so easily. I feared I would face some crucial moments. But that did not happen. Perhaps Obhut needed me no less than I needed it? The corridor was full of gray people, as if they lacked any personality, unlike those tough guys I met in Łochów. Would I meet their kind again at the military base?

On the way to Okęcie, I asked myself how to go through registration at the base office. It was no ordinary military unit but an airfield of the German air force. I believed I would manage to slide through this dire place and land myself in some quiet corner.

I remembered RWD was a small aircraft factory for light planes.[1] Their construction was conducted solely by Poles—the nation's pride. One of its planes, led by Captain Żwirko, twice won the European Challenge competition for that type of light plane. Following the second race, on their way home, the plane crashed, and both the pilot and one of its developers, engineer Wigura, died in the accident.

141

Gossip said they both drank heavily before the flight, which was the reason for their crash. Nevertheless, they were both inducted into the national heroes' pantheon. What were the Germans doing in this factory? I'd never been there, and I'd never been to Okęcie. The fact that no one knew me there was an advantage.

The office that issued the working certificates was humbler than I imagined. An armed air force sentry stood at the entrance, next to an Obhut sentry armed with a pistol. The latter explained to me that I had to start with the office tending those who were not German, which was nearby. Miss Iza, who dealt with issuing the certificates, told me to bring a photo of myself in uniform. Meanwhile, she would issue me a temporary certificate. That's it. As simple as that. And once I was outside, without any curious eyes inspecting me, I examined the paper in my hands: a small palm-sized carton document in a transparent cover that could be inserted into a coat pocket. It was orange, with a black vertical line along its center, headlined "*Nichtdeutsche*" (not German) in bold Gothic letters at its top so that there could be no misunderstanding. The certificate's title was the unit's name: "Luftwaffe Fliegerhorst Warschau," followed by my personal details, my duty, and rank, all of which were signed by the officer in charge—Hauptmann Schnabel.[2] A round seal indicating the German eagle clenching the swastika in its claws was stamped onto the paper. This paper, even without my photo on it, was so surreal that I stared at it every few minutes in order to convince myself that it was indeed I who possessed it.

The Germans changed the RWD enterprise's name. It was located nearby the airfield's main entrance. The road leading to it was desolate and covered with a thick layer of snow. The Germans had erected several cabins on the road-sides in order to meet the constantly growing logistic needs.

I found Malescek, in charge of the guard, in a small room at the entrance to the factory. He was awaiting me, but I didn't know what they told him about me on the phone. That was not how I imagined a sergeant serving in the Polish standing army—a Ukrainian. I guessed he did not identify himself as a Ukrainian in the army. He was about 45, a slow talker. He asked whether I knew how to operate a gun and remarked that their Mauser rifles were not new, and most importantly, he stressed that they should never be loaded inside the guard room, only outside. He explained there were only patrols surrounding the factory instead of guard posts. He used German words as he had heard them from the Germans. Clearly, he did not know any German and often heavily mispronounced the words he used. Although keeping his distance, he did inquire whether I'd had lunch, and I did not disclose that I had yet to have any meal that day. He said one of the guards would soon finish his shift and take me out to eat. He even asked whether I had a place to sleep. He was prepared to ask one of the guards if he could offer me his place for the night as he did with previous guards who needed accommodation. I had lunch together with the air force soldiers. They were later transferred to another dining room. It had been only seven months since I'd left the ghetto, and I could not believe what had happened since then. I was sitting down having lunch in a dining room designated for Hitler's soldiers, dressed up in German uniform. Was this really happening? The alarm bells immediately rang in my head: *Do not get intoxicated with success! Keep a clear head!*

That evening, I rode to the old city with an RWD worker who had offered me to share a room with another tenant. I explained I hadn't yet brought my luggage. "Never mind," he said. "My wife would know how to solve any problem." I was very tired since the day exhausted all my energies. My new address was 48 Parta Street. The landowners were a childless elderly couple. It was a two-room apartment with a kitchen. My roommate was a man of about 50 who worked somewhere as a laborer. He did not look like a laborer and had a "singing" accent typical of the Wilna area. Was he a refugee too? I did not ask any questions. He didn't ask any questions either, and that helped us maintain proper relations. I dreaded the possibility that I might talk in my sleep, but the strict prohibitions I imposed on myself subconsciously probably worked. In the morning, my roommate contently remarked that I did not snore. The landlady brought us warm and thick soup. I settled for a cup of coffee substitute.

I traveled to Sokołów, where my brother was waiting with a package of clothes, most of which were donated by the sympathetic Maliniaks. In one of the times, he saw our aunt. It was a distressing sight. She looked bad, neglected, and exhausted by the hard work. She said she feared her end was near. Arthur was devastated. How could he talk about it with the Maliniaks? They might say, "If you don't like it, you can take her back." We were completely helpless! My brother continued to travel through the villages for his work. He was soon due to attend a course in Warsaw for about a week, luckily enough, just one week.

The work in the RWD factory appeared to be conducted quietly and serenely. They were manufacturing motorized skis to be used in Russia's snowy outlands. My landlord remarked once that they were mostly busy fixing. He used to work there before the war and had known its managers. He spoke of engineer Wigura as a technical genius. I got to ride to work with him once; it was inconvenient. My colleagues informed me that one of our privileges was riding the front of the tramcar, which was reserved for Germans, designated as "Nur für Deutsche" ("for Germans only"). It was less crowded and also suited my needs since it guaranteed I was less inclined to meet people I knew. I tried to stick to the corner at the front door where I could not be seen from within the wagon, mostly standing next to Germans. They were no threat to me. It was paradoxical but true.

Among the sentries in RWD was a German from Silesia, whose face was always gloomy. There were also two Ukrainians, one of whom was cunning and aggressive toward Poles and everything that is Polish. The rest were Poles, the eldest of whom was quiet, experienced, and level-headed, often replacing the cunning Ukrainian, who was too "busy" to get to work. In return, he would get a bit more money and an additional meal. We liked each other. He took me to lunch on my first day and gave me some advice. He didn't talk much but introduced me to the new landscape. "You should fix your uniform," he said. "You don't have to look like a fighter, but you are young; girls will look at you. Perhaps you'd want to go somewhere and do some smuggling; a man must make a living somehow. If a man takes care of his looks, people look at him differently. Get yourself Sparkie boots.[3] They are made of thick leather, nailed soles, hoofed heels; they do not wear out, and they are incredibly cheap." I listened to his advice. He advised me how to dress up as a "fighter," yet, he himself looked terribly wretched. His shoes looked as if they were made of paper. Before going on every shift, he would pad them with newspapers. Still, I valued his advice and appreciated him, as did many other sentries.

I asked my older friend why many sentries carried the German eagle emblem on their caps while others, including himself, wore a different bird symbol with a ring on its claws. "It is not a ring," he answered. "It is the letter O—the Obhut company emblem." Germans and Ukrainians wore the German *Adler* (eagle) on their caps in order to distinguish them from the Poles, who until then were forbidden to wear it. Lately, there were fewer Germans around, and Ukrainians were also being drafted into the army. Our guys found out that it was easier to move around with the "Adler" on your cap and began wearing it too. The Germans know it. They forbade it before, but now they didn't mind, even welcomed it. The German belt could be bought in any market; emblems and badges were bought in the German shop at the Bristol hotel. I asked whether those accessories were sold to all, including sentries. He looked at me with pity and said, "Remember well: if you demand something from a German, it means you have the authority to do so. You should know how to speak to them. There were guys like you before in that store, but they didn't know how to speak, and you do."

145

I bought Sparkie boots. I also bought a belt on whose buckle was an inscription that read, *"Gott mit uns"* (God is with us). I fixed my uniform at the tailor's and changed my coat for a nicer one as well as the beret for a cap, on which I attached the Adler with the swastika. My landlady determined: "One can see you were promoted. They gave you a nicer uniform. Too bad it's not one of ours."

While walking the streets, my boots stomped like those of soldiers. I felt safe. The passersby kept their distance.

I spent whole days in Okęcie. I wanted to experience the place and get used to it and let others get used to me. The meals were important too when you're penniless. I did my utmost not to hang around Warsaw. How many people here still knew me? And yet, how could I not take a look? It had been a long time, and I missed it. Now I could not ...

This wasn't the same city. Warsaw's streets looked gray, not because of the early morning or early evening winter hours I usually saw it in. The trade at the city center was carried out in the streets. In other boroughs, Warsaw was an "occupied," sad city. Once I came across Yurek Leiman in the city center. He was my friend from high school and a neighbor on Sienna Street that got me into the resistance organization and introduced me to Stephan Weinberg. He burst with joy as he saw me, hugged and almost kissed me. His joy was authentic and honest but ignored the safety rules and drew the attention of passersby. I was also very emotional but somehow had to curb his enthusiasm. I did not succeed. He made me go to the nearest coffee shop with him, where Rishek Edelberg, another school friend and underground colleague, was waiting for him. I gathered one could meet many such underground members there. It was an absolute breach of the secrecy rules, but I joined them anyway. Apart from Rishek, there was also his brother and other familiar faces from the ghetto. Some were speaking loudly. People who were sitting at other tables looked at them curiously. I guess it didn't take much to figure out their identities. It was all odd, incomprehensible. Only later did I come to understand that this loudness covered up much lack of confidence and confusion generated by fear. I did not attract much attention since I was not wearing a uniform. I wanted to depart as soon as possible, but they didn't let me go. They told news about themselves and wanted to hear mine. They all lived in rented apartments under fake identities, at times bizarre ones. None of them worked. They sustained themselves on money they managed to take out from "there" (the ghetto). Yurek mentioned only in my ears that he was financed by a one-time business partner of his father's. His father owned several cinemas before the war; among them was Capitol cinema, Warsaw's largest, located on Marszałkowska avenue. He was also a partner in various film studios.

I told them I was looking for a job in a firm that operated for the Germans in order to obtain a certificate. They comprehended my words sympathetically. They meant to obtain Kennkarte. They assumed that in the coming weeks, it would be impossible to move around without it in your pocket. One could buy a fake or original Kennkarte; it was just a matter of price. I had no idea concerning these issues. On this occasion, they warned me that many Jewish Gestapo agents were roaming Warsaw looking to hunt Jews that were hiding after having escaped from the ghetto. One cannot let one's guard down even for one minute. You must not give your address to anyone nor keep any notes, letters, or registries. They talked this way but were themselves very uncautious. They mentioned a young man from whom I was advised to stay away. He was the fiancé of a beautiful blonde, the daughter of a famous gynecologist. She was at the café as well.

I stumbled upon this guy a few months later. I was lucky again, and I was with no uniform on. He told me that one could get out as part of an operation organized with the Gestapo. They gathered the people at the Hotel Polski. I responded that I could not afford to join the operation, and immediately he lost all interest in me. After only a few months, we all learned of the "operation:" several hundred Jews had been concentrated there, mostly wealthy ones, from among all those who had managed to escape the ghetto and hide. They were driven to various places from where they even sent postcards and were finally exterminated.[4]

I met with Yurek three or four more times; we had a close relationship. I disclosed to him where I was working and how I got there. I insisted that he not tell anyone, including Rishek, and he promised to keep silent.

I wrote a letter in German to my uncle in the Netherlands, with no introduction under an alias. I informed him that Arthur and I were alive and in touch with our aunt in Węgrów. I wrote that we both worked and hinted that our aunt was in hiding. I enclosed my address. In previous letters, we corresponded in Polish. He would read the letters to my aunt without understanding a word. She could not have read them since she was almost blind. Among all the brothers and sisters, two of my aunts were partially blind, and one uncle was completely blind. Only the eldest sister and my mother, who was the youngest, had healthy eyes. The illness was allegedly a result of a marriage between two first-degree cousins some generations earlier. My uncle's response arrived very promptly. His letter was so full of love that I couldn't conquer my emotions. He was cautious but asked numerous questions. First and foremost, he inquired whether we had anything to eat and wear. I felt it was dictated by my aunt. He wrote he was not living with her on a regular basis, but they saw each other. She, too, was forced to live in hiding. He asked whether it was possible to send a parcel to my address. I was happy: we had a family. Our contact with Uncle van Oyen had always been restricted since they lived abroad, and the language differences made it difficult to communicate. For some time, he had been angry with me for having neglected my music lessons. He himself was a professional

148

violinist in the Königs Wusterhausen radio symphonic orchestra in Germany until he was laid off because he was married to a Jewess. I once told him I do not play because I lack the talent for it anyway. I was about 12 or 13. He replied seriously, after having reflected on it, that in order to gain accomplishments in music, one needed two major qualities: a musical ear and determination. Of all the performing musicians, only a few had been blessed with true talent. All the others had invested hard labor to achieve their goals. But one must love music. If only he had known how I loved music! I had proven it through an adventure I was too scared to talk about even to my brother.

In the village, once I had no longer felt in immediate danger, I was filled with longing for my relatives, our past life, and music. It was always an inseparable part of our lives. Throughout the terrible hunger period in the ghetto, I felt I had to go to concerts. In Węgrów or Ksawerów one could not even think of classical music. It was nonexistent. In Warsaw, already in the first week, I discovered advertisements announcing upcoming classical music concerts at the Lardly café on Polna Street.[5] The orchestra was conducted by Adam Dulgicki of the Polish national opera before the war. Although inside the café only a limited number of musicians could play due to lack of space, it was the only place in Warsaw one could listen to good music. I couldn't let go of the idea and finally gave in and went there, thinking that if it were possible, I'd go inside. I wore civilian clothes. The hall was packed. From the windowpane, I could observe that not all attendees really took an interest in the music. Most were businessmen, the regular café's crowd. Outside it was dusk, and inside, the lights were dim. I went in. At five o'clock, the orchestra took the stage. There were 10 to 12 players, followed by the conductor, who was greeted with applause. I sat next to a tiny table in the corner; the waiter stared at me; I was a new face there. I ordered coffee. The waiter asked if I would like "real" coffee, which he could get me. I replied that everyone's regular coffee would do. I gave up dessert too after the waiter said it tasted like rye bread. We both laughed. He brought the coffee while the orchestra was already playing, so he didn't get the chance to take a closer look at me.

The playing was fabulous. While most musicians had been unemployed, only the best could be handpicked to play in such events. The conductor performed as if he was standing in front of the full cadre of the national opera. A few Germans in uniform who sat there were very enthusiastic. I dove into the music, although I could not allow myself to forget where I was. I felt the waiter was "inspecting" my face from a distance. They played pieces of *Peer Gynt,*"a waltz from Faust, and I think the *Vltava* too.[6] Not even one Polish music work. Was it to not encourage nationalist feelings in the crowd? I wanted to listen to music, and I finally did. The traders left the hall, and the seats were quickly taken by music lovers. After seven o'clock, the waiter came to charge the bill. "You will be soon leaving, too, sir?" he remarked. "Soon, many Germans will flock to the place and take any seat left free." I gave him the impression this didn't make any difference to me, but I left after a few minutes. Let sleeping dogs lie. The music kept playing in my head long after the concert. Going to the German-infested Lardly just to hear music was unbelievable madness as well as insolence. Still, I was proud of myself.

My command of the German language was not enough. It could be useful for small talk but not in order to conduct a free conversation while riding the front of the tramcar among Germans. I wasn't used to introducing myself as German, but why make it easier for them to "decipher?" In that period, there were many sentries at the airfield from the Poznań and Pomerania areas. Most of them spoke freely with the soldiers. I was also seen as from that area, so I had to try and fit the mold. I had to come up with an idea of how to fill in the gap in my German knowledge. The Germans themselves were no threat since they could not identify Jews without the locals' assistance. The number of Volksdeutsche was dwindling with each day because they were all gradually being drafted into the German army. Polish citizens, such as my landlords, were not occupied with the issue of whether a foreigner from the Reich, like me, was more or less of a German. I didn't deem it terrible if I had been suspected to be affiliated with the German nation. I presented myself as a Pole to whoever I needed to but never disclosed to others who I really was. The German occupation administration recruited conscripts to the German List (*Volksliste*), thus designating new categories of being "Germanic."[7] Until then, there were only the Germans citizens of the Third Reich (*Reichsdeutsche*) or Germans citizens of the occupied countries of German origin (*Volksdeutsche*, after 1939). Now there were also the German Descendants (*Deutschstämmige* or German diaspora). They brought Germans from the Baltic States, the Ukraine, and the territories across the Volga.

As a fake German, I had to speak German. I bought a book to learn German, *Tausend Worter Deutsch* (a thousand words in German), which was quite common at that time. It was divided into 12 thin booklets. I could keep one of those in my coat pocket and take it with me to the patrol, taking a look at it every once in a while. My patrolling path circled the plant and its cabins. There were about 30 Polish workers there apart from some technicians, supervisors, and two engineers—all Germans. On the lot between the factory's buildings and the fence laid dozens of motorized skis. They resembled a pickup truck with an open crate. There were rumors the whole project failed. The "cunning" Ukrainian said it didn't add up too much. The financial administrator was a tall and quiet man. He never reacted to a salute and never noticed anyone.

When the winter wind blew fiercely, the skis proved most useful for the sentries; you could take shelter behind them for a few minutes. At night you could sneak in and warm up a bit. Although this was an offense, I had done it once or twice. I held on pretty well in the cold, but my clothes definitely were not suited for a temperature of minus 10-15 degrees Celcius. At night I used to get in between the skis, more often equipped with a small torch and the booklet. While reading, I could recognize some German phrases I heard at home or at the airfield. My hearing helped me distinguish between the accents of lay or educated people or even those of various districts. I learned all the grammar rules, including the irregulars, and with every day, I could speak more fluently.

After a few weeks, all of a sudden, Maliscek became interested in my religiousness, of all things. He often cited verses from the Bible, those of the apostles or the prophets. I was amazed every time, yet kept silent. Until one day, he bluntly asked me whether the gospels interested me at all. I replied that it interests me just as it does every faithful Catholic. That sufficed for him to take a New Testament out of the drawer and hand it to me. "This is a gift," he said. "It's good for anyone." He asked that I read a bit, and then we would talk a little. I began suspecting a provocation on his part, but on that day, my elder friend asked me, "Did he start with you as well? He's trying to convert everybody here; it's his duty." I asked, of course, "whose duty?" He answered, "Jehovah's Witnesses; who do you think printed the book you were given? In a few days, he will invite you to pray with him." The old man laughed, and I was furious but decided to wait patiently.

The old man's scenario was precise. After just a few conversations regarding what I have read, Maliscek reached the conclusion that I was ready for the "higher knowledgeable" level. He invited me to a dinner organized by their organization. "This is not mass," he said. " No preaching, only singing Psalms together and rejoicing with each chant." A meeting with a group of strangers who would examine my face was the last thing I needed, but I couldn't refuse. The event was held at a small hall in a residential building downtown. I did not get there early on purpose, and when I did, I found about 60 people. Maliscek did not hide his happiness that I was present. A man in the officer's uniform of a German technical military unit spurred special enthusiasm among the guests. They knew him, patted his shoulder, and then all sang together. I was given a songbook so that I could join them. In fact, they didn't pay much attention to me. I was invited there twice more but succeeded in evading. Shortly after my arrival in Warsaw, the health administration organized a course for the disinfection unit managers. My brother and Yulek Suchetzki were dispatched to the course from the Sokołów district. The course went on for a week uninterrupted. This successful week filled Arthur with much optimism. He got a diploma that was not worth much, except that it was another authentic "Aryan certificate," which was so important at the time. He tried not to stand out, and yet, the girls were impressed. One of them asked him to visit her in Radomsko and then sent him a postcard with her address.

We tried to keep in constant touch, yet, not too often, because we did not live together and the landladies received our mail for us. My brother wrote me more often. I usually did not know in which village he was staying. We decided that should something crucial happen to any of us, we would send a telegram to the last known address. But only a few letters arrived, and there were no exceptional events.

One day, the landlady handed me a telegram. It arrived before noon. My brother wrote: "Basia is very ill," and added a question: "What shall we do?" I didn't know what to answer. We had no possibility whatsoever to take our aunt from Węgrów. Dear God, I am not heartless, but ever since I had left the ghetto, I had learned to think cool, no emotions involved. That faded once these two's fate was concerned. Our aunts were no ordinary aunts; they were like mothers to us, and we were their "boys." I knew we were faced with a problem that had no solution. I had no means to take my aunt out and hide her elsewhere. Not just because we had no money, but also because there was absolutely no one I could turn to, even for advice. We were all alone, all alone!

Much later, when I could think more calmly, I comprehended that our lack of means helped us much more than damaged us because it forced us to find legal solutions to our housing and employment problems. But nothing could help change our half-blind aunt's fate. I knew I had to find an immediate solution for my brother; what happened to our aunt could put him at immediate risk. Rumors spread quickly, and the Germans will get him too.

It was Monday. I planned to get a short leave from work and take the afternoon train. The telegram was sent from the post office in a small train station between Sokołów and Kosów. I hoped to get there by evening so we could decide together how to act. In the worst case, I would take my brother with me. I couldn't think of what to do next. My head was empty with ideas. I was afraid to bring him to my apartment on Parta Street. Our being together would accentuate our Semite traits, but I could see no other option. My leave got approved, but before I set out, I got another telegram: "It's all over. I'm awaiting the worst."

I traveled dressed up in my uniform. I disembarked at the midway station at 9 p.m. The station was a wretched cabin manned by one worker who was the cashier, moved the tracks as well as operated the means of communication. I was the only one to get off at that station. There were about 5 kilometers to the next village. I started walking and thinking about what to do. People in the village told me where the head of the disinfection team stayed. He wasn't there. He was visiting the head of the district's daughter with a group of youngsters. I knocked on the door. A young woman stepped out dressed in a surprising manner. I explained I was looking for my brother on a pressing matter. She invited me in, but I preferred to remain outside. My brother came out. Although it was dark, I could see he was pale, and he told me what had happened. Two gendarmes came to take the aunt. They entered the cop's house; they knew the house and its inhabitants, and they knew exactly who they were looking for. They marched her to the nearby Jewish cemetery and shot her in the head. Arthur did not know where she was buried. No punitive measures had been taken toward the family for having hidden the Jewess, and Maliniak continued with his work in the police force. "And you?" I asked. "What could I do?" he answered. "Only wait for them to come for me too." I elaborated on my action plan. He would announce in the room that his brother had arrived suddenly to tell him our mother had died in the Reich, and he got two permits to enter Germany in order to attend the funeral. In an hour and a half, there would be a train to Siedlce, and from there, we would take a train to Warsaw. There, we'll think about what to do. He tried to object, saying we stand no chance and we would both be caught, whereas alone I have a chance to survive. I didn't give up. And I had another idea. "Surely you won't be able to return here, it's too dangerous. But you could look for work in another place, for instance, in the town where the girl you've met in the course lives." He wasn't easy to convince, yet, after two days of waiting for his death, he heard there could be a way out.

Once in Warsaw, we had some difficult hours. We didn't look like the "almost German" residents of the western districts. Luckily enough, the landlady's imagination was not that vivid. I looked like a "half German" to her, and her ideas and opinions of me were shaped based on that notion. In Warsaw, I did not tell the story of the funeral. I just said my brother is going away for a vacation in the Reich.

After Arthur had left, I waited impatiently to get any news from him. A letter arrived after a week. Danka, the girl from the course, was of greater help than we could have imagined. She was astonished and proud to see that he had come to stay with her. She had connections that helped him go through the district office bureaucracy. He notified me that he was stationed at the town of Żarki in the Radomsko district; he would elaborate on the details when we meet. I went to Ksawerów to get his personal effects. They did not ask anything. They took my uniform as a joke, which saddened me, but I did not stay long enough to reach the confession stage. Zosia recalled that my Obhut episode began with meeting her friend in Sokołów. I sent Arthur a package by mail. I was the only one to know his new address.

There was unrest in Warsaw. The Germans worked hard to cause it, and the manhunt was underway every day. At times passersby warned that around the corner lurked a *"boda"*—a truck—its rear disguised with a canvas bolt in order to hide the people forced inside it. Most kidnapping operations were conducted by soldiers supervised by civilian functionaries, who usually hid behind the building. They detained anyone who fell into their hands and rarely let go those who had some certificate from an important institution. Most people, men and women alike, were transferred to Germany for forced labor. A document like mine was usually enough to avoid being detained, but on occasion, some diligent soldier would decide to arrest a sentry too. He would later be released, but before that, he would go through a medical check. Such an exploit would have had a deadly end as far as I was concerned.

The Reich ran out of laboring hands. The Germans were all recruited to the military. The dwindling military units as a result of the war were now replenished with fresh cadets who only yesterday were found unfit to be conscripted. Their place at the offices, transportation, and communication, was in turn taken up by women. An influx of slaves kept coming in each month from the occupied countries in order to keep the industrial and agricultural production lines going.

Those places in the General Governorate abandoned by the Germans were manned with substitutes such as Obhut. In actuality, substitutes like me. Who would expect a Jew to find himself there? Wearing a uniform and armed with a rifle, he was out to guard them. This foreigner sustained himself well, wearing his uniform properly, his shoes shined, and he spoke German pretty well. Does he look any different? Sure! That's because he hails from the Reich. The soldiers usually welcomed "non-Germans" to join them, while most German citizens were hostile since they felt they had to display loyalty to the Reich and the Führer, which manifested itself in disliking the "occupied nation."

One day, as I showed up for my shift, I learned some Jewish workers had been brought to RWD. Until then, they had been employed only in Škoda Works, at the other end of the airfield. Now, some 15 young guys were brought in by a soldier each morning and returned to their dorms in the afternoon. On Sundays, they would return to the ghetto. The sentries had no contact with them, but I was no less fearful. I feared a spontaneous reaction in case I met someone I knew among them. I subsequently met two of them. They were digging a tunnel along my route in order to lay a pipe in it. One of them remarked he had a rifle just like mine in the army. He said it out loud for me to hear it, awaiting my reaction. I thought it would be wise not to avoid a conversation. I asked him about his military service. He replied he completed a reserve officers' course and was released as a sergeant destined to become an officer. I knew that from among the Jews, only university graduates, medical doctors, or pharmacists were accepted to this course. I asked whether he was a doctor, and that was a wrong move. He stared at me curiously, wondering how I was so proficient in matters so specific to Jews. I managed to get away, adding something like "so I've heard." He asked where I was from. "From Środa near Poznań," I said. Chances for him to be familiar with this town were low. I found him interesting. He wasn't tall and was six to seven years older than me. He spoke fluent Polish, so it was evident he spoke it at home. He said he didn't know why he was taken to an officers' course because he wasn't a university graduate. He spoke of the ghetto in a restrained and reserved manner. He tried not to ask questions that were too personal, although he did inquire whether there were only Germans serving in my unit or rather Poles too. My response did not help him reach a conclusion. If not for Yurek Leiman, I wouldn't be mentioning this meeting.

Yurek and I were to meet once again. This time we didn't go into a café. I told him briefly about myself, about my life, and of the loneliness. He understood it well. He envied me for having work and keeping an authentic certificate, not a fake one. He was already in possession of a Kennkarte but warned me not to buy one; it was clearly forged. I replied that he shouldn't worry; I don't have money for such pricy expenses. When I told him of the meeting with the worker from the ghetto, he gaped. He asked if I could do him a favor.

The love of his life remained in the ghetto, Dana P. She worked in Többens' shop. The manager, a middle-aged German, was the master of life and death. He demanded that she become his mistress, and when she refused, he raped her. Yurek knew she was in a terrible emotional state and wanted to get her out from there at all costs. He asked that I deliver a letter to her through a man who was returning to the ghetto. I had heavy doubts about this. The danger in divulging my true identity was great, but I could not refuse. The next day Yurek brought an open note, written so that only the recipient could decipher who it was from and what about. The "almost officer" received the letter, no questions asked. I told him a friend had a friend who knew the girl and was worried about her. I asked for him to keep it discrete. He deemed it necessary to add no one would know of his mission. I was calm. How could I explain that there are certain things one could feel are safe? After having returned from the ghetto, he brought an oral answer. There was no resolution. She had questions that she promised to deliver by different means. Yurek was disappointed, desperate. He immediately wrote another note and asked the messenger to deliver it. The latter smiled sadly. Who knows how much time is left to organize anything? After hesitating, he added that he, too, has a big request, "Can I try and find a room at a family's house for a traveling couple going through Warsaw?" Of course, it's about him. I said I would try and inquire among friends. I actually meant Yurek. I met Yurek once more and asked him to find a room for a "traveling couple." He invited me to visit him in Żoliborz, Warsaw's northern district but asked that I come without uniform so as not to alarm his landlady. He promised to inquire regarding my request. I did not receive another message for him from Dana. Jewish workers did not arrive at Okęcie any longer.

I went to him with mixed feelings. I was not in uniform and did not feel confident. On Sunday afternoon, the street was empty and quiet. I rang the doorbell at the house near Wilson square. I stood and rang for a long time. At last, the door was slightly opened, and a woman's head appeared from behind it. I noticed the woman was petrified.

She looked at me with great fear and almost whispered, "Sir, you must leave immediately and never come back." I did not understand. "Can you tell me what happened to him?" I insisted. Even today I cannot grasp my sheer idiocy. The answer was unequivocal: "He's not here and will never be again." The door was shut.

After almost a year, I met Zanka Natanson. She knew details of Yurek's capture. She didn't say from whom she knew it. It was unacceptable to inquire about ghetto refugees in those days. She said Yurek and Rishek had been arrested at a cinema on Chmielna Street. Someone informed about them, probably the usher. Before the war, the cinema was owned by Yurek's father. I knew my friends were not cautious enough, but like that?

Yurek was my friend. We spent time together in summer camps several times. He used to confess to me about his infatuations, and I to him. In the ghetto, we grew even closer. Again I experienced the loss of a loved one.

1943

I had no contact with Jews or with the ghetto. I had no idea what went on there. I met a few refugees outside the ghetto. They knew more than I did, either because they left it at a later time or because they had information from relatives still living there; or, unlike me, they stayed in Warsaw after leaving the ghetto. They, too, did not know much. They tried not to stay in contact for too long.

In my conversation with the Jew who had worked in RWD, I raised a dangerous subject, yet I excused it as a favor to a friend's friend. I spoke as little as I could, but the danger was imminent. It was not an appropriate time to inquire about what went on there or how people lived there. The Jewish workers watched me from afar. Only seldom did they hang outside. My encounter with the Jews in Sokołów taught me to keep my distance. I couldn't help them anyway.

The worker that delivered Yurek's letters was discrete, unlike the girl from Sokołów. For a long time, I could not understand her motives. What made her tell hostile strangers I was a Jew. Jealousy? Perhaps because she saw no chance for herself to flee while I was free?

Anyone in hiding knew that in such conditions, the only thing one could do was to try and survive. As time went by, only a few survived of those who fled the ghetto—those few who succeeded erased any trace as they slipped away from their pursuers. They began to build themselves new lives through a sophisticated conspiracy. They knew many were awaiting the opportunity to end their survival. Those who had survived due to a tremendous effort and extraordinary luck were looking for a way to avenge the loss of their loved ones and their people. However, chances of joining one of the resistance organizations were nearly nonexistent. Any contact or communication entailed knowing the right people who could be trusted and, most of all, it required time.

Each morning, when I embarked on the tram near Krasiński Square, I saw the wooden ghetto wall along Bonifraterska Street. Only a few passed that way. One afternoon, I neared the ghetto wall. A minute before, two people were talking from both sides of the wall. At that spot, one could move loose planks in the wall, so that's what I did. On the other side of the wall, I could see the face of a Jewish cop. He noticed my uniform and asked hesitatingly in German what I was looking for. I was equally embarrassed. I found it hard to get used to the idea that they saw me as a German. I was no longer looking for my relatives, so I asked him whether he knew the Gutman family from Berlin. There were Jews from all over Europe locked up in the ghetto. No, he didn't know. Not many were left from among those who once lived there. I asked if he needed anything. How silly of me. How could I have helped him? He was surprised by my question. I got the feeling he was beginning to understand who I was. His German wasn't fluent, and I said only a few sentences too. He smiled and said he needed nothing; they already took all his family. He advised me not to stand there for too long. I went, almost ran away. Once again, I grasped how helpless I was, unaccounted for, irrelevant.

I didn't know about the armed resistance in the ghetto. These stories only reached few people outside the ghetto. I only heard from Yurek, who had left the ghetto much later, about hitting Lejkin and Szeryński, the Jewish police commanders.[1] The very fact that there existed a force implementing rage and revulsion and executing verdicts boosted morale. However, in the face of the genocide in process, it was too little too late. The predominant part of Warsaw on "this" side took no interest in the ghetto. The inhabitants expressed no interest in what was going on beyond the walls. It was impossible for them not to know that the ghetto was being exterminated, that its inhabitants were being transferred to the death camps. This indifference, this apathy, was amazing. It was hard to determine how many were there that actually dedicated some thought to these events. According to rumors, the leaders of the Polish resistance groups did take a stand and perhaps even tried to help the ghetto. These operations were carried out under heavy confidentiality. Nevertheless, the street was silent; when not indifferent, it was hostile.

But the ghetto's voice was heard.

That day I returned home in the late morning hours after a night shift. The tram driver was not in the habit of conversing with the passengers who stood next to him. As soon as I meant to disembark on the corner of Miodowa and Długa streets, he turned to me and said, "Pay attention to that corner; until an hour ago, it was prohibited to linger there." It came as no surprise that he spoke Polish to me. He was familiar with his passengers and with the various types of uniforms. But what did he mean by "prohibited to linger?" The answer was yet to come.

Next to the street corner, just across from Karsinski Square, a machine gun had been deployed, and soldiers were lying next to it in a firing position. The machine gun barrel was pointing in the ghetto's direction. When I disembarked, they were not firing. The sergeant was standing behind the soldiers and prevented passersby from stopping there. He screamed at me, too, "Get on, either here or there!" and added an "explanation"–"*Scheisse!*" (shit). There was no point in asking anything. The man was furious. I asked a lady who was on her way, as I was, to the old city. "Don't you know?" she said. "The Jews have been shooting since the morning. They said they killed many Germans among those who tried to get into the ghetto. So now the Germans are shooting." It took my breath away. Who would have expected such a twist after the ghetto had been emptied of several thousands of its Jews?

At home, the landlady had been worried for her husband. I promised I'd accompany him, but he arrived back safe on his own. He knew nothing of what had been happening until he heard some details on the tram. There, it was not as silent as on the front of the tram. People knew that flags had been hung on the ghetto's buildings, including Polish flags. This made the landlady angry: "What right have they?" My roommate began to comment on the events, saying it was very important. They were convinced I could be trusted, so they spoke freely, saying this had shamed the Germans greatly, so now they would retaliate. As for the Polish flag, we would soon know whether there were Poles inside too.

We went to sleep late, and my head was filled with thoughts. I understood the goal of the uprising was the mere fact that it was happening. The rebels knew they were going to die, and they were prepared for it. This was utter bravery. And what about me? I was here saving my skin. These were not easy thoughts. But God almighty! What good would it do if I died with them?

After midnight, there was the sound of soldiers marching in the street. The landlady knocked on our door, asking if she could take a look through our window. Only she looked outside. Then she asked that I take a look as well. On the pavement across our street marched a column of combat soldiers. I immediately recognized the Waffen SS unit uniform. Apart from their personal rifles, they also carried machine guns and flamethrowers and tried to keep quiet, as if someone could have warned the rebels. There was something arrogant, nonchalant about their march as if they wanted to declare: soon you will have a taste of German power; you will witness what becomes of whoever raises their hand against us. The landlady whispered, "Well, now the Jews are kaput; it will be over soon now." We took turns watching through our window. The military force disappeared, and we returned to our beds. After several hours, their marching was heard again. The Waffen SS returned. Again, they marched in a column, but no longer in the exemplary order so typical of the German units; their coat buttons were undone. They carried several wounded; their colleagues bore their weapons for them. It was already dawn. A few hundred meters away from our house, the SS soldiers boarded the trucks. The landlady said, "Looks like it won't be over so fast."

Two days went by. No gunshots were heard in Parta Street. The battles continued, but they were fading into the distance. They did not obstruct daily life on the Aryan side anymore. I tried to inquire what went on there, and each time I found only few cared. Before the burning down of the ghetto houses began, I had left the old city and moved to Okęcie.

One more thing preceded this change. After having refused again to join the Jehovah's Witness gathering on some pretext, Malishcek's attitude toward me had changed. He wasn't hostile but no longer as positive as before. One night, he found me in the ski compartment reading a textbook under a flashlight. He made furious arguments against the elite intelligentsia. I was most preoccupied with the thought that he suspected something, but it didn't happen. In the morning, he announced that he did not want me under his responsibility anymore. I should return to the office; Brzozowski would decide what to do with me. I was troubled, but I reacted as if it didn't bother me. The "old man" encouraged me. "They won't do anything to you; they need us just as much as we need them. It's just a pity because I grew fond of you." He told me that in Warsaw, there was a new company competing with Obhut. He was wrong about that, the old man. Argos was a company dealing with night guards. They did not work for the army, and their certificate was regarded as less safe than that of Obhut.

Brzozowski lashed out, "Malishcek has gone mad. What does he want? What happened there?" I told him that I entered the skis in order to pull up my socks. He didn't believe my story. "What for? Couldn't you do it in the guards' room? You really don't need this mess!" He later added on a calmer note: "I will send you to the airfield. There are posts there for which you need to know German. One of them is near the main gate and the other near the entrance to the Skoda factory. This main entrance is our business card. Be there often and try not to cause trouble; I have enough of my own, and anyhow, we need to talk about a few things."

The next day, I showed up at the airfield at commander's Alfred Zeigner office. A young man, approximately my age, a German from Pomerania. Before the war, he studied at a Polish high school, and I came to think he was trying to avoid the draft into the army. But he did not succeed. After several months, he, too, was in uniform. He welcomed me with sympathy. Malishcek already called him and told him to keep an eye on me because I was not responsible. But Brzozowski called him too. Zeigner explained that the man in charge here was the senior officer (*Oberwachführer*) of the watch, Messinger, a German from Łódź. Since he was away a lot, he, Zeigner, was the acting officer. He also said the work there wasn't hard, but the demands were punctilious. The sentries were required to maintain a neat appearance like soldiers. Obhut was about to gain new contracts, and this unit was considered their most presentable, their business card. Various representatives came here and sometimes took photos of the guards in the posts. That's all I need now, I thought to myself.

Already on that day, I began to work. Prior to that, Zeigner suggested that I ride a service bike between the posts in order to see where they were situated and what work was entailed. I was ready to do that while thinking about the sudden changes in my life. I wasn't preoccupied with what Brzozowski meant regarding the talk we must have. Some of the guard posts looked tranquil, like a peaceful stroll along the railway tracks, which I don't recall ever seeing in use. One post was nearby the air force auxiliary unit's women's hostel. One could sit there in a well-kept garden, and the sentry's job was to forbid the entrance of "unqualified" people. Throughout most of the day, the place was empty and desolate. In the evenings, in order not to "bother" the sentry, the guests entered through the ground floor window. Naturally, there were also posts with some substantial work.

At the airfield, I hardly met any Germans and Ukrainians among the Obhut workers: only Poles, some from Poznań and Pomerania, the rest from Warsaw and its surroundings. This could have been dangerous, but what could I do? I quickly befriended some of the Poznań guys. Stephan Malinowski, a butcher's assistant from the town of Wągrowiec, immediately declared there was not much sense in working in Okęcie and living in the old city. He suggested I move in with him. He had a room in a long and gray building on the main street. "We will both pay less, and it will be more convenient for you." I agreed. He got the landlady's approval to bring me in. Thanks to this move, I was spared the sight of the ghetto going up in flames. This sight felt tragic even miles away in Okęcie and brought on sad thoughts.

The new room was like on another planet. Stephan kept it exceptionally tidy. The landlady was mostly away, and her husband, a "blue" policeman, served far from home in the Kielce area.[2] She visited him often and made a living from food smuggling. She was young, and she seemed to examine me with sympathy. Another Poznań guy that also took an interest in me was Theodor Balchinski. He claimed he was a professional butcher, but his stories indicated he dealt with various jobs before the war, such as a tradesman and a horse seller. Stephan didn't like Theodor and kept grumbling that he was not quite a butcher but a horse thief. I was first shocked at this, but later I learned that butchers and horse thieves could become good friends.

Theodor, so he demanded to be called, was married, and was soon to become a father. He was rather new to the General Governorate but managed to go through a lot. He had lived in Lublin for a while, where he married a girl much younger than him. He declared we should not go on earning the wretched pennies that we did but try our luck in trade. We should start immediately, with me playing a major role. I was troubled that he may have suspected me as qualified in trade, but it turned out he meant something else. "You Yashinek," was how he called me, "are not suited for slaughtering pigs. Stephan and I will do that. You must carry the merchandise by train. This is where we need to use your head. In some stations, the train police conduct checks and confiscate meat and lard. God forbid if they should find tobacco. In case they bother us, that's where you come in. You will have to convince them to leave us some of the goods." The plan was ready. If only they knew how many doubts I had, but I decided to give it a try. My brother gave me my part of the initial funding for the deal.

The initiative was very fruitful, much beyond our expectations. The pig, after having been butchered and divided, was packed in wooden chests ordered especially for that purpose. They were stronger than ordinary suitcases and seemed like military equipment. Each one of us carried two such chests, which were hung on the arm by a strap and weighed between 30-35 kilos. I couldn't believe I would be capable of carrying such a load for a few kilometers up to the train station, but my friends thought I was "tough." At the station, we jumped on board the train, sometimes even on a military one. In order to make it stop at the station away from the inspecting eyes of the gendarme or the train guard, we had to bribe the worker in charge of the railway tracks. In return, the traffic light at the crossing got "stuck," and, strangely enough, the mishap endured for a minute or two until we managed to load our cargo onto the train. When the train stopped, we jumped onto the nearest wagon while I was giving commands to my "team," such as how to load the chests, not to place them in the aisles, etc. Should someone ask us to identify ourselves, we would present the certificate from Fliegerhorst Warschau (the military airbase in Warsaw). A money note folded into four was inserted underneath the plastic cover, on the *Nichtdeutsche* (not German) inscription. The tactic enabled us to bypass the "inconvenient" stations since the military trains stopped only at a limited number of stations.

On the one hand, the idea to stop a military train in an open field was unsound. Had the soldier on guard noticed that the train didn't stop at a station, he would have opened fire at intruders like us. The military trains' passengers feared the partisans and placed a guard on each wagon. On the other hand, the war was already at such a stage that both the train commander and his passengers were eager to get home for a holiday as soon as possible, and minor mishaps didn't even count. However, it did happen that the commander threw us off the train.

We used to converse with the soldiers on board on their way back from the frontline, responding to their questions while presenting ourselves. It helped me make progress in learning the language; my friends were content—I did not let them down. All that helped forge our friendly relations.

Sales in Warsaw, as well as purchases, were Belchinski's responsibility. He was familiar with all the restaurant owners who used to sleep in their restaurants, and at the early morning hours, we arrived on the site with the merchandise. They bought it all. If they did not need a certain item, they knew who to pass it to, and the deal was worthwhile to both parties. We had breakfast there and returned home with the money. At times, when our uniform and our affiliation with the air force did not come in handy, our cargo, or part of it, was confiscated. The train police and the Gendarmerie at the Demblin station were especially aggressive and uncompromising. Our uniform did not impress them. They had an airfield on the site, and they openly confiscated the passengers' food for their own private use, which accounted for their outstanding diligence. We were also familiar with the Koluszki station. The train guard commander was a red-haired fat guy who never compromised. Smuggling was a felony, and the smugglers were considered criminals and faced heavy penalties.

Once, after having completely emptied our cargo, leaving us penniless, I decided to take action. I stepped into the redhead's office and complained that his personnel had taken all our cargo. He was shocked; he had not yet been confronted with such audacity. I told him I had been deported from Warthegau, that I was the sole provider for my mother and sister, who also needed to eat.[3] I could not believe I was doing this. He stared at me for a while, and instead of kicking me out, he ordered half our cargo be returned. At last, he added he was doing this for the sake of good relations, suggesting that we do not go through this station for a month or two. He then asked me for my name, where I was from, and we parted with a handshake.

A few weeks following our initial trip, I was informed that Mr. Brzozowski wanted to see me. "I heard you began sightseeing the land," he began. "You must know that we have a law according to which, if a worker abuses his uniform for illegal activity, he cannot continue working here. On the other hand, once you are on your way, you might as well provide us with the service of passing on something." I could only guess what he meant, but I could not ask him who he meant by "us."

Time went by, and no one asked me for anything. After a few weeks, I was provided with a tiny package by an anonymous messenger, which I was asked to deliver "in case I go to Chełm Lubelskie." I had no plans to go to Chełm. I went there briefly alone and returned after 24 hours. My friends knew nothing of the trip. I waited for new instructions, but they were yet to come.

I began to assimilate into my surrounding, or at least I thought so. Though I knew I mustn't trust my instincts, I was simply forced to rely on them. This ongoing vigilance was most exhausting.

I missed constant contact with my brother. Instead, I began to correspond with my uncle in the Netherlands on a regular basis. He sent letters abundant with love. I always wept while reading his letters. He also sent packages with surprising grocery items: coffee, cocoa, chocolate, sugar-coated nuts, as well as warm linen, scarves, gloves. In one of his letters, he asked whether we had winter coats. Although I replied that we were fine, he sent a package with a winter coat. In fact, just half a coat. It was unraveled along the back so that "it wouldn't be stolen in the mail," the letter said. A month later, the other half of the coat arrived. It must have been my aunt's idea. After the war, they told me in Holland that my uncle used to call on friends' homes and just take items he thought we needed. "For my boys," he explained. His friends didn't quite approve. There was a war going on in Holland, too, and no house had many commodities to spare. My aunt was hiding in one of those houses.

One day, I met Messinger, the watch senior commander, a native of Łódź. He was a small man with a protruding belly who moved swiftly, almost impulsively. His face reminded me of his German origins. Right from the start, he did not conceal his sympathy for me. For a quick minute, a thought went through my mind. Maybe he was ... I reprimanded myself for the mere thought. Impossible! How could it be? A German who continued to live in his native town, Łódź? He told me he was staying for the past two months in the Obhut center in Breslau where, as he stressed enthusiastically, they were preparing for several new bases from the military to be transferred into their responsibility.[4] He then remarked that there would be many more opportunities for the talented, such as myself, to prove themselves. He asked me whether I would be interested. I did not provide a clear answer. Following this meeting, Messinger disappeared and never again showed up in Warsaw. After Zeigner's draft into the army, they

171

announced a new commander would arrive. This time he would be Polish.

A few years after the war, I had heard from a Łódź woman that she had resided in an apartment previously belonging to a Jew named Messinger. She said he fled and, according to his friends, lived in the General Governorate and in the Reich as a German. He kept his original name. That's all she knew.

My regular position was at the airfield's main gate. I stood there with a soldier from the guard company. I had a pistol; he had a gun. His job was to check and identify the military personnel coming and leaving the airfield while I was inspecting the civilians, mostly Polish. I also managed well with the Germans. The German sentry was amused to see his folk rage over the fact that they were being checked by a Pole. The soldier would reply indifferently that everything was carried out according to procedures. He would remark to me half-heartedly, "If his highness demands to be greeted by a German, he should join the army, so there will be enough manpower for that too." A touch of entertainment.

I knew all the men in the company, both privates and NCOs. We bonded quite quickly. Some of them expressed interest in my family and origins. Some of them became really close friends. We could not converse at the post, but since we often stood together for many hours, one could draw information even without long conversations. Some months earlier, there was an exchange of the guards' company. The rather young folks were replaced by older ones, around 40 years old and over. Among them were many Austrians as well as Bavarians, Silesians, and others. Some of them were members of the Nazi Party, but that did not matter since their attitude towards the Poles who had served with them was positive. At first, they felt lost, missing their homes more than the young folks whom they had replaced. Their sons served on the front lines, and they were very proud, at least on the outside. In private conversations, they admitted their concerns. They shared with me their Catholic customs. They were surprised I

172

didn't fast on the designated days; others did not understand why I did not know the names of the Catholic holidays in German. How could I not know what the *Verkündigung* was?[5] Do I not hail from the Reich? It was not easy to explain that this Reich was, until recently, part of Poland. I conversed with them freely; I felt safe. They could not tell the difference between a Jew and a Pole.

One day, I was strolling bored along the railway tracks—one of the quietest guard posts. I could think and dream peacefully, luxuries I didn't often allow myself. A man in uniform suddenly appeared riding a motorbike. He had two stars on his shoulder straps—a senior commander. He smiled at me but did not stop. I saw him for the first time, but his face seemed very familiar to me. He reminded me of my gym counselor from my Warsaw Jewish school "La'or." I thought to myself that I was not likely to ever recover from this "illness," thereby hurting myself and the victims' memory.

In the guards' room, I met the new officer in charge, Witkowski. He introduced himself without much detail, but within two hours, I already knew that he was a reserve officer hailing from the Lvov area, which had been recently annexed to the General Governorate, and that he had a brother, an officer, who was in a prison camp. He was married to a tram conductor. The easiness with which he disclosed his personal details was odd. But he was very cordial, and the team liked him. Except for two new Volksdeutsche, no one there knew any German, and the Poles were proud of the fact that they were commanded by a Pole. Witkowski and Brzozowski had a cordial relationship. Witkowski was in charge of all the Obhut guiard positions in Okęcie. He was different in that he had a friendly relationship with the field officers, especially with a captain who was officially the military advocate-general officer (*Gerichtoffizier*). He was in charge of the field police as well as guard procedures such as that of our post. The military police consisted of several NCOs who dealt with internal investigations. I didn't know what the problems with the soldiers were; however, the investigations concerning the

Polish workers dealt mostly with theft of material and equipment and were carried out with discretion. I never heard about trials since the cases were often resolved by reaching a settlement. The soldiers didn't like the policemen, as they were commonly disliked elsewhere.

The new watch commander implemented new procedures: the place was manned predominantly by Poles, which made relations between the commanding officer and his subordinates more cordial. Witkowski's military background affected the special wording of his orders: "Do it the right way, so they wouldn't think only they get it right." People loved him. Some of them, among them three butchers from the town of Żyrardów near Warsaw (butchers again! I never understood why so many of them were fond of that place!), asked him occasionally to move their shift to another day. They were often heard saying, "I have a chance to help in 'operating' a cow," or, "they ask me to prepare a multicolored cow-head roast since no one else knows how to prepare it."[6]

Witkowski was the only commander. Messinger and Zeigner worked together in the alternative shift. It wasn't an easy job for one person to look after everything, and gradually discipline procedures began to loosen. Many problems began to pop up: someone was ill; another suddenly asked to change shifts. The Germans imposed new instructions every day. A new officer showed up from the north. His name was Henrik-Heinz Zrodelski from Pomerania. He spoke fluent German and Polish. He said he was sent to help Witkowski but wasn't sure he would stay. He asked me whether I would be prepared to fill in as commander. I was shocked. Messinger had already mentioned the idea before. I didn't want to think about it; I didn't need this. I needed peace and quiet. It would be better to step aside. This job would force me to get involved with many people, thereby creating unnecessary tension. Most of them wanted to change shifts and prepare sausages. I asked Witkowski some time to think about it, but he refused to wait and announced, "Listen, had someone from the locals tried to dodge this task, I would understand that he hesitates because of his neighbors and so forth. I know some of them change their clothes before getting back home. You do what you have to survive. But you hold this certificate while waiting till you go back to your town. This promotion could only help you." I preferred not to look for hidden meanings in what he said. When he added that we were at a sensitive location, I gave in and agreed. On that same day, they announced that a new *Wachführer* (watch supervisor) was appointed—me. I visited the store at the Bristol hotel again. I attached a silver star to my shoulder straps. The new salespersons at the store spoke Polish and asked me what unit I was in. Only a few were knowledgeable regarding the various units' uniforms.

We continued our smuggling trips, but the requests from Brzozowski's messengers became more frequent. These trips entailed not just time and energy but also high expenses. I turned my colleagues' attention to it and from then on got reimbursement. They once remarked that I should use the second class (at that time, there were three classes on the train) since it became my rank and stars. The packages I transferred were small and inconspicuous. Because of these trips, I hardly had time to hang out with my friends, who were growing impatient with me. But then Witkowski interfered and suggested they would wait for my return, and then he would join in. I was surprised he knew of Brzozowski's affairs, although he never mentioned it. He liked traveling with us. The profits were good in spite of a few failures. He once remarked, "I wonder what the military advocate-general officer would have said had he known where the lard I feed him with comes from." In order to avoid gossip about our trips, we spoke about it very little in the guard room.

I no longer lived with Stephan. He found me a new room. The landlady's husband was suddenly arrested, and his wife hardly went to visit him. She began visiting my roommate when I was away. After a while, he informed me that they found a new place for me. "It will be more convenient for you, Yashinek; you do understand," he said. I did understand.

The new place was indeed more comfortable. Here, too, the landlady was a young woman, the mother of a five-year-old child. Her husband served in the Polish army established in Britain. Every two months, a parcel would arrive via the "Red Cross" containing a variety of delicacies, such as dates, raisins, and compotes, which were luxuries for someone who didn't even have bread. On those days, she would close herself in her room, sobbing alone. Later on, almost daily, an *Oberfeldwebel* of about 45 used to show up and bring a bit of butter, a horse-flavored sausage, and candy for the child.[7] He used to stay the night and completely ignore my presence. He knew I wasn't her taste. That's what Stephan declared the day he brought me there, and it suited me well.

At that time, the authorities pushed forward the process of issuing identification documents for all citizens with no exceptions. The police, supervised by the Gestapo, began to stop trams and conduct Kennkarte checks on all the passengers on board. If someone failed to produce one, he would be checked on a surveillance list in order to inquire whether he had ever applied for it. This check could have been crucial for me. In one instance, the police detained and checked a tram just a second after I had disembarked from it. No doubt I had to obtain a Kennkarte without further delay. In order to apply at the Warsaw population registration office, one had to provide a birth or baptism certificate. But I had already given Bobby Gutman my brother's certificate in the ghetto. So I still had the coachmen union's certificate, and I believed it would suffice. Now I was facing the dilemma of how to attain a birth certificate.

As always, the solution came across by chance. One day, I stumbled into Ella A., my mother's good friend from Kalisz. She was a decade younger than my mother; she was blonde with a straight nose and nice legs. In other words, she caught the eyes of passersby in the street. I hadn't seen her for years since she didn't live in the ghetto.

We knew she lived with the Kalisz rowing-club trainer named Gunther or Gerhard. Now I learned that "he had always been a German" and worked for one of the German offices. "Not the Gestapo," she insisted. It was an emotional meeting; she inquired about Mom, Dad, and the family. She didn't ask about me; she could see for herself. It turned out that she could obtain a birth certificate for me. I wanted to give her my personal details. "No need," she said. "We shall fill them out ourselves." I had to prepare 1,500 złoty and call her within a week; then, she would tell me where and when to come. And that's how it was.

Ella lived in the German quarter in a modern and elegant studio apartment. The landlord was away. She laid the documents on the table: a birth certificate from a community in the Wilna (Vilnius) area, carrying the seal of the local priest in charge. I wanted to fill out the form, but she said it had better not be in my handwriting and filled it out herself. I watched with growing concern as I noticed that her handwriting was not neat. I knew that the community offices employed special calligraphic writers for such purposes, but it was too late to object. In one instance, she wrote the mother's name "Katirzyna" instead of "Katarzyna." I cried with despair, but she, in perfect calmness, corrected the mistake and wrote the right letter over the wrong one. Such a birth certificate was unprecedented. I declared this document would not do and asked her to prepare another form, which I would fill out. "Impossible," she said. "The gentleman who brought me this form said he had none left." I was desperate. She was, too, but what had been done could not be undone. I left carrying a useless piece of paper.

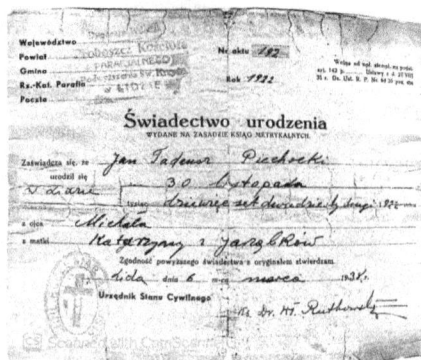

The forged birth certificate with the spelling mistake

The hunt for the "Kennkarte evaders" in the streets continued, and with each day, the danger grew. I was racking my brain, figuring out what to do. An idea came to my mind to ask for a notary copy of my certificate and submit it in place of the original one. But how would I present it to a notary? Finally, I convinced myself there was no other way; I must take the risk.

I remembered there was a notary office on Miodowa Street. Near the house gate was a bilingual sign indicating Adolf Keller's notary office. I stepped in. Whatever will be will be! The small corridor led to a hall whose walls were lined with the clerks' desks. Across the entrance was a large desk behind which sat an old man with white hair. I approached him and said I had a birth certificate and I needed a copy in order to preserve the original. He looked at me. I imagined he was examining me carefully. "No problem," he said. "Please sit down." He took the paper and read it attentively. He turned to one of the clerks and asked, "Could you please lend me your typewriter?" She was astounded and said, "But, magistrate, I can type whatever you need."

"No, no, I'll just do it myself," he replied.

She placed the typewriter on his desk; he inserted a few copy sheets and began typing. It was a very short document, but to me, it seemed to take forever. I felt the eyes of the curious clerks examining me. I looked to my sides, searching for a way out in case I had to escape. The notary, probably a retired magistrate, continued to composedly type my certificate. As he finished, he put a seal and tied a red ribbon on the document, confirming its match to the original certificate. After completing this ceremony, he handed me two copies as well as the original. A third copy remained at his office for filing. "You pay ten złoty," he said. I was surprised, "So little?"

"Yes," he answered. "Notary and legal fees remained as they were in 1939."

I paid and took the receipt. He reached out his hand. "If you ever need our help again, you are welcome; all the best, sir." I muttered something about being thankful and left.

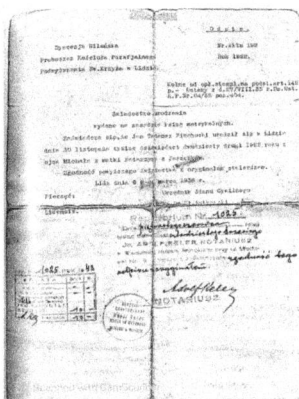

A notarized copy of the forged birth certificate

I went to the population registry office only after a few days, fearing someone may inform them of a suspicious type who came by. After having calmed down from the visit to the notary, it was time to apply for a Kennkarte. I went there in uniform. The female official studied the paper and asked, "Are you Polish, sir?" I smiled kindly and explained that this unit employed non-Germans too. She was surprised but issued the paper confirming I had submitted all the necessary documents. I had to return in two weeks to get the certificate. As a matter of fact, with the temporary paper I got, I could already move freely. After three weeks, again not at the designated time, I arrived to take the desired paper. The official looked for it for a few minutes and then awkwardly announced it had yet to return from the registry office. She did not know why. It was uncommon, but it may happen occasionally.

I returned again a week later. And, once again, my Kennkarte was not there. This time I asked to speak to the office manager. He accepted me immediately. "It's strange," he said. "But it's a mess there too."

"Where?" I asked.

"At the police headquarters on Szucha Avenue," he replied. "We transfer the certificates to be signed by the deputy police chief, Mr. Weidmann. Your paper must be lying there somewhere," he said.

"So, what do you do in such a case?" I asked.

The response was: "Sir, I would have suggested that anyone else wait, but it might take a long time. Therefore, I suggest you go there directly and let them search for it."

I asked whether there could be any reason other than a mess. I wore a uniform so I could afford to ask such a question. He simply didn't understand my question.

"Listen, it may also happen with Germans. You see, at the time of war, they don't always recruit professionals."

Everyone knew which German institutions were located on Szucha Avenue.[8] The Gestapo headquarters lay there, the bureaus of investigations and the torture facilities. I didn't know the deputy police chief's office was also in that terrible compound. I left the municipality building ready to go to Szucha Avenue. If they had been looking for me, they must have had my address and workplace long ago. Anyone showing up at the police chief's office expected to be treated well. And, ultimately, I just had to get that Kennkarte!

I took the tram and got off at the avenue's corner. The street was empty, almost sterile. I marched, and the sound of my boots thumping on the pavement was heard all over the street. I arrived at the address and approached the police sentry at the building entrance. He straightened up after seeing the stars on my shoulder strap, but he, too, had no idea which uniform it was. He asked what I was looking for. I said I was here to see Mr. Weidmann. Upon hearing the name, he straightened his stature even more and told me to go up to the second floor. I entered a fine-looking building. Nothing there indicated it was a place of torture of so many people. At the hall were two middle-aged secretaries. They asked in German what I was looking for. I said I needed to see Mr. Weidmann personally. They asked me to come in. I knocked and entered, hearing *"herein"* (come in) when I was already in the room.

In a large room with three tall windows, behind a heavy wooden desk, sat a man of about 45 years old, wearing a fine suit. He looked at me curiously, and it seemed to me he wasn't quite used to visitors and was even pleased with my sudden presence. He asked me to sit down. I began to talk using my best German, which I had memorized on the way, explaining that I work at the airfield. I applied over a month earlier for a Kennkarte, went to the registry office three times, and still, no certificate could be found. Each visit to the municipality involved a day off from work. "Would you be able to help me?" I asked. Instead of answering me, he began asking questions: where was I from, how did I acquire my German, which language was spoken at home, which school did I attend. I made an effort not to disclose too many details. But my response indicated I was a Pole hailing from the areas where German was widely spoken. I attended a Polish school where many Germans studied too.

He listened with open sympathy and then started talking. "Sir, issuing a Kennkarte would take less than 15 minutes. The thing is that you should obtain a German Kennkarte, not a Polish one. You are a native of the Reich; you speak German at home. According to our laws and criteria, you are a German. There's no reason to treat you otherwise."

I was careful not to disclose my feelings at that moment. With a calm smile, I thanked him but said I considered myself as a Pole, and I didn't think it would be right to identify myself as a German. I felt he liked my response. He replied that naturally, a decision like that is not taken in five minutes, but I should reflect on his proposition and get back to him.

"We'll take care of it in a few days. Meanwhile, I will give you a note for the registry office manager, who will issue a Kennkarte for you there and then." He took out a business card and scribbled a few words on it and gave it to me. "I wish you luck," he said and shook my hand. I exited the building with a feeling of euphoria. Again, I said to myself, *The world belongs to the brave.* As usual, the warning sounded in my ears again: *Do not lose your senses.* The handwriting on the business card said: "A certificate should be issued immediately for Mr. Piechocki", signed by Weidmann.

I was surprised a certificate could be issued there and then. If so, why did they send me to the police headquarters?

As a matter of habit, implementing my safety measures, I didn't go to town that same day but on the next day. Again, I took a day off work, but the Reich would survive somehow. The department manager said, "Yes, I thought so; for people like you, they take Kennkarte from the reserves." I didn't understand. He explained they had several signed documents for urgent and exceptional cases. I was such a case. The official who attended to my case, outside the queue, remarked that I must belong to those non-Polish folks who are issued Polish documents. I reprimanded her, but she went on to smile like a secret partner and said, "It doesn't matter what you say; I know the truth."

I was completely legal. All that was left was not to raise suspicion. That was even harder than calling upon the deputy police chief on Szucha Avenue.

LIFE IS NOT ALWAYS GLOOMY

Everyday life is dull. I know it sounds ridiculous. How many refugees like me would have considered such dullness as endless happiness? But it was hard to detect other colors in the feelings I had at that time. The gray color reflected just another day gone by with no troubling events. No one looked at me; I did not attract anyone's attention, and at night in my bed, when I summed up my day, I could find nothing that could have caused any distress. I like the color gray even today. These habits left their mark on me for years to come; some of them are part of me to this day. I tried to avoid illuminated places as best I could. I preferred the short days of autumn and winter to the long days of spring and summer. When I walked into some public space or office, I stood as close as I could to the wall; from there, I could watch the whole place without being noticed. I subconsciously noted all the escape routes, possible ways out. I had no ambitions to become an "Agent 007," but rules were determined only by the course of life regardless of my intervention. I lived underground, since evading predators on a constant basis is a life underground, even when your camouflage is a successful one.

The sentries' company in Okęcie consisted of a variety of people. Most Poles considered the certificate as a guarantee of relative safety, enabling them to engage after work hours in random activities, which often became illegal during the occupation. Many among them were broken people who, for some reason, lost their families and homes—very common events during a war. There were also lost intellectuals, artists who dedicated their shifts to reading while being provided with a warm meal or two as well as a uniform—benefits that freed them from the hunt for food and clothes. This human landscape became predominant once the German and Ukrainian soldiers disappeared from the service. They were recruited to the army while their jobs were given to non-Germans.

Most ordinary Poles rejected the idea to serve the German occupation, especially with a gun in their hand. Many of my friends diligently concealed their workplace. But there were others too. One could identify their patriotic motivation and the feeling that they were there not by chance. A supervisor such as Witkowski certainly induced that atmosphere.

There were two people there by the name of Kaczor. The first, about 40, quiet, almost tight-lipped, came from the town of Grodzisk. When Stephan introduced his plan to move to another room, Kaczor intervened and said that he could arrange a nice room for me. "You can find a room at educated people's homes and not too far from work too." I did not take up his proposal, but we became close friends, "old" Kaczor and I. He once mentioned privately to me that one could get arms. I immediately replied I was interested. I had been thinking of it for quite some time. He explained that the arms were not new and that I shouldn't build up my expectations. Someone took out a gun that had been hidden in the ground for a long time; we'll take it, but it's not "brilliant." This did not deter me. He brought an old Steyr pistol, 7.65 millimeter, wrapped in rags; the prolonged time it spent in the ground left its mark. It had five bullets, and I paid a small sum of money for it. Kaczor warned me that the cartridge-spin could cause trouble, but that did not intimidate me. I soon learned that the cartridge-spin rarely worked and that I could shoot only after having had loaded one bullet at a time. I kept my pistol between my underwear in a suitcase beneath the bed. I felt better when I knew it was there. I didn't carry it on me.

At work, I was positioned at different posts. Nearby, the warehouse was an armory, and I knew the sergeant who worked there. In fact, he started a conversation with me. At first, I thought he spoke Polish, but it turned out it was Czech, and I didn't quite understand what he was saying, but that did not stop us from conversing. He hailed from the Sudetenland and did not see himself as a German; nonetheless, he was conscripted to the army.[1] He thought it was due to his profession, since he graduated from a technical school at the Brno arms factory. He was employed at various workshops for arms maintenance. He was about my age and talked a lot about himself. We spoke Czech mixed with Polish, and when we could not understand each other, we moved to German. He told me about his school and his love of sports. His cousin was part of the Czech athletic team. I told him I saw the Polish-Czech athletics competition in 1938 and that I remembered his cousin. He was very moved. We met a few times, and he said he felt comfortable speaking Czech. One time, I could not restrain myself and asked him whether he knew how to fix a cartridge-spin. "There's nothing easier," he replied and asked me to bring it to him and that I would get it back fixed the next day. He was not surprised. He must have thought that if I had a pistol, it must be licensed. I brought him the cartridge and meant to ask that he keep it discrete but gave up on the idea. After a day, I got it back with a new spin. "If you need any more fixing, let me know," he said. "Your pistol must be very old. Just don't tell anyone I helped you out because they write down each fix, and I didn't register your cartridge." I told Kaczor I had fixed the cartridge. He was pleased. "Listen, boy," he said. "Keep this friendship close. We may need it. Even if your Czech guy can't do everything, he could surely get us material." I did not respond. I understood who he meant by "us" and what he needed my "Czech guy" for.

There was another Kaczor—a younger one. Zbyszek Kaczor was from Warsaw. He was a robust guy with golden curls, who claimed the curls caused him problems with the girls. We knew each other when I was still living in the old city. Once, we returned together from a shift onboard a tram. Zbyszek suggested we go into the *Soldatenheim* (soldiers' recreation center)—that's when I heard for the first time that we were allowed to enter the soldiers' club (or restroom). I did not appreciate the Germans well enough. They respected a uniform, even that of an auxiliary force. I didn't know that Soldatenheim was located at the YMCA building. There were others across town too. It didn't cross Kaczor's mind that although I'd never been to the YMCA building, I was familiar with that neighborhood, which housed a few theaters. I asked him what exactly we were looking for in a soldiers' club. He made no effort to conceal that it was not for the black-flour cakes or coffee substitutes that he wanted to go but for the pretty German waitresses. The latter didn't necessarily set their sight on soldiers alone, having probably grown bored with them.

I was amazed to find out the place belonged to the Waffen SS.[2] Once I discovered that, it was too late to withdraw. We entered the coffee house hall, which was almost empty. Apparently, the YMCA continued to serve as a hotel, serving both the Waffen SS and Wehrmacht soldiers passing through Warsaw. We sat at a table. A waitress approached us. She knew my friend well, and they liked each other. She didn't mind his basic German, and they kept talking and laughing incessantly, showing their white teeth. After a while, another young girl joined us. She was pretty and more delicate than her friend. "Did you bring a friend?" she asked Kaczor. "Yes," he replied. "He's new, not from here, that's why he needed to visit the Soldatenheim, in order to meet pretty girls." She asked me where I was from. She was from Bonn, Beethoven's town. "My name is Ursula. They call me Ushi at home. Do you know who Beethoven is?" she asked. "Because he," she pointed at Kaczor, "didn't know who he was." I knew who Beethoven was. But I shouldn't overemphasize my knowledge. Still, I made her curious. She sat at the table. "This isn't my shift," she said. "I can only sit for a few minutes."

Kaczor responded, "Be careful who you flirt with; he's a *Jude*."

I turned to stone but continued to smile. It was a result of my ever growing self-control.

She turned to me and asked, "Are you really a Jew?"

I continued to smile.

Kaczor recanted, "Well, it's only a joke so that you will notice me, not him." She thought his explanation was tasteless. She got up and told me, "Next time, come alone, best before noon while my boyfriend is still at work."

As we left, Kaczor explained that all the girls serving there belonged to the Waffen SS auxiliary unit, and almost every one of them has some boyfriend. Ursula's boyfriend was Unterscharführer, the swimming pool's manager.[3]

I asked Kaczor how this nonsense about me being a Jew came to his mind.

He laughed, "Why, can't a person joke anymore? The truth is, when you arrived, people said that there's something Jewish about you."

I shrugged, "Well, you sure have some sense of humor." I had something to think about. I knew that sentries talk and gossip. I hoped my companion's opinions worked to my benefit. My journeys' companions could not talk much about our trips, but a remark about my achievements here and there must have had an impact. I knew I had to be cautious, but I equally had to find out who it was that started the notion about me being a Jew. I was troubled over the idea that had someone suspected me as a Jew even once; this suspicion might resurface again. How would I react? What would I do? Would I run away? Where to? Life wasn't always dull.

What surprised me most was that the new "instructions" were different than before. The package-delivery operations' proxy arrived and asked that we step outside. He wanted to speak freely. He wandered around as if the place was familiar to him. He instructed me to report in uniform at a street corner in the southwest of the city before the curfew hour. There I would receive further instructions. "Ah," he recalled. "I heard your gun already operates. You might as well bring it with you." Time and again, I became breathless, discovering how much other people knew about me while I didn't even know who they really were. They were routinely informed about me, but by whom? Only by Kaczor? By Witkowski too? Brzozowski must have been involved in this.

I got there on time. One of the two guys who approached me mumbled, "My name is Wojcik." Maybe it was another name; I don't remember, but that was the password. Later, with no further talk, he instructed me to turn to a side street. I was told to wait by a store in a half-burned-down house. They entered another building about 150 meters away. A broad-shouldered fellow walked around there with a dark coat, and I was supposed to signal to him if I saw a military or police officer approaching and walk to the main street. It was already after curfew hour. The streets were empty. I had no reason to signal him since no one intruded. After about an hour, the people who brought me there returned and signaled me to get back. They walked right past me. I walked toward Narutowicz Square in order to catch the night tram back to Okęcie. I was bothered by the idea that a German patrol could have detained and interrogated me and even conducted a body search. It occasionally happened at night, even to many permit holders. The pistol would have complicated matters even more. In our next meeting, I told this to the proxy. I didn't even know his name. He quietly agreed with me that it would have been wiser to have gone without arms. Since then, I allowed myself to express my opinion every time I got new instruction. I was astonished at how feeble they were at times in conveying their orders. I was yet to have been sworn in, but I knew it was Armia Krajowa—AK.[4] For a long time, no one had told me that expressly. I also guessed that others in my surroundings were carrying out various missions on its behalf. "Old" Kaczor sometimes hinted that and was the one to introduce me to Brzozowski's messenger. Brzozowski himself behaved as if nothing was happening. He spoke about his journeys but never mentioned a word about his ties with the resistance movement. Witkowski was simply silent about it as though the subject was nonexistent. However, he gave that impression so that one could "guess" it. Several times I had said to myself I was going to ask him straightforwardly. But immediately I had doubts. What if they demanded to know about my origins, my family, etc.? I had no guarantees that disclosing my origins would not devastate me. That was why I continued to fulfill instructions and waited for the right minute. I suspected I was being put to the test on different occasions. Even the visit to the soldier's club might have been such a test. Often it turned out that I was wrong; other occasions remained unclear.

Toward the end of 1943, Theodor and his wife, Halina, asked that I accompany them for a visit at their friends in a village near Okęcie. It was a rather sizeable farm. Before the war, they used to grow vegetables, which was a profitable business due to the short distance from the city. It was less profitable during the war, so the energetic landlady found another gainful occupation: she took cows and calves to an illegal slaughter. It was a risky business, but it worked out for her. A village woman leading a cow with an ear tag through the fields did not raise suspicion (the Germans marked and numbered all the farm livestock; cows as well as pigs wandered about with a numbered ear tag). This occupation enabled them to live well. At the head of the table sat the husband, but the wife wore the boots in the house. We were raising glasses for our hosts' sake in the hope that the war would end soon, when a young girl joined in. Basia was her name, an only child, her parents' pride. Soon I learned that I was invited in order to get introduced to her. She was pretty and smart. She said her mother didn't want her to work growing vegetables. "My mother makes every effort for me to go to university after the war. That is why I devote most of my time now to studying."

Her mother began to inquire about me and asked, "Where do you hail from? What does your family do?" I tried to disclose as little as a few words, but she insisted. Her questions embarrassed Basia, and she turned to her mother and said, "You ask so much; perhaps Mr. Yanek is embarrassed." Everyone laughed, including me, and Halina remarked, "Mr. Yanek should not be shy. He will probably be interested in Basia's dowry." This time I was the only one to laugh, and Basia blushed, which made her even prettier. Her mother said with determination, "She has everything that's necessary, even more than enough. But what matters most is that she has character and God at heart." I did not expect such a declaration. The girl was nice. She inspected me closely. This house, this family, this girl, all appealed to me. The tranquility there made it feel as if we were on a different planet. It was so different from everything I was immersed in during the past year. It was nice to find shelter there, even for a short while, to recover from the nightmares, to rest a little. I could only dream about it. I regretted that their heart's wish remained impossible for me.

It was a pleasant visit. We were invited for Christmas, but Theodor made it clear that they were going away to his wife's parents. I preferred not to come on my own, so I announced I had to visit my family on Christmas. When Basia repeatedly asked that I come for a visit, I promised to do so after the holidays. Her mother seemed content with my response. I later met Basia at the Belchinski's house with his neighbors, and it was their idea to match between us.

The Belchinskis had a new baby, and they invited Basia and me as godparents for their son. Basia had two requests: that I come in a suit and not in uniform and that I agree to let her pay her share in the present for the child. I agreed to the first request. I showed up in the suit my uncle sent me from Holland and which was fitted to me by a local tailor. Basia was modestly but elegantly dressed. She looked beautiful and blushed upon hearing the usual remarks made at such events: "If the godfather doesn't touch the godmother, he will go to hell." The priest sprayed some holy water on the newborn baby and chanted the blessings. Then the genitor approached with a tray at hand. Being so tense, I didn't remember to put a money note on the tray. Basia did it for me and whispered, "You silly little fool; couldn't you see it's that only thing he cares for?" I already knew what the tray was for, but at that moment, I was so anxious. I was nervous about my role and played it with no previous experience or rehearsal. I bought the child a delicate gold cross pendant. Both the parents and the godmother were happy. I assessed my appearance at the event as successful. It looks like the occurrence at the soldiers' club was coincidental. A person suspected as a Jew is not invited to be a godfather at a christening. I came to the conclusion that I could not let my relations with Basia become serious. I was sorry for it, but it was inevitable. Just then, things got hectic around me.

My relationship with Henryk Zerodlawski, the other shift's commander, was fine. He was two or three years older than me and with higher seniority. He perceived this as a reason for his authority over me. I didn't ascribe much importance to it, and it didn't affect my everyday life anyway. I made sure I had no quarrels with him, and our meetings were short enough to avoid any unpleasant situations. When our talks did resort to personal issues, I avoided disclosing information as much as I could about my family, my town, and so forth. I always had an answer ready: "You know very well how it is down there, how we used to live there, and what life there is like now. It's no use talking about these subjects over and over again." Zerodlawski asked much, but never talked about himself.

Looking at the way he comported himself, one might have thought he was German. He spoke excellent German, especially on the phone, calling himself Heinz. I once hummed a tune, and he immediately asked, "What's with these Jewish melodies?" I calmly replied it was a tune from the latest German movie, and I recommend that he see it—it's funny, has nice music, and pretty actresses. He let it slide, but his expression indicated the subject was not closed.

One day, Henryk intervened in a conversation among the guards. They exchanged the usual opinions about the extermination of the Jews. Zerodlawski surprised many by saying, "They say that Poland must thank Hitler for relieving it from the Jews. It's not that simple. The national radio is also against it. The Germans themselves claim Hitler never ordered the Jews killed. *Mein Kampf* only called for forcing the Jews to become productive." His words were meant to prove that he was knowledgeable with what the Polish government-in-exile determined, as well as with what the Nazis determined regarding the final solution. Everyone hushed. They had their own opinions, but they didn't wish to argue with him. Who knows, perhaps he was more Heinz than Henryk after all. I was troubled with the looks Zerodlawski gave me occasionally throughout the conversation, as if he was waiting for me to intervene in this dangerous and slippery discussion. I listened with apathy. I had already heard "the Poles owe Hitler thanks for 'relieving' them from the Jewish problem" many times before. Many had spoken this way, even educated people, the so-called "civilized" people. I had already been immune to this and could display indifference toward these convictions.

I kept my distance from Zerodlawski as much as I could but could not regain my self-confidence. I had sleepless nights, wondering how I would run away in case something happened. Where to? I could find no answers to these questions. It was a tense period, and Zerodlawski kept on making provocative remarks on various occasions. People looked, listened, and undoubtedly, with each day that went by, the situation had worsened.

I met with my brother; I wanted to consult with him on what to do. Each time, we had to find a new place to meet—not in any of our living places, since it was too dangerous. We once met in the famous church in Czestochowa, full of pilgrims, not far from my brother's workplace. We "prayed" and talked. I already knew my brother was linked with the left-wing resistance movement *Armia Ludowa* ("people's army") and asked him if he could help me join them. He was amazed and said, "They will instantly see that we're both Jews!" I didn't understand: "But you said they were socialist." His reply was decisive: "If only you knew what they did to Jews they found in the woods, you wouldn't have said this nonsense." We parted. I returned to Okęcie.

And suddenly, Zerodlawski disappeared as if the earth had swallowed him. He hadn't been seen for some days, and then the word was out that he had left to the General Governorate. It turned out he had been trying to join the Todt Organization for some time. It was an auxiliary unit to the armed forces, mostly dealing with construction and fortifications works on the front line. He was finally accepted and sent to France.

———

Many years have passed, yet I still cannot define what fear is. I was naturally afraid, even very much afraid. The fact that I was brave did not change that. Both can exist simultaneously. Fear is, above all, a feeling of uncertainty. I could sense the situation I was in, not assess it. A certain sensory receptor in my head could intercept a transmission and activate an alarm: someone is looking at you, talking about you, suspecting you. This paralyzed me, but only for a short while. I automatically scanned my history and checked whether I'd left any footprints to my brother, an indication, a note. I learned the addresses by heart. I carried no photographs; I simply did not have any. The landlady knew I was receiving mail from my brother and uncle—quite seldom, though. The letters did bear the sender's address. If one was very curious, one could have inquired into the postmark. My top priority now was to protect my brother. I could not harm my uncle. I myself was cautious but unwilling to subdue to fear. I felt that running away would be the end for me, a dead end. I was fearful but at the same time calmed by the dim notion that I would make it. I convinced myself: I must keep cool and calm. I often pleaded for help from the heavens. In fact, I didn't know any prayers in any language. In retrospect, I pulled myself out of countless dead-end situations. Was it my brave heart? My impertinence? No. I do believe in an almighty power.

Brzozowski's people occasionally sent me on trips, mostly to guard activities at dusk, pasting announcements, painting slogans, distributing leaflets concerning verdicts to traitors and women who befriended Germans, as well as murders of the Gestapo. My job was to warn about upcoming risks and to serve as a cover when necessary. I once escorted "workers at a beer brewery" on their way to an operation. One evening, a group of guys and one girl, who had no idea who was guarding them, began escaping when they saw me approaching. I had to call them to come back, but not too loudly. The girl recognized me since we were once together in a similar operation. Once again, I had topics to discuss with the proxy.

On one of the winter days, a young and energetic woman entered the guard room in Okęcie. She was dressed in a heavy coat and was looking for one of the guards. She said she had to see him. The guy was out on a mission and was due back within an hour. She decided to wait for him. I felt uneasy about her waiting in a room full of guns and telephone rattles, but I could not dismiss her due to the freezing weather outside. She started conversing with me. She was carrying a message to her friend from his mother. "I am Halina P.," she said. "And I live in Piaseczno." Perhaps she thought I was German since she emphasized there were many Germans in her community. She later added that she, her mother, and her family are Germans. I was surprised because she spoke perfect Polish. The guy she was looking for was Polish and strongly patriotic. When he returned, they went outside to talk. After she had left, he came back in and said they had dated for a long time and were about to be married, but eventually separated. I asked him whether he would have married a German. He replied that they had known each other since they were kids. He knew she was German, but she was sympathetic. She used to share hard times with him. He also noted that she asked about me. After a few days, she returned again, this time asking about me. She knew when my shift was over and asked that I escort her home.

"Where to? Piaseczno?" I asked.

No, she was to spend the night at her aunt's in Warsaw. Rejecting her could have held me up to ridicule. She was waiting there for a while letting everybody know it was me she had on her mind. I spent that night in an apartment on the rose avenue, a fancy southern Warsaw neighborhood that had been turned into a German quarter. I also heard stories about her mother, who fell in love with a young German officer during WWI and traveled with him to Germany in 1918. Halina was born after a few years. Her parents were not legally married. Halina mentioned she did the same—she too has a daughter outside wedlock, raised by her mother. The child's father is the sentry she came to see—my friend. They never married but remained good friends. He was the one who persuaded her that I was the "best catch" and that she shouldn't let me slip away. She told me about her parents. Her father was a university graduate. They lived a difficult life. There was a great deal of unemployment in Germany, and they were poor. Finally, she and her mother returned to Poland. The parents kept in touch. Her father had joined the Nazi Party at an early stage and quickly rose to power. He was appointed a minister in the Reich government: Dr. Hans Lammers, the Chancellor's Bureau Chief (*Chef der Reichskanzlei*).[5] He took care of her and her mother's affairs and tried to improve their living standards: "Though we don't need anything, we endure well."

I was shocked at this confession. It was hard to swallow the details, and I said so to my partner. Every common Pole would have felt the same. She agreed it was quite astonishing. "But..." I didn't understand. "There's something different about you from the guys I know; you are more delicate. Anyhow, from the first minute, I felt you had something to hide." I tried not to turn to stone. As usual, I reacted with laughter. In this situation, I could not get out or avoid another meeting. I stayed. Halina did not remain silent about her affection toward me. I did not want to leave her either.

One evening, she was telling me about her school friends. She mentioned some Jewish names and claimed that if she could, she would have done much to help these girls. It was a clear attempt to put me to the test. I could not but reply. "Listen," I said. "If you are telling me all this because you assume I'm Jewish, I have to prove you wrong. You made up a spicy fairytale—the daughter of a Reich minister and a Jew—but it won't do because I'm not Jewish. If I'm gentler than the other guys you met, I can only conclude you've met the wrong guys. Anyway, you're a nice girl, and I really don't mind you being a German." She laughed, but after a while, she raised the issue again. This time she said that it really didn't matter to her whether I was Jewish or not. Even if I were a Jew, she would have liked me just the same. I replied decisively, even bluntly, and then tried to be kind.

We met numerous times but always within the realm of the apartment. In our many conversations, she proved to be smart, gentle, and sensitive toward injustice. We just never spoke again about Jews. And then something happened that forced us to stop seeing each other.

One of the guards asked for a day off. As always, I tried to meet his needs by rearranging the shift schedule. In order to help that guard, I had to cancel another guard's day off. The second guard was intolerant, despite the fact it was his second or third request for a leave in a short period of time. He stated his demand with a resolute, almost insulting tone. When I refused, he lashed out at me, "That's what happens when a Jew is in charge!" The people in the room were astounded by the unprecedented accusation. I only knew this: I had to retaliate aggressively. I stepped up to him and, with utter calm, slapped his face vigorously. He did not expect this. I felt like that was the only choice

I had. Clearly, the subject was not closed. I did not run, though my brain stormed. How should I act in order to prevent an investigation in this case? I decided to wait for Witkowski. I sensed the atmosphere in the room was explosive. I stepped outside and walked near the windows so that I could be seen.

Witkowski arrived. I invited him for a walk so we could talk alone. We strode along the railway, where I met him first. I told him about the incident in detail. His face became gloomy. He looked straight at me and asked, "I have to know the truth: are you a Jew or not?" I answered simply, "Yes, I am." He turned away, and we continued to walk in silence. After a while, he stopped and said, "We'll go back to the guard room, and I'll announce that, at your request, we are going to the airfield doctor in order to check you, but we won't go. After we return, I'll announce that you had been checked and had been acquitted of any guilt or suspicion. You will then order vodka for everyone and drink heavily. Then you'll go on a rampage so that I will have to throw you out. We will then think what to do next."

I immediately recalled the time I did go on a rampage as an alleged drunk in order to clear my brother's name. This time I was playing for my own fate. I played along with Witkowski's scenario up to the tiniest detail. As a result, I was forced to leave Okęcie a few days later.

About two weeks before the Polish uprising in Warsaw, I was notified that Witkowski's wife was asking to see me. I didn't know why. I suspected some misunderstanding between him and his wife because he used to cheat on her often. I had money to deliver to him after my last smuggling trip. I took it with me to give it to her and set out to meet her in midtown Warsaw on the corner of Marszałkowska and Aleja Jerozolimskie. She was nervous and frightened and told me immediately her husband had been arrested at the airfield. A new military advocate-general was appointed, who suspected his predecessor and Witkowski were involved in corruption. She was helpless and hoped I could tell her something about it. I knew nothing. I was certain Witkowski did not participate in any corruption; he was too smart to do that. His position was too important for him as well as for the resistance group, which I was convinced was behind him. He received an apartment from the former advocate-general officer in the German zone since the airfield held several such empty apartments with no one to give them to. Witkowski also convinced his captain friend to give him a gun license. It was easier than getting an apartment and was completely formal. I told his wife that I could only assume, hope, that everything would become clear soon and her husband would return home. She almost burst into tears. "Yes, but meanwhile, he's in jail. They allowed me to bring him some underwear, and he said I can calm down, but it is a jail, cells, showers, toilets, all common." I still did not understand. "If he said you can be calm, it means he believes he will be released soon." She looked at me as if I fell from another planet. "Yanek, good God, don't you understand that Juli (Julius) is a cat?" I felt as though I was drowning. The ghetto refugees used the word "cat" as a codename for a Jew.

After a week, Witkowski returned. He was released without any investigation. In our meeting, he pressed me to forget what his wife disclosed. Our next meeting did not take place until after the war. I was an officer in a unit temporarily stationed in a town in which he was the police chief. For some reason, he didn't feel comfortable when we stumbled into each other. We didn't keep in touch. God knows why.

After having raised hell as a drunkard, I wanted to disappear from Okęcie. I was waiting to be transferred to another base. I had time on my hands to travel for a few days and was asked—as was customary—to urgently deliver a "small package" from Chelm Lubelski. Someone would bring the package there from another town, and my job was to transfer it to Warsaw. It turned out that on the ride back to Warsaw, I was to be accompanied by the girl who brought the package, and it really angered me. When I was traveling alone, I could go into the Germans-only cabin. It was easier and more convenient. But, with her, I had to force my way into the regular cabin. And anyway, if she was going, then what was my role here? I didn't know what she carried and where she stashed it away. The girl, a redhead who talked a lot, seemed very confident until we boarded the train; then, she turned to stone. After a few questions, she admitted she was also smuggling for her private needs: 2 to 3 kilos of tobacco. I was mad. Her stupidity could have caused us a needless investigation and inspection of every pocket, as well as a body search. I asked whether she knew what they did to tobacco smugglers and whether she kept "my" package with the tobacco. Luckily enough, she kept it in a small case with her clothes. Without further discussion, I took the package from her hands and told her that if she didn't get rid of the tobacco, I would move to another cabin. She almost burst into tears but left the "merchandise" in the toilet. When we arrived in Warsaw, it was no longer there.

I asked my instructor again why they asked me to carry out the task when the redhead was on it too. I told him about the tobacco. He was bewildered. He didn't know about the redhead and promised to check the mission's every detail in the future. He added that I would not be able to go on any mission in the coming weeks since I was going to a course. It was important since it meant the whole affair in Okęcie, and the medical check did not change the attitude toward me. I asked the instructor, whose nickname was "the miller," whether I would be participating formally in the course. He knew what I meant: I had to take the oath. He suggested I do not waste my time on "things which are due to come." Meanwhile, the course is a "serious business." At that time, I was appointed by Obhut as the new guard commander in a new airbase in Bielany, a Warsaw district. A unit serving the small airfield near the city was located within the institute for physical education in this Warsaw suburb. I asked whether I could get some days off before beginning my new job. Brzozowski was absent, and his officials didn't know why. I had doubts, though the new place appealed to me. Yet, I didn't want to give up the course. The next day, after speaking with Brzozowski, it appeared I could get a week or 10 days' leave.

I preferred not to be seen in Okecie. Although I could not disappear, I tried very much not to stand out; so much has happened there lately. I managed to find a room in northern Warsaw, near my new base. It was a pleasant room in a neighborhood of small modern houses built before the war by a socialist cooperative for the working-class families. My new landlady wanted to know whether I was Volksdeutsche or "something else." I replied that I was Polish and was welcomed with a smile as if saying, "Well, you can't really tell the truth, can you?" I did not leave my room in Okęcie. I declared to my former landlady that I would continue to arrive less frequently since I was now working outside Warsaw. The course was about to begin shortly.

MEMORIES WITH NO BRAVERY

Here too, I will not speak of courage. I was no hero. I had no ambitions to be one. Maybe I had some in the past, as a child raised on fairy tales of bravery, but that also was gone with time. Nevertheless, I didn't act like a coward. Sometimes I was too brave, and that may account for the numerous times I got into trouble in school and the reason I was known as a stiff-necked trouble-maker.

After having fled from the ghetto, I used to act at times on the verge of insanity—more than anything, to prove to myself I was not afraid. Today, I believe that was precisely what saved my life several times. In the first months, the survival problem had been intertwined with the idea of fighting the murderous occupation. The world around me was determined to kill me, and I, in return, had to do everything in my power to evade the forces combined against me. It frustrated me that many thought I was a German, and it brought about various thoughts. But it was as if Obhut was made for me. I could hardly have hoped for a safer haven. It was no coincidence I had met so many people there who, each for their own reasons, looked for shelter in that place. It later became known that the resistance, too, used the place as a convenient acting ground. Like all those who hid away, I yearned for the day when I would come out of hiding, take off my guise and meet people to whom I'll tell the truth—about me and about those who weren't as lucky. I could never imagine what this moment would be like. It always remained vague.

The will to strike, to act, to avenge was conceived in the ghetto, and after I had left, I always looked for ways to realize it—first, in Ksawerów, but at that time, the resistance was not interested in candidates like me. I had no chance of making such contacts. A year later, I was in a different position. I had the potential that could be exploited, and I could carry out various missions. I was not always aware of the possible dangers involved in those missions, and sometimes I was astonished to find out how dangerous it was and how close I was to a real catastrophe. Once, we came across a paper check by the gendarmes and SS officers of civilians wearing a uniform. I was called in for a check as well, yet, just at that time, I was equipped with an official travel order (*Marschbefehl*). I was surprised and found this coincidence hard to believe. But the missions I had undertaken were not enough for me, and I wanted more.

Battles with the Germans appealed to me. Several times, I was just about to ask my proxies for a real mission, but then the question always crept up: what if those that will have to decide will be less friendly than Brzozowski. What if they discover my secret?

The course I was about to participate in was postponed. Meanwhile, I was ordered to change to a position in the base located within the physical education institute. We were supposed to protect the factories, warehouses, dorms, and, most important, the kitchen. The base was not big, not at all like that in Okęcie. It was a temporary base "Until it is changed once again." I was ordered to report before a very young *Hauptmann* (captain), a combat pilot who had recently been appointed the unit commander. He made it very clear he despised his administrative job, looked through me as if I was transparent, and told me to turn to his subordinate, a major. I was not surprised by this order of rank. In spring 1944, there were strange events in the army too. This unit arrived from the Kiev area. The commander was a famous combat pilot. Here he was quickly promoted to a major, left his base, and went back to his air-force wing. His subordinate major was an elderly man, who was also reluctant to deal with guard jobs and told me to go to the base's *Hauptfeldwebel* (master sergeant). Spiess, who was the highest-ranking officer from among the NCOs, was amazed to discover I was not German. He was told there would be Poles in the guards' shift, but they didn't tell him the officer in charge would be a Pole too. In the place they had been stationed before, there was a German hailing from the Volga region in this position. He didn't know any German except for a few words, so that I had my advantages. The master sergeant said the unit would not be stationed there for long and demanded a meticulous military appearance. To my surprise, we were equipped with helmets, up-to-date Mauser guns, hand grenades, and ammunition not counted properly.

When I got to the base, the guard team was already there—most of them younger guys than me. I noticed many of them already knew each other, although they had only been recently accepted to Obhut. They had been waiting for me for two days. They were told by the head office that a young Wachführer was about to arrive, a Pole, one of "ours." That's what they told me when I introduced myself. I was embarrassed. I wondered who arranged this "business card" for me? I said with indifference that we were here to get the job done, and we got paid for it. Whoever had questions would get answers.

Within a few days, it became clear that certain sentries were joined in some common interest. They willingly accepted the tasks, tended to their arms, and they very much liked the fact that they possessed hand-grenades and helmets. I didn't know what tied them together, so I decided to ask my proxy. Already before my transfer to Bielany, my "instructor" informed me that he would keep in touch with me. Now I was waiting for our meeting.

I divided the bullets, 20 to each gun. The guards were supposed to return them with the gun after every shift. After designating the posts and shifts, a small blond guy approached and asked to speak to me privately. He wanted to turn my attention to the fact that we were in the woods and here anything could happen. "The situation is changing, you see, so it's better not to restrict the amount of ammunition." He recommended the "guys" be warned about engaging in any follies or unruly behavior. And as for the hand grenades, they should be treated with caution and without insolence so that a hostile eye would not detect us. He did not indicate who was supposed to give the orders, but it was crystal clear. He also suggested I ask for an instructor who would train us in hurling German hand grenades. These were indeed different types of hand grenades; they had long wooden handles.

In the east Warsaw train station, where trains pulled in from the Russian front, one could have bought almost anything from the soldiers passing by there on their way to vacation. Not only uniforms and boots (many of them had a reserve pair of boots), they also wished to get rid of ammunition and bayonets without hesitation. It was harder to obtain firearms, but occasionally, soldiers agreed to "get mugged" in return for an agreeable amount of lard and ham.

The master sergeant promised we would be getting an instructor the next day. And, indeed, a young German *Unteroffizier* (staff sergeant) who had just been released from the hospital appeared and taught us each day how to use hand grenades. The idea was to hurl it through the barbed wire behind which was a firing position or insert it through the bunker embrasure so that it would explode inside it. The base was surrounded by barbed wire. Every 100 to 200 meters was a bunker designed to protect the soldiers in case of an attack. We guarded the bunkers from the outside and did not go inside. The little blond guy became a master in hand grenade hurling. He befriended the instructor, and they even went together to meet some girl. The German hailed from the east, where he said he spent too much time. He said he was happy in Warsaw, happy to "return to Europe."

One night, after a few weeks, gunshots were heard near the base's fence. I ran there fast. My sentries were all shooting indiscriminately. "What's going on here?" I asked. "Can't you see? There, to the right!" I couldn't see anything, not on the right nor to the left. I stopped the fire. We laid there for a while, watching and listening. I counted the ammunition. One hundred bullets and two hand-grenades were spent, although I could swear, I heard just one explosion. The sergeant on duty arrived after 15 minutes and wasn't at all alarmed. He moaned about having gone through such indiscriminate shootings in the eastern front, and it was no big deal. I was confused. I asked them why they didn't tell me they were planning to stage this event. The reply was surprisingly honest: "Sir, you would have interfered. You'd better explain it to the Germans and protect us. We have to take out what remained from this operation—some bullets and one grenade." I took out the grenade myself. On the other side of the Warsaw-Danzig train station, the blonde guy stood waiting for it. It was a stupid and unnecessary affair. It could have been organized with more sense, but that's how it happened.

I was ordered to join the course with no further delay. I was told to say I was not quitting my job, just a few hours off for a few days. It was a theoretical course, a preparation for field experience. I was ordered to get to an apartment on Marszałkowska Street. Within 10-minute intervals, two other guys arrived. One guy got there before me, so there were four of us. I got the impression they were from Warsaw. The instructor was an older man who appeared to be an intellectual. One would have never guessed that was what an explosives expert looked like. The apartment was large and empty. The participants were numbered, and the instructor called each of us by his number. I was number three. I had reason to believe my colleagues were in the resistance for some time, all having been sworn in.

I decided to be patient. The person who had sent me there introduced himself as the "miller's substitute." He claimed that the fact that I didn't go through all the formal procedures was not because of a mess but because there was no time for procedures in such crazy times. It was a two-week course with only five meetings, and we were not allowed to write down anything. We had to keep in mind every detail. Only once did the instructor display the actual materials. In the outside surroundings, the police manhunt was constantly underway. After the course was done, I never saw any of its participants again.

Every day brought news of the nearing frontline, and in the Bielany base, the atmosphere was growingly tense. From among the Germans, I mostly saw the NCOs. The privates were transferred to a barrack in the airfield, and I only saw them when they got to the infirmary and the warehouses and seized the opportunity to get a proper shower there. We were preparing for an evacuation, and some services had already been transferred to the Reich. They now allowed themselves to say things they wouldn't have dared to say only weeks before. One guy remarked it would be difficult to stop the Bolshevik offensive. They were promised numerous times that the offensive would be halted! But once they got to the Reich borderline, it would all be over. Then, the people would have had their say. Not "Jupp the lame" (Goebbels), nor "fat Hermann" (Göring), but the people themselves! I had never heard such bitter expressions before. They were undoubtedly said from their hearts. One of them knew where I was from. He said, "You must be waiting to get back home. What do you think will happen here once we're out of here?" I answered it was no secret the Poles wanted liberty and sovereignty. "Do you believe," he asked, "they will let you have your own state without the Germans or the Russians?" I disrupted the conversation. "That's politics. I don't deal with it. Had I dealt with it, I would not have been here." These conversations fueled my thoughts: at last, the Germans stopped believing the false slogans they had been fed with for so long. The bombing of German cities by the Allied forces had also weighed in its heavy part.

We continued to "slaughter pigs." It appeared as though something had changed; the gendarmes and the train police changed their skin and became more moderate. They continued to confiscate merchandise but left over a great deal as if making sure the "business" didn't die down. We took advantage of the situation; we all needed money. Theodore had his own "shopping list:" for the fast-growing child, for his wife. He said a young woman could not always wear the same rags. Stephan discovered suddenly he didn't have enough clothes. We hit the road whenever it was possible.

When a German soldier, in a train filled with soldiers on their way to vacation, found out his seat neighbor was a non-German (I once had to take off the note covering the inscription "non-German" in my certificate in order to prove I wasn't German), he instantly became talkative and asked numerous questions. They asked about everything. They returned from the eastern front, and all the horrors taking place in the Reich now had been censored in the letters addressed to them. Nevertheless, they did know what was happening. They also knew their families were hungry due to the shortage of food. The news reached them mostly by friends returning from holidays at home. They were eager to know what was happening in our parts since we were part of the picture. They were curious to hear our opinions about what was taking place. They were probably looking to hear from us what we heard on Radio London.[1] They had a determination that replaced the stern discipline that prevailed only a year ago. Our answers always initiated with: "What can we know?" And yet, we used some phrases to describe the poverty and hardship in an occupied land. It had left its mark on them. Suddenly, after four years, they comprehended their situation, and ours was quite similar despite their "victories." But first and foremost, they wanted to bring food to their homes. They sold whatever they could. Once, I saw a soldier at the train station taking out a gun wrapped in a towel. The buyer held a bag full of ham and pork loin wrapped in rags.

I visited my former base in Okęcie. I met some old friends as well as many new people. Most of them were intelligent people who until recently avoided working in a place such as Obhut. The guy who was the reason why I had to leave Obhut was no longer there; he was allegedly sent to Germany for forced labor, but I could not figure out how all this had happened. Among the new ones, I identified two with a Jewish look. I felt it. I met them both after the war. They never divulged whether I was right. After the war, I met Jews who survived the Holocaust but chose to go on with their lives as Christians. After all, they had gone through, they were still afraid to identify themselves.

"Old" Kaczor asked me if I would like to exchange my pistol for a new FN. Of course, I wanted! I got a tiny pistol, a 6.35mm that could be carried in a small pocket, even inside a boot. It only had two bullets, and Kaczor promised to get me more bullets, but the circumstances did not enable it. I was now holding a new little toy in my pocket. It was hazardous and unnecessary, nevertheless...

One day, I came to arrange something in the Obhut office on Ujazdów Avenue. The office was spacious and occupied the whole ground floor of an elegant building. A young man bumped into me at the entrance to the hallway. I wanted to scold him, but at that moment, he hugged me cordially and whispered into my ear, "My name is Stanislaw Zawada." It was Alexander (Olek) Leshno, a Jew who was two years my senior in high school. He was excellent in gymnastics and in the school's top team. He played the violin well enough to perform in school events. He was excited, and so was I. It was as if he was resurrected. Brzozowski, who witnessed the meeting, asked, "Do you know each other?" I immediately said we competed in sports together back in high school. He smiled and said, "And who won?"

"Of course he did. You can tell," I said.

We went out. Olek, despite the need for cautiousness, asked that we meet again. We decided to meet the next day at the gate of the house he was supposed to visit. We conversed there for an hour. We didn't have time to go into details—family, friends—but he did ask what happened with my brother. He was evidently happy to hear he was alive. He knew him well, while I was just a kid in his eyes. He had been working in Obhut longer than I had. I could tell he did not live off a sentry's salary. He was the son of a famous tailor who made officers' uniforms for the military. This was quite a profitable job. Funny enough, another tailor who worked for the military was also a Jew, so the common talk was that these two held all the officers' names in Warsaw and the area. Olek asked whether I was in the resistance. I answered frankly, "I am and I am not." I executed some tasks for them, but I didn't belong to a specific unit. At the same time, I was to attend a field-engineering course. He simply said, "Don't make an effort to change your fate. You'll never know where you'll end up and what you'll find there." He also said he was accepted to an organization whose name he didn't know. After a few months, he was told its name was NSZ–Narodowe Siły Zbrojne.[2] The organization's members didn't like Jews, and many among them were nationalist extremists. Nobody knew he was Jewish, yet, he thought nobody would have hurt him had they known the truth. He befriended many of them, and after having many doubts, decided to stay. Leaving, by the way, was not simple and sometimes not possible. He finally came to terms with the fact that they, too, were fighting the Germans. We met nearby a house where he had participated in a course.

After the war, I learned a few facts about him. Olek Leshno—Stanislaw Zawada—completed a course in the NSZ, probably an officers' course. He was a sergeant in the "Bashta" battalion of the

AK, and participated in the 1944 summer uprising in Warsaw, and was killed in action.

I had another surprising meeting at the Obhut main office. I talked with Witkowski and Orishek, a "fresh" Volksdeutsche, who admitted frankly he was wrong to sign the Volksliste—the document determining he belonged to the German nation. Already in the coming days, he would have to leave his elegant apartment in central Warsaw and look for a new home in the west of the city. His German neighbors had already begun leaving. The problem was they were not returning to the Reich but to the Poznań and Warthegau area. Luckily, he was not being recruited to the military. I listened and almost laughed inside. What had it come to? A Volksdeutsche was sobbing and complaining he played a lost game. I listened to his stories like a confessor. He thought that Witkowski and I should have been glad we didn't have to pack up and take our families to the unknown.

A young couple passed us by. I recognized the man. He was the Jewish worker from the RWD, the guy who had passed Yurek's letters to Danka. He saw me and stopped. I approached him, and the surprised woman stepped back a little. We were both happy to meet again. I said it was good to see him healthy and sound. He remained discrete and did not ask questions; he congratulated me on the promotion. Had he known the truth about me, he hid it well. It was a pleasant experience for me.

At last, I was ordered to join the practical part of the course. I was told it would last for ten days, but the commanders could keep me there longer "if needed." I understood it all depended on the operations taking place. Demolishing and damaging the German train and communication lines were daily events. I was surprised to hear that I must return to my "home unit" in Warsaw. I wondered whether I've ever had a "home unit." I was told not to expect any formal procedures and that things would clarify as we went along. I was instructed to report at an agricultural cooperative in a town south of Lublin, and from there, I would be transferred to the base. The name of the town was Bychawa—unbelievable! It was the same town where we had stopped on our way to Warsaw in 1939. The locals there offered my father to hire a truck and buy petrol from the local teacher. I was startled by the thought that I could run into this person again. I didn't know what to do, but there was no place for regrets. I decided to go. I could meet people I know everywhere, and I must be prepared for it. I planned in my mind how I would react if I saw that antisemitic teacher again. I took the pistol and two bullets with me.

I arrived at my destination and was offered a place to sleep. Early next morning, I was called to the cooperative for a meeting with the unit's messenger. The latter informed me too many people had arrived for the mission so that they would have to give me up. He promised they would direct me to another unit. I didn't say that to my hosts, but I must admit I was relieved to know I would not participate. I disliked this town, with the memories associated with it. Finally, I didn't take the practical course dealing with explosives.

The front line was rapidly approaching us. Even the German military headquarters' formal announcements admitted their divisions were retreating all along the front line, from the Baltic Sea to the Black Sea. We calculated every week how long it would take them to reach us. I wrote to my brother to get ready to come as soon as he got this telegram. Earlier on, we decided that it would be better to leave before the Russians arrived at the Wisła's eastern bank. The battlefront might be halted at the river banks.

While waiting, I was ordered to join an unexpected assignment. I was to return to Chełmno in order to deliver something, so I thought it might be the last opportunity to earn a few pennies. One never knows what the future holds. I convinced Theodore to join me and get a piglet—not too big so it wouldn't be too heavy to carry. It all went as planned except that on the way back, the railway had been bombed at Świdnik, nearby Lublin. We stood and waited until they fixed the railway. We weren't impatient nor bothered by the fact we may need to discard our merchandise due to the heat. All that mattered was that we could hear the sound of cannon fire coming from the east. The Bog River was coming under fire, perhaps even conquered. Theodore sighed because his wife asked him not to leave her alone with the baby. I could not let go of the feeling that if I stayed there, the German occupation might be over for me within a couple of days. Yet, I was resolved not to part from my brother. From previous experience with my father, I knew what it meant to separate during wartime "just for three weeks."

A train came in from the west to carry the soldiers who left for vacation. They were joined by other passengers who were delayed by the bombed railway. We carried our suitcases for over a kilometer. My friend was happy he was returning home. I felt like I was committing suicide. Suddenly, I saw a familiar face. I tried to recall where I saw this face. It was the girl who took the clerk course with me in the ghetto! Before I could say a word, she came up to me and kissed me on both my cheeks. Theodore looked at me with astonishment. The girl grasped the situation. She didn't say much, just that she was living with a female high-school friend. From the friend's name, I figured she was Jewish too. I remembered her; she was exceptionally beautiful. The girl whispered to me she had decided to return to Warsaw because she didn't want to leave her friend on her own. I nodded my head: no one could understand her better than me. We had no reason to prolong our conversation. I never met her again.

The base at Bielany was undergoing a rapid evacuation. The master sergeant was happy to see me. He was looking for me and was told that I was out on an assignment. The base was to move to Środa near Poznań, and he suggested I should leave with them. I thanked him but said I had someone I could not leave behind. He accepted. The Obhut headquarters ordered me to return to Okęcie. Orishek, who got my job, had already left with his family to the west. Witkowski was "temporarily" away after having been arrested and released shortly afterward.

Warsaw's streets were packed with columns of trucks and carts. The Germans had vacated their offices, institutions, and bases. They also took their massive private possessions with them. The inhabitants stood on the pavements and watched the exodus in process. There was much tension as well as hope in the air. Many had been much better informed than me; I could gather that finally, the long-awaited change was coming.

I was embittered that no one informed me what was happening. I recalled Olek's words: don't try to handle your fate. Two days earlier, when I reported about my trip, I asked what to do. My new proxy didn't know. The planned operation in Bielany was canceled. The base was evacuated, and the gear was taken out. He promised to find out and notify me where to report.

I sent a telegram to my brother, who was in Radomsko. I wrote carefully but unequivocally that he must come immediately. "Should the aunt's visit be postponed—come back home." I waited for two days, and he didn't show up. Lublin had already been conquered by the Red Army, so I could not figure out what could have detained him. A neighbor told me people were moving to the Praga suburb or another area across the Wisła River. They were not necessarily escaping into the Russians' arms, but they feared the battle over Warsaw might be long and cause severe losses. After the third day, I boarded a train to Radomsko. I got there in the afternoon and went straight to the family's address where my brother lived. They were shocked: he got the telegram the previous night and left that morning. I immediately boarded the train back, hoping he would be waiting for me. I got off at Warsaw-west, nearby Okęcie. I was in uniform and hoped that although security was stricter, they would allow me to get to Okęcie. As I was leaving the train station, an air raid began. The British planes finally found their way to Warsaw. The bombs were falling quite far from the train junction. After a long wait, a tram arrived, and I reached Okęcie well after midnight.

I found my brother in my room, and we decided that, in the early morning, we would go together to Praga with no baggage at all, only with handbags—from there, to Józefów, and then we would see. We talked a lot. We had a lot to catch up on since we hadn't met for several months. The next morning, we woke up late and left. Already from afar, we could see the street was empty. Someone warned us there were gendarmes on the bridge checking people's IDs and packages. If you didn't live across the river, you had to explain why you were going there. That was a blow. It was too late. We decided not to risk ourselves. We would try again the next day.

An uprising against the Germans began in the evening. I got my orders in the afternoon through the guy that lived next to me and worked as a laborer in the airfield. I was ordered to report to the company whose commander was "the miller"—my proxy. I was to arrive at the end of Opachewska Street in southwestern Warsaw. I left all my money to my brother. I did not have any food, but I carried two bottles of vodka in my suitcase—they were better than money.

I could only advance a few meters ahead since the Germans had already taken all the surrounding streets and prevented people from getting closer by frequent gunfire. A few young men entered a small house, so I went in there too. There were a few officers there too. I was asked who I was and where I came from. I relied on my orders from the "miller." I heard them whispering, "Ah, he's the one from the stove-builder." I didn't know any stove builders, but they asked no more. The commander asked me if I had any weapons. There was another guy there with the same pistol as mine, but he had no bullets, so they told me to give him one of the two bullets I had. I gave it away with a heavy heart. Only a few had weapons in that unit, and there was no hope for more since all the supply lines had been disrupted. At midnight they announced that anyone living in the vicinity should try and return home. We could not leave

214

through the main road but only skip through the eastern and southern exits, through the fields and the backyards. A few left, me included, and on my way to Okęcie, I was all alone. We were instructed to join any fighting force we should come across. They could not determine where exactly the battles were taking place. They only had partial information since they lost contact with headquarters.

After leaving, I moved my pistol into my pocket, not in order to draw it but in order to throw it away in case I bumped into the Germans. As long as it was dark, I stood a chance to get back to Okęcie through the fields and the backyards. I knew there were no German posts along the way, perhaps only in Sigalin's cowsheds.[3] That was a large industrial cowshed that had produced Poland's best cream and kefir before the war. Since its owner was Jewish, the Germans took over the business in 1939 and continued production for their own consumption. I assumed the Germans would not be in the city during the fighting. I was lucky, and until it was dawn, I was already back in Okęcie.

I did not find my brother at home. He was among those who gathered in the house near our apartment. The guy, who broke the news to me last time, returned and said that since I hadn't left yet, I might as well join the local gathering force. My brother went in my place, and I joined later on. They, too, were without arms and cut off from headquarters.

In the afternoon, the signal operator sneaked in; he was a friend from primary school in Warsaw. I tried not to stand out, but it was hard in such a small place. He looked at me once and wanted to approach me but changed his mind; he probably wasn't sure about me. He was called into the commander's room. They later announced there were no weapons left and no chance we would be supplied with any. We were disconnected from headquarters, and the uprising continued throughout some of the city's neighborhoods but was unsuccessful at ours. Whoever lived nearby should return home, one by one. My brother and I had left the post. The others were left there, cut off and hungry.

After three days, a gray-haired lady came by. With no further talk, she asked that I put my uniform on and help her deliver some flour to the bakery—"for bread for our boys." Someone told her to turn to me. She introduced herself, but I don't remember her name. She said, "Everyone here knows me. You're not from here; that's why you don't know me. But I know you'll do what I asked you to despite the risk." The lockdown and the curfew continued. The Ukrainian unit raged around Okęcie, Kaminski's SS unit. The residents were too frightened to open the windows. The streets were empty. The grandmother carried two sacs full of flour in a cart pushed by a 14-year-old. She helped the child but scolded me when I tried to replace her: "Don't you dare touch the cart! You are only leading and supervising us." Once we were at the bakery, she kissed and thanked me. This warrior-grandma is engraved in my memory.

As far as I was concerned, the uprising had already finished in its prime. In Okęcie, the Germans allowed the inhabitants to leave their houses; Kaminski's rapists and robbers had been moved to another region, although they turned up surprisingly several more times. People tried to get back to their jobs: either to private business or to the German-owned factories that still operated. Some of the equipment had already been dismantled. Some of the workshops at the airfield had been disassembled and moved to the west. My landlady had taken her son and a suitcase and declared she was going to her family. Her Otto had been transferred westward before the uprising. She gave us the keys and asked that in case we went away too, we should leave the keys with the neighbor. We were left all alone.

In the streets of Okęcie, the people moved carefully. From time to time, the gendarmes of the Kazakh and Georgian units who collaborated with the disintegrating Reich army patrolled the streets. "My" soldiers had been assigned to guard the airfield, especially the evacuation of equipment.

A huge cannon (more than 60 centimeter in diameter) was placed on a platform that stood on the railway surrounding the airfield. Its shells had shattered numerous windows hundreds of meters away. The howling noise the bombs made on their way to Warsaw's houses granted the bombs' nickname—the "cows." Another platform served as a center for gathering the bombs that had been transferred by a crane.

A day or two later, we were woken up by punches on our door. A sobbing woman stood at the door, the wife of the baker who baked the bread for the AK friends in the hide. Her seven-year-old son had taken the dog out for a walk, and a German machine gun entrenched some hundreds of meters away shot him. The boy jumped into a pit and couldn't get out. Each time he tried to move, the soldiers replied with fire. She asked that I save the child. I knew most of the soldiers on that company and wondered why they decided to kill the little kid. I figured the "old folks" that finally were given an assignment were eager to "do their best." I put on my uniform and beret—the stars on my coat sparkled. I left with the woman toward their house. The machine gun was entrenched 150 meters from the house. I called out to the kid not to move and began marching toward the fire positions. Someone there was too enthusiastic or got a stupid command; suddenly, a burst of gunfire was aimed at me too. For the first time in my life, I heard a bullet whistle. I began shouting as hard as I could while using all the curses I knew, and it probably worked because the shooting ceased. I approached and kneeled by the soldiers in the trench. All were familiar faces. They asked how it was at Bielany and whether I had stayed in Okęcie. I replied they probably didn't want me to stay because they almost killed me. "No way!" they laughed.

217

"Ludwig shot, and he only hits the sky." One of them asked suddenly, "Have you participated in the uprising? We talked among ourselves and concluded you must be a partisan." I turned the question into a joke. I pulled the kid out of the pit—he was still carrying his dog.

After a few days, my brother and I left Okęcie southward. We first thought to approach the Wisła River to see if we could be lucky enough to cross to the eastern side. But soon, we were told it would be suicide. The front line had extended all along the river, and all access to it was well guarded. A stranger walking in there was sure to be caught by the Gestapo. My brother returned to Radomsko. Us being together for too long was too perilous.

There were two months of waiting left.

Once again, I returned to thoughts of when all this was going to end. When would liberation reach us too? Strangely enough, for people who lived under cover as I was, this time was easier than before in many ways. In the south of Warsaw, masses of refugees were on the move, expelled by the Germans from the capital, which was on fire. In the villages and towns, I did not stand out as a stranger. Like me, there were thousands roaming around. I could no longer wear my uniform, and I tried to look like an average Warsowian, with regular clothes, not catching anybody's eye. I remained for a few weeks in a village near the town of Rawa, and the landlord, a wealthy farmer, was happy to gain a worker for free during the potato-collecting season. Several months later, he was declared a *kulak*.[4] Work was especially hard. One had to collect potatoes in accordance with the progress of two pairs of horses carrying the plowing machines. However, I held on and won the farmer's appreciation.

One evening, a group of partisans arrived at the farm. They were looking for a place to sleep, having fought the Germans unsuccessfully so far. It appeared they lost contact with their headquarters. They also lacked medicines and tried to treat their wounded with "homemade medicines." According to the whispers of the soldiers, their commander, a young second lieutenant, hailed from a noble family. He was interested in the residents of the farm, me included. He didn't like me, but the landlord guaranteed that I was a friend of his cousin. It was partly true. I had to confess and told him about the explosives course I attended, and he said he would pass on the information. I tried not to get into details in my conversation with him. His soldiers admitted that they were about to conclude their fighting. The uprising in Warsaw was dying out, and people spoke of unprecedented heroic acts, self-sacrifice, and thousands of victims and injured. The partisans left after a few days. Some days later, we learned that the Germans had killed all of them in an ambush. Only the commander managed to escape this fate.

After having collected potatoes and picked the winter apples, I stayed in the neighboring village. My signal operator found me there and led me to the resistance commander, as I was an "expert on explosives." They were very few, without uniform, mostly from the surrounding villages. The situation was now different. Unlike six months earlier, when nobody contested the need to actively fight against the Germans, now the uprising in Warsaw had failed and left a burned-down city and thousands of fatalities. The battlefront expanded along the Wisła River, and there was no doubt as to how things would turn out. I wasn't enthusiastic about playing the hero in an operation, which was more political than military. The commander—who demanded he be called "Cuba"—wore civilian clothes and disregarded the fact that I didn't complete the practical course. I was ordered to assist "a long-time expert." Eventually, he failed to arrive since his unit was dismantled after a fight with the Germans. Cuba demanded that we prepare the "operation," and he would assist us. We didn't quite know what to do with the explosives. The guy who joined me had also been recruited unwillingly. I suggested that we blow up the narrow railway between Rawa and Biała Rawska, just as an experiment. Cuba was angry and said we were wasting time. At last, he consented, asking that we spare the train passengers since they were almost only Poles. This made the task easier. The experiment turned successful.

After a few days, we drove to the main railway line bound to Silesia. We were anxious and insecure, but we had a surprise in store: the long-awaited expert was there. If he was there, what was I needed for? Headquarters instructed to bring in only the experts and rely almost exclusively on local forces. But this was a serious operation: no more sleepy train line on a narrow railway; this time, we blew up a major railway and hit the engine. One of the team members muttered, "Too bad about the engine—it's ours," and said he was going home. I informed Cuba I was going to see my family. He admitted there were too many German ambushes lately and that he suspected I had no previous experience with explosives. "But you learn fast and were of help," he said. Well, then.

I never imagined that such experiences would take place after the Warsaw uprising. For weeks and months, I had enough free time to think and analyze what I intended and what I had actually achieved. I couldn't forgive myself for not going a day earlier to bring my brother. Everything would have turned out differently. I did not regret not having stayed in Świdnik, on the other side of the Wisła. [5] Not for a moment did it cross my mind that I should stay there and leave my brother, but the long-awaited liberation was already within reach and then lost again. I had waited for it for so long; I dreamed and counted the days and weeks, and then...

I recalled Olek Leshno's words: "You should not force your fate." It was completely the opposite of what I had done and how I'd lived after having fled from the ghetto. And yet, his words made much sense.

I did not forget the idea that once it was possible, I would tell the world. Everyone must know how things had happened, how a nation had been murdered, how only a few survived to tell and testify.

I did not tell my story right after liberation—only once, and not all of it. He was a Jew from Russia, a military doctor, and he wanted very much to know how the Jews had lived in the ghetto, how they were exterminated, and how I was saved. He interrupted my story about my hiding in Warsaw, about the attempts to fight the Germans; he closed the door and said, actually insisted, "Never mention your contact with the 'nationalists' and your part in the resistance during the uprising; for your own good." For years I had not talked about how I survived. My part in the nationalist resistance had haunted me for a long time in postwar Poland.

INSTEAD OF AN ENDING

The avid reader who has reached the end of this story deserves an explanation about what eventually happened to the narrator.

So, the occupation had ended; the Red Army had finally arrived with the Polish Army established in the USSR. The initial encounter with the Soviet soldiers who brought about Poland's liberation was a lot less dramatic than what I had imagined throughout the years. They did not impress me—putting it mildly—not in their appearance, dress, nor in their conduct. I myself had a hard time grasping that I had become a free man. I needed time to comprehend that I was no longer a refugee from the ghetto, since the war had amplified the notion that I was not "like everyone else."

I immediately enlisted in the Polish Army, just in time to participate in battles against the Germans. I became an officer with distinction and was awarded The Cross of Valor decoration.[1] In May 1945, after the battles had ceased, I became submerged in some kind of fainting; it took me a couple of days to understand that this time was really over. Since I was a soldier, I was spared the need to decide what to do with myself or where to go.

I cannot tell of my new lifestyle e as a direct continuation of the occupation, hiding, and resistance period. The new life was entirely different. However, again, there was one thing I was forbidden to talk about: my "affair" with the nationalist resistance organization. I had learned fast enough that I was not alone; there were numerous issues that could not be mentioned in the new Poland, secrets that may have put the teller in conflict with the new regime.

Polish army officer, Cavalry Corp 1945

Following two years of study in the military academy as an honorary student, I was expelled due to suspicions that I had been affiliated with the "wrong" resistance movement. This had disrupted my military career. I was lucky they had let me complete my university studies.

After several more years, I left Poland for good.

Hiding outside the ghetto quickly became an impossible mission for many who had fled the ghetto. The occupying force worked intensely to trace them, using a close network of agents, informers, and snitches. The ferocity and diligence invested in their operation were beyond imagination. They often seemed to be acting on behalf of an ideal—if one can designate hate an ideal.

Those who survived often managed to do so thanks to the help of decent, quiet, humble, and invisible people, who not once had put their own lives and that of their families at risk.

I have no illusions. Besides those who extended a helping hand, many others, who had looked at me, decided not to see, not to know, not to think who I was. That was a lot too.

I had left the ghetto determined to help my brother and to avenge. The manner by which I had carried out my tasks leaves my conscience clean, though a clean conscience does not necessarily grant peace of mind.

ANNEXE

My name is Yohay Remetz—previously Tadeausz Piechocki, but in Israel, they thought that Jan Piechocki was enough, even too much. Even before all this, when I was born, I was named Tadeusz Grausaltz.

I did not like this name, maybe because my surroundings did not favor strange and misunderstood words, and maybe simply because it did not comply with my way of life and what I had identified with. And yet, I could write so much just on this subject. This subject actually refines the very central question of my life (and the lives of us all!) until the beginning of the war. But this is not what I wish to write about.

As a matter of fact, the most fitting name was and remained Piechocki since it had served me for a long period of my life.

I had written a book about my experience as well as several articles. Each of these texts obviously had to be confined in length by the identity of its readers or listeners, by the circumstances that led to its appearance. Therefore, on several occasions, I had omitted one or another detail or a whole event. I would like to write about some of these details, but first I'll begin with some personal reflections.

A man is a complex creature; otherwise, it wouldn't have been possible to explain why I had so often stubbornly rummaged through my character and deeds during crucial moments. Well, I'm a complex person, and as such, I shall stay. I must admit that as a boy, and even in later periods in life, I had been designated as hyperactive. In those times, these terms had yet to be known and hardly been thought of how to be dealt with. The simplest thing was to say about such a kid that he has pins and needles, but in order to make him sit tight in class, he had to be severely punished. In my case, no one had made a special effort, so I had to be frequently shamed.

That is how I had to acknowledge that my elder brother was the Goody Two-shoes while, unfortunately, I was not and that I'd been wasting my talents with my unruly behavior. It took years to arrive at the conclusion I was not at all unruly. Perhaps some Ritalin, of which no one had heard of in those days, would have helped. But after all, my self-control had been put to the test many times while in hiding during the Nazi occupation. The one thing that had bothered me most was my belief in my above-average talents. Only after many years did I realize I was not much above average and that that too is enough, provided you are prepared to work hard. Since I mention my advantages and disadvantages, I must note my memory. It did not always prove to be an advantage in school, but I'm a fast learner of languages. I also tend to forget them fast if I don't use them daily. Nevertheless, events, persons, names, and details related to a person are engraved in my memory forever and almost never fade away. That, too, weakens with age, but I still surpass most people of my age. It is sometimes a nuisance but is a benefit when it comes to telling my story.

In the past years, like many older people, I delve into my memories. I obsessively return to my recollections from the occupation time and the war; I study and examine deeply all I know about Holocaust history. I hereby intend to tell things a man would usually keep to himself.

A few months into the war, at home, they still believed all this was temporary, and by spring, it would all be over, that we only had to sit down quietly to survive, etc. In 1940, my friends and I began discussing how to evade persecution as Jews, since as Poles, we had all been already victims of the same edicts. But not being able to go out to the street because the ribbon on our arm exposed us to various aggravations, that was a totally different thing. One cannot imagine the extent to which the Germans went to persecute and bully the Jews even before the establishment of the ghettos and the total extermination that came afterward.

The end of 1939 and the beginning of 1940 was a time of settling in for the conqueror in the subdued country. The easiest thing was to confiscate apartments or offices owned by Jews. First, they would "vacate" the owners of the property and then refurnish and redesign the place according to their personal taste. Furniture could be taken from any apartment or office belonging to Jews. All one needs is to send a soldier or two to hunt down a few people with Star of David ribbons on their arms to serve as carriers, cleaners, or installers. However, should those captured had been well dressed, for instance, wearing hats, etc., then the task would have been even more appealing, not to say amusing.

In order to avoid being captured, one had to obtain documents that would turn, for example, Bornstein into Borowski or Rosenberg into Rakowski. In the beginning, it was even quite easy. Near our school secretariat, which lay in ruins following the German air raids, was a pile of scattered office papers rolling on the pavement. In it were also some of the students' personal files. And so, within a short time, I became Sverin Skoblo—but only for a short while, since gangs of youths began to appear. They were more than happy to turn the Germans' attention to this or that person not wearing the ribbon as required. It turned out, a document was not enough; one must have the "proper face" too. Among my friends, I was considered to have an average look, not quite "the proper face."

Yet, from the very beginning, I was resolved not to take risks. I still did not know why, but I felt we were about to go through a storm that only a few of us would survive. I could not explain this to my family, but I remained adamant. I did not use the Skoblo document—the name seemed too harsh to me—first Grausaltz, then Skoblo...

I moved with my mother to the ghetto, but when my brother returned from Lvov in 1941, I begged him that instead of working as a rickshaw carrier, he should check how we might manage on the Aryan side. For many reasons, he did not find this feasible. Escaping with mother was impossible—her semitic looks would compromise her anywhere, and there was no place that could hide her outside the ghetto. Luckily, a friend from school I bumped into had obtained permits for both of us as rickshaw drivers. He got them from the Warsaw drivers' union, where he was officially employed. Like many other high-school refugees, this union assisted its members with jobs that would prevent them from deportation to forced labor in Germany, which had begun to gain momentum already in those days. That's how I became Jan Piechocki, and I kept using this name for some decades later until I "gave in" when traveling from Israel on an official delegation as Yohay Rememtz.

I admit that my previous name, the one that had been changed, is much dearer to me than my present name. As a Piechocki, I had survived the most terrible years, and I can safely say that I feel proud about the manner by which I did.

Not once had I found myself in dramatic situations under circumstances that were beyond my control. When I was writing the book, I had to choose from among all these incidents. I had to take into consideration how it would be accepted by the contemporary reader many years after such extraordinary events had taken place, if not daily than frequently enough to make it hard to imagine today. As a matter of fact, I myself did not remember these events but recalled them later under different circumstances, and until today various incidents occasionally come back to mind. How could some of these incidents not be defined as miracles? Today I know that such miracles had happened to all those few who had endured. These people, who in the most difficult moments did not believe they would endure but eventually had survived. These miracles were so unthinkable that it's hard to believe they had actually taken place. Meanwhile, of course, many rather trivial incidents had been happening all along, as if by chance. Thus, during most of my many travels (which for a long time were carried out under an anonymous command), I possessed no formal document indicating the purpose of my trip. After all, Obhut was not a military or governmental institution. It never crossed my mind to ask for an official document such a Marschbefehl (a journey ordinance). But in 1944, the restrictions had been worsened, and as a result, there was a surge in the number of defectors from the various units. That motivated my supervisors to issue me a semi-military certificate confirming I was traveling under the authorities' command. I did not think much of that certificate. I shoved it into my pocket and then forgot about it. Up until then, no authority had ever taken interest in my presence on the train. And then it happened.

In Rejowiec station, where I had to change trains, all men wearing a uniform (and the Germans had many of those) were ordered to enter a hall. In that hall sat an SS officer and a few of his subordinates, reinforced by a few men in civilian clothes, probably from the police force. They called upon each of the uniform wearers in his turn and examined their papers carefully as well as their luggage. The three young infantry officers, who were dining on the table next to me, were very alarmed when they were called into the hall.

When the SS Sturmführer noticed their reluctance and fear, he loudly declared that he and his men demand, not ask, to check everyone—no exceptions. The young officers had no other choice but to approach the table and hand their papers. I understood that this might be dangerous for me. And then I suddenly recalled that I had that journey ordinance in my pocket. It was authentic, and I wasn't worried about the impression it would make, and it made me feel better. Just before my turn came, I was told that Obhut employees did not have to approach and that I could leave the hall. Shortly before that, I witnessed how they had detained two Todt corporation employees for "further questioning."[1] I admit it moved me.

A few months prior to that, the tram I was riding was boarded by German policemen accompanied by two civilians, who were undoubtedly Gestapo agents. They checked all the passengers' papers as well as the pockets of some of them. I had been confident that my pistol, a large and awkward Steyr, was in my pocket. Until this day, I have no idea why I carried it with me. In the tram, it was clear that I would be checked despite the fact I was wearing a uniform. My ID and my "German" identity were neither a problem nor a surprise to them. When they almost got to me, I reached to feel my pocket and realized that on that day I had left my gun at home in a suitcase. This incident was such a marvel that it exhausted me mentally.

But there was yet another incident that was even more jaw-dropping. In August 1944, after my return home following my attempt to join the rebels, I spent a few days with my brother in our apartment. We tried to go out as little as we could because we knew that once we were seen together, an immediate suspicion arose—who are they?

Where are they from? Maybe they're ... In the initial days of the uprising, this caution was less disturbing, but now... anyhow, how long can one sit in isolation? The fact that all Okęcie residents shared those hard times and lack of food made it no easier. In addition, in Okęcie and its surrounding appeared various military units, who were supposed to impose order for the Germans. Those units were predominantly composed of ex-Soviet prisoners, Kazakhs, Georgians, Uzbeks, and others. But this area had also been raided by bandits from the Kaminski brigade (*RONA*—the Russian national liberation army).[2] These were professional bandits who mostly engaged in pillage and rape. At first, the Germans turned a blind eye to their deeds, and only following many weeks, put an end to it, arrested Kaminski, and executed him with a gunshot. By then, the residents of Okęcie were too scared to step outside their homes.

I concluded that it was better to identify myself again as an "almost German," therefore, I went out wearing a hat with an eagle emblem. I hid my pistol and a single magazine in my boot. If, God forbid, they had checked me and found the gun, at least my brother, whom no one knew here, would have been saved. After several days, a patrol of soldiers with a Georgian emblem on their uniform sleeves came into our house. Only the commander spoke a little German. I guess they had a specific reason why they came into our house and examined me. Someone must have remarked something, perhaps even without asking to put us at risk. Following a few questions—who I am and what I do—they demanded I take off my boots and, of course, discovered the pistol. It was no longer the heavy Steyr but a small and novel FN 6.35, which I managed to obtain shortly before the uprising broke out. They were surprised and, for some minutes, were at odds with what to do with me. I kept explaining determinedly that it was the airfield's gun, that I was a senior sentry, and that I carried it in my boot so that the rebels would not find it. A staff sergeant from some engineering unit burst into our yard (wearing a black brim hat). He heard the shouts in German and came to see what it was about. The Georgian officer explained that it would be best to hand me to this

233

sergeant. He told him in broken German that I hid the gun in my boot and refused to give an explanation. The German asked me about it, and I explained again that I was an airfield official, that I was at home because of the recent events awaiting orders what to do next. He replied briefly that he would take me to the airfield; they would surely know what to do with a rebel. He also asked what kind of an armband I carried during the uprising. I pretended not to know what he was talking about. He was near 50. I assumed he was recruited because he was some technical specialist. Clearly, he would take no risk. I began to pray aloud; I must have cried too—not for fear, but for anguish that I had tried so hard to stay alive in vain. And as for Arthur, did I bring him all the way over here just to get him killed because of me?

We entered the guard room. My captor was astounded at my being welcomed there. Most of the guards in the shift were my friends or colleagues. A few of them were those from whose hands, only days before, I had rescued the little boy with the dog. Now they were amazed at my arrest. When they heard I was carrying a gun, they insisted it was the airfield's and that they had seen me with it before. The technician was told I would be transferred with the incident's details to the guard supervisor in the morning. He was content, like the Georgian officer, that he was rid of this affair. It was evening, and I was hurled into the customs room. They put a mattress on the floor and asked if I wanted water. Then they locked the door. I cannot describe what it was like to spend that night; I was in shock, yet, I felt that what I had said was fruitful. In the morning, the door was opened by a soldier who wished to clean the room, and therefore told me to step outside.

Around 9 a.m., the shift commander checked in on me. It was evident he knew nothing about the case. He didn't ask about the gun. He inquired why I was actually arrested. I said I was outside the apartment, and the Georgians insisted that it was already curfew time. It seemed to me this shift commander had been preoccupied with something else, not me. He was a newcomer to Okęcie; I had never seen him before. He said that he would report that he sent me home and that in the future, I should refrain from arguing with German-speaking authorities. When Arthur saw me, he turned to stone. He had been busy all night thinking of how to find out about me.

We sat at home constantly thinking about what to do. Now that they had mistakenly freed me, would they be coming to correct their mistake and arrest me "for good?" So after a couple of days of nonstop contemplation, I decided to go to the airfield. On the contrary! Let them see me there. I would even try to go back to some kind of work. There was havoc all around, and I assumed I could just show up there as an Obhut delegate.

I arrived at the office of the administrative officer, in which there were also Obhut guards. Hauptman Schnabel's signature was still stamped on my *Wachführer* (shift supervisor) notepad, but the soldiers informed me that he had already left. In his place was a major named Schlacht. I asked that they inquire what I was supposed to do as an Obhut shift supervisor. Perhaps there was something else I could be helpful with. The petty officer went into his room with this question, and a few minutes later, I heard the roaring reply, "Let him come in!" I went in. At the other side of the desk was an elderly man in a major's uniform. He asked for my name, and I got the impression the Polish language was no stranger to him. He asked a few questions regarding my previous employment and then began to talk. There's no need to supervise workers because there are no workers left. That is the problem. The airfield is dismantling all the buildings that had been built there for years and was transferring them elsewhere. For that purpose, about a hundred workers were required daily. Yet, the Polish workers are afraid to leave their homes. They must be gathered and must understand that this was not forced labor but a well-paid job. They would get a daily salary as well as a hot lunch. They would be picked up and returned home each day at an agreed location. Will you, Herr Piechocki, undertake this task?

After a quick thought, I agreed to take on the job. Maybe, in the beginning, I would not be able to pick up a hundred laborers, but after a few days, having realized it was safe to leave home, get an honest salary and even a hot meal each day, the people would agree to come, and we may well gather the necessary manpower. The major was satisfied with my reply. We were set to begin the next day.

I said I needed a written power of attorney confirming that I was operating on behalf of the airfield authority and exclusively following his orders. Of course, he said. We shall immediately write such a document. He would also inform the delivery manager to prepare the right number of meals as well as the right number of trucks.

I could not believe my ears; in my wildest dreams, I could not have imagined such an outcome to this affair. The most unbelievable thing about all this is that no one had raised the question about my gun. For me, it was a mere miracle. After only two days, more than a hundred job-seekers stood waiting for the pickup trucks to the airfield. The work was supervised by a *Bauleitung* (construction manager) while I was in charge of the entire operation—mobilizing the workforce, registration, and payment.

Unexpectedly, thanks to the dining room manager, who declared he could not feed the soldiers as well as the Polish mob, a professional cook had to be recruited. Once we did, a separate dining room could be designated for my men. I already had an assistant who was a jack-of-all-trades from Warsaw, who could be trusted to find as many cooks as we need. The next day we had a new professional cook, approved by the authorities. I later learned that he was, in fact, a senior "blue-police" officer who had also fled from the burning capital. But he sure knew how to cook. He had a well-prepared bunch of assistants, and "one could find as many women as necessary for peeling potatoes."

I became the airfield's entrepreneur, a personality. That is precisely the reason why I wasn't enthusiastic about it.

I was managing the workforce registry myself. Every week, the staff sergeant brought a folder full of banknotes, and after two to three days, he collected the signed registries and the leftover money. Some workers were late in registering for payment, and I had to run a separate list for them too. I added to this list other names as well, thinking the Reich would not go bankrupt because of me. After all, someone had to think about my salary too, since Obhut no longer existed in Warsaw. Still, I operated most carefully.

The airfield's officials looked upon me as Schlacht's assistant. The major himself asked later on whether I could send him a dozen workers to the airfield in Boernerowo, at the outskirts of Warsaw. They asked for help after having heard about his exemplary dismantling project in Okęcie. But here was a problem—the workers did not want to leave their families, not even for a few days. Therefore, the trucks picked them up in the morning and returned them home again in the evening. Sometimes, parts of a cow that had just been slaughtered had been distributed, and the workers each took themselves a piece of meat. The truck drivers didn't mind the stops, as long their vehicles were kept clean.

Sometime toward the end of September or the beginning of October, Stanislaw Zawada came to bid farewell. He thought the dismantling project came to an end. The rest of the Warsaw population had been evacuated from Warsaw, and the area became even more dangerous. One just had to watch how the Red Army was preparing for the offensive. Stach (Stanislaw) had a cousin, a wealthy farmer in the village of Wilków in the Grojec district, and he intended to go to him. He proposed that my brother and I join him. I presumed he needed my presence in case he ran into Germans on his way. On the other hand, I feared a too long exposure together with my brother. Yet, here Stach offered both a pretext and security because he appeared more Jewish than the both of us. So we set out together. Just before that, I encountered a serious problem. Since the workers' payments had been conducted in recently printed banknotes of 500 złoty, I gave a group of workers a joint sum which they were supposed to split among themselves, thereby owing me a few złoty. As a matter of fact, I had a cover for these differences—the airfield's accountant received the exact change—as it appeared from the documentation. So I needed no further delay. I announced that I urgently needed to go to the Reich. We left on Sunday, which made it easier for us. At the time, Major Schlacht was at the Środa Wielkopolska airfield, and I was to transfer there.

I opened a new chapter. A few dozen kilometers from me, freedom was at hand. Yet, I had missed it and almost paid the dearest price of all.

EPILOGUE

February 1992

In December 1991, Helen and I traveled to Poland. We made the decision to travel following a great deal of hesitation and doubt. Helen consistently refused to go for years. She changed her mind after seeing an interview with Jan Karski on television.[1] In this interview, he spoke about what he had seen in the Warsaw Ghetto and how he tried to convey it to the administration in Washington in real time. One of them was the Jewish minister in Roosevelt's government, Felix Frankfurter. Generally speaking, we were quite familiar with the West's conduct during the Holocaust. But when you hear it from a person who had been there and saw "both sides," the load of shame somehow divides differently.

We were determined to ensure the possibility to leave whenever we may encounter something dissatisfying. We rented a car from Germany, and it wasn't at all an easy task since most rental companies refused to allow a western vehicle to cross "eastwards" for fear of robbery or theft. We drove from Munich to Karlovy Vary (Czechoslovakia), where we vacationed for a few days, and then drove to Poland through the Karkonosze Mountains. On our way, we passed through Kalisz. I wanted very much to see this city, Pulaski road, Józefina Boulevard, the town center, the schools, and the park. Until then, I never felt the need to see it. I didn't have time to see everything. It was raining, and my wife did not understand what could be so interesting in old and unbelievably crumbling-down buildings, even if it's a big city. At that time, all its streets had been dug inside out in construction works. It was a city that became a district's capital only thanks to a bureaucratic whim. And yet, I managed to visit the street and the house in which I was born, as well as in the Kempners' (my uncle) house and office on Kazimierzowska Street. I even peeked into Grandma Kempner's window on St. Stanislaw Street. The way to the city was blocked due to construction works, but I watched it with its entire splendor from the market square. We also drove along the well "near the church," described by the novelist Maria Dombrowska. I can testify that even today, its water is the best for tea making.

The state of those houses and places gave us a hint to what we were expected to find in other places: on the one hand, a construction impetus seemed intentionally ugly, and on the other hand, extreme neglect alongside some disproportionally fostered buildings. This annoyed us; I could bet that the house I was born in hadn't had a plastering since we had left Kalisz in 1933.

The people were mostly neglected, busy looking for an income, a possibility that suddenly had become open to everyone upon the fall of the Iron Curtain—but with one condition: that you already have money, a lot of money. But the population was penniless. Unemployment rose as the governmental factories closed one by one due to diminishing demand. People were now paying the price for years of a communist economy. The euphoria that came with the Solidarity Movement now gave way to despair and often apathy. Not many people detected the opportunity for enterprise by seizing the time of the fall of the old regime in order to make profits easily and quickly. The masses needed time to adapt to the new order, which was just on its way.

Under these circumstances, how can one find traces of Jewish life? The traces of the occupation inferno? After months of profound contemplation on the matter, I concluded that had it not been for those who survived and dwelled on their past, no one, literally no one, would have bothered to deal with this problem. We must not forget that the Polish writers who deal with this issue are predominantly Jewish or affiliated with Jews. That is why dealing with the Jewish culture or history in Poland is now greatly in fashion.

[*Clearly, looking back at 1992, that is not the case today.*]

It was clear to us that we would not find Warsaw as we had remembered it. Helen left in 1950, when the greatest part of the city still lay in ruins. By contrast, I left it in 1957 and had experienced not just the W-Z Route,[2] but also the renovation of the old city, the MDM face-lift project,[3] and the building of a great part of the Powiśle neighborhood, near the Łazienki Gardens.[4] The first apartment I got right after the war was on Nowolipie Street. Of course, it had nothing to do with our last apartment in the ghetto, of which the entrance was from Nowolipie Street, and from its windows, one could overlook onto Milna Street's evangelical church.

All meant little since I found almost nothing.

After having settled at the Koters' house, we went out on our search—at first on our own. We started in Mokotow. Only after disembarking too early from the bus did we realize that the Sadyba neighborhood where the Koters live is, in fact, outside the Warsaw we knew. We marched a long way to get to Kazimierzowska Street. We found it. It turned out to be the only place we visited in Warsaw that hadn't changed at all.

241

Helen managed to locate the Woidat family's window.[5] She showed me the place at the house's backyard, today covered in grass, where the fallen rebel-fighters (from the Warsaw 1944 uprising) had been buried in a mass. Then she found the basement windows where she, her mother, and her brother Marek hid when they were "not allowed to stay alone at the apartment." When she spoke of it, her voice trembled for a second, after which she recuperated and remained restrained, though not cold. I, for my part, was moved. For long, I had tried to understand how it felt to be a boy, then about 11, who constantly lived in fear, day and night, and could never escape because he had nowhere to go to and could not do it without his mother and sister.

We didn't get to Eva Woidat's apartment. An unfamiliar name was written on the placard in the building entrance. No one answered the doorbell. The passersby looked with suspicion upon the strangers peeking through basement windows, pointing at bushes in the yard, and taking photographs.

We crossed Asfaltowa Street. There was no sign here indicating that "in this 'elegant and comfortable' single room apartment lived Jan Piechocki." Those were really good times. The interest taken in me by the military authorities had been long gone and done. I lived off an executive's paycheck (quite a good one) and enjoyed the life of a young man. Man indeed lives from work but also enjoys theater, a concert, and opera, vacations. But there's constant learning. Indeed, until my very last months there, I had not thought about leaving until that day. I don't know why I didn't want to get married "there."

Central Warsaw left us dumbfounded—an alien, noisy, and crowded city with heavy traffic. It was alien also to those who lived and worked there. The endless bazaar extends from Nowy Świat to the Science and Culture Palace and the adjacent plazas, including the underground passage leading from the eastern part of Marszalkowska Street to its western side. This subway was unpleasant, filthy, and allegedly full of pickpockets. Warsaw was never a clean city—

242

perhaps it was only in the days of prime minister Slawoj Skladkowski. Now it left the same impression on me as when I walked for the first time in downtown Haifa, near the port, right after my arrival in Israel. And also sometime later when I was introduced to the Carmel market in Tel Aviv. That's when I felt for the first time the shock of the Middle East. Now I got this same feeling in "my" Warsaw. Furthermore, the traders, especially near the Science and Culture Palace (you could hardly see the palace behind all the stalls), had multiple specialties. It was a remnant of the Kercelak.[6] Everyone was trading with everything—not just in stalls but also on canvases spread out on the ground. There was nothing you couldn't get there: from kitchen appliances to clothes, screws, batteries, and even Red Army ornaments, including Order of Lenin medals.[7]

We tried to find the buildings on 50 Złota Street and 33 Sienna Street, but we could find nothing. The houses were still standing in 1957 but were later torn down to make space for the Science and Culture Palace. And now they were building a new one—each regime had its urban-financial preferences. Naturally, this area was very expensive. Real estate entrepreneurs and others exerted a great deal of pressure to undermine the palace's architectural significance in order to erect office and commercial buildings that would surely yield more revenue for every square meter.

In the place where my house stood on 50 Złota Street, ended the new building of the Pewex pavilion mall, which was intended for foreign currency paying tourists. At 33 Sienna stood various warehouses and shops, which appeared quite temporary. There was not a trace left of the building nor of the other buildings. Only house, No. 41, was still left standing, and from there, I could try and calculate where our apartment was, the one we moved to from Złota Street, in order to get "close." At the time, mother agreed with the family with whom we exchanged apartments that all would return to their original apartments as soon as "all this is over."

All this was once. Some of it still existed after the liberation and up until I had left Poland. At that time, I once went to take a look at our house. This was a big effort for me. The facade of the building had been destroyed during the uprising. The two inner courtyards were still standing. I watched from a distance the part of the building where our apartment had been located. The porter stepped outside— the same one we had in 1939! He looked at the army officer observing the ruins from the other side of the street. He didn't recognize me. Now there was nothing here. There was some commerce around, but nothing to remind me of the peaceful cultural gem that prospered between the streets of Sienna, Złota, and Sosnowa, and later in Śliska. This was my daily route to school on Prosta Street and back. Today, Prosta turned into a major road leading to who knows where. What did it have in common with my Prosta Street?

The Traders Union Gymnasium was the pinnacle of Warsaw's high school education before the war.[8] It hosted some revolutionary educational experiments, such as the "half-boarding school," but all that belongs to memories. A few years ago, there was a graduates' reunion event of this school array. I didn't know about it, and I doubt if I could have participated. And who would've remembered me after having gone through so many homes and family names? Too bad! I have always missed that school and those people (Who had survived? how do they look today?). The older I get, the more I return in my thoughts to these times. I now better understand Zygmunt (Heidelbaum, a close school-friend), who, after 60 years, can still recite the class's pupil list.

We continued to wander around the city until late afternoon. Endless changes and alterations are salient for someone who has been absent for 35 years. One needs not much imagination to understand where this is all going. In one stall, or rather, in a car's back-loader, a guy takes an expert's look at a dollar note, changes the money with no registration or forms, no checking of passport, no questions asked; if you want, he can provide you with some factitious receipt. Some efficiency...

Today's Polish language is quite odd. It is more standard than in the offices, newspapers, or radio. There are many bizarre language innovations; it seems they are trying to quickly get rid of Russian and other foreign influences. Yet, the dictionary is getting full of strange words which have no source in Polish. For instance: the verb *dominovac* (to dominate) is, of course, obvious. The adjective *zdominowany* (dominated) already has a Polish word for it (*opanowany*–restrained, reserved). But this *dominowany* word kept haunting me wherever I went on this trip. And this is just one of many examples.

As we recall from our "great teacher's" teachings, language evolves, modifies, advances, and adapts. This had also been the claim of many humble researchers before him. Words like *wszelako* (however) and *natomiast* (alternately) were not really part of the everyday language yet were considered original Polish. These days, you wouldn't find an educated person who would use the phrase "on the other hand," while any beer seller will use "alternately." To me, it sounds pompous and pretentious. It must be the generation gap. But when I heard a candidate for parliament speaking on TV, I realized that language too has been exposed to many changes, and not necessarily good ones. The officials and wheeler-dealers of the Communist Party, especially in the beginning, lived in conflict with the Polish language. They learned with time. By the way, the Polish language spoken by Jaroszevic, Bierut, and Cirankevitch was utterly pure, with neither borrowing nor foreign influences.[9] On the other hand, Lech Walesa's assistants shocked me with how inarticulate they were. They couldn't even conjugate nouns properly. Well, I guess the motto "lacks graduation but has ample goodwill" is not enough anymore.

Throughout our stay in Poland, we had not encountered any antisemitic expressions. This could also be attributed to our hosts, the Kotters, who did not leave us for a moment, as if they were guarding us. The Polish we spoke remained pure until this day, with no foreign influences nor foreign accent (I happened to talk to a Pole who had left Poland not long before I have, and his language... God forbid...). On the whole, only once on Sienna Street did we notice graffiti, which has since been covered, "Kikes" and something else, and in Mokotow, one that hasn't been covered: "Jews out!"

Except for the policemen guarding in Umschlagplatz and then around a synagogue on Yom Kippur, and if not for the anti-Jewish script on the monument in Umschlagplatz, that has later been carefully erased, I could not point to any antisemitic sentiment. Indeed, we did not travel by train, we didn't hang around in the suburbs, and in the ghetto area, we were not alone. And yet, Helen's ethnicity is so recognizable, and on the bus, youngsters got up and offered her their seats. And as for politeness: Poland can set a good example to all of Europe, especially regarding road manners. In almost two weeks, we've heard someone honk only once; slow-driving vehicles stepped off the lane to let faster cars drive by. (*To be honest, on our visit four years later, I could not distinguish the Polish drivers with such excellence... Tempora mutantur*[10]*... Poland had become one big traffic jam on the road to Europe, which also reflected in their driving*).

We did not go on this visit to Poland as regular tourists, and certainly not for pleasure purposes. Nevertheless, we went to see precisely what we were missing. Just before leaving, we briefly visited Łazienki Park. I find it hard to describe my feelings, but more than anything, I wished to be there on my own.

The Kotters took us to Wilanow, just a walk away from their place.[11] Both the park and the palace are beautifully maintained. I was there last with Leshek several weeks before I had left Poland in 1957. Now the park looks even more spacious. The palace is full of visitors, and the guides speak other languages than Polish. In my time, there were still renovation works taking place in the palace and the town square. Łazienki and Wilanow were some of the city's staple sites.

What else? We could not forget Helen tasting Marysienka Café's cheesecake with cream near that square. She'd had cheesecakes all over Europe, but this one, called Sobieski, she keeps mentioning until today as something outstanding.

We strolled around the Umschlagplatz area with Leshek and Marek up to Mila 18 and the rebels' monument and bunker. Following the scandal after which they've closed down a gas station that was located near the Umschlagplatz gate, the city leaders are trying, successfully, to turn it into a historical monument and to assign wherever possible informative placards as well as stone-like monuments.

But the ghetto is no longer there. It had vanished in 1944.

I crossed the street named Nowiniarska. It is about 25 meters wide, perhaps more. It is composed of ugly-looking all-white residential buildings. How could I find there my grandfather's house, which was between Swietowjerska and Franciszkanska Streets, which was about 8m wide and during 20 hours a day was bustling with streetcars rattling and vehicles honking? With houses so old, in whose stairwell you could already smell the intolerable scents of kugel and sauerkraut in the air.

We then walked to the corner of Żelazna and Chłodna streets to find the house in which, until 1939, lived Yisrael and Luba Brenner (Helen's parents) of blessed memory. We found it. It indeed didn't look the same because it had been renovated after having been partially burned down, possibly due to an airstrike. After the renovation, it no longer looked like it used to. Helen recalled there was a gate that was not there anymore. The building's veteran resident verified to us that there was indeed a gate there that had been installed in another part of the building. But the apartment remained in the same location.

The building's present residents asked how the lady knew about that gate. After we had explained, we were immediately met with the question, "Have you come to reclaim it?" In spite of the calming reply, they remained uncertain and kept wondering what was behind our visit, especially since I kept filming the house and the yard on my video cam. So what's the problem? Obviously, no rich people live there today. Yisrael Brenner wasn't rich either, but together with his sister, he owned a small stocking factory on Bonifraterska Street, which provided for both families. It was from this factory that they took him to a transport in 1942. And exactly there, on August 1, 1944, the Warsaw Uprising caught Marek Brenner, Yisrael's son, and Helen's older brother. His mother sent him to check whether the retreating Germans had taken the machines with them. The 14-year-old has not returned to Mokotow since. A totally strange family embraced him, and he stayed with them through the uprising days. After the uprising had been suppressed, he was sent with the family's father to a labor camp in Germany, where he was discovered as circumcised and immediately shot. This family looked for his mother after the war and told her of his fate. It seems to me she never overcame some kind of guilt feeling for having sent the boy and having never seen him again because of that. However, she had never mentioned it.

On her gravestone in the Holon cemetery, the inscription says: "In memory of her husband Yisrael and her son Marek, who had perished in the Holocaust; May God avenge them."

Even before 1957, I knew the ghetto did not exist anymore and could not be restored even with the strongest imagination. The Germans had probably succeeded beyond their imagination with erasing any memory of the Jewish existence. Wandering about in the streets that still bear the old names (Stawki, Muranowska, Kremlicka, Nowolipki, Smocze, Mila, and many more), which look nothing like the original ones, is not even close to exhausting. It first comes as a surprise, then it is annoying, and finally, it is saddening and leaves you baffled. Meanwhile, new life evolved here, another life. It evolved over graves, and it's not even especially pleasant, beautiful, or successful—this new life. It is quite gray and depressing. No one remembers the lower stratum, the abysses over which this life came to exist. Nothing here reminds me of the past, except for the placards with the street names on the street corners. These streets were usually built on an entirely different grid in those days. Somewhere, the Nalewki Street disappeared and was gulped in the seam between Długa Street and the Krasinski Palace. Try saying that now to the thug from ONR[12] in the university, who had "fought" for the segregation known as the "bench ghetto"[13]; who in 1938 screamed at me, "Jews to Nalewki!"[14] That too was a sort of compromise because they usually shouted, "Jews to Palestine!" or "to Madagascar!" how could I have explained to him today that I haven't even found Nalewki (or perhaps I did not look that well...)

This embarrassed both Leshek and Marek, who had been accompanying us the whole time. Without them, we wouldn't have ever managed to see all the places we wished to see within the time limit we had. They led us in accordance with the familiarity of the locations, the distances, order of importance, etc. They had prepared their "homework" perfectly. They knew every alley, stone, sign, and its details and history. I assume they did not "learn it by heart" for our sake but must have learned it for themselves, as well as the history of the Warsaw Uprising and details regarding the later era of communist oppression. Such is the endless curiosity of intellectuals.

We strolled across the old city, as was necessary after the ghetto impressions. The colors of the old city, which Helen never witnessed since its renovation took place after she had left Poland, had been so lively in the '50s but had since faded. This is normal. But a few weeks later, when we saw Munich's fresh colors, clean and ready for *Oktoberfest*, I had to admit that this "normal" process of fading polychrome plaster in the old city is not at all unavoidable everywhere.

The old city was exceptionally busy, like the city center—all crowds and bustling commerce. There is commerce everywhere in everything: from ragdolls to ambers and Soviet decorations. This liquidation sale of what remained of the communist trademarks accompanied us all along the journey: from Krakow and Zakopane up to Budapest. There, on the Elizabeth Bridge, one of the sloppy-looking youngsters tried to explain to me in English that these stamps will one day be worth a lot for collectors. He had a pretty grim look, seemed intelligent, and had probably not been a trader for long. I said I was prepared to pay two German Marks (that's all the change I had at that moment, and it wasn't at all a small sum back then) and not take the Order of the Red Star for which he asked for five marks. He dismissed me nonchalantly and wished me a safe journey.

The highlight of our journey to Poland was Treblinka.

We are both tied to this place more than to anywhere else. Here, most likely, almost with certainty, perished the people who were the closest to us both. (I was not successful in finding evidence to the story about Helen's father's escape from Treblinka. I will elaborate on that later on).

Here, on this soil, among the villages of the Podlaski voivodship, which lie close to Treblinka, precisely here, ridiculously enough, where I had been roaming for about nine months after having fled the ghetto. Here I had to organize myself the new life I had hijacked under the Germans' nose. I used to know every road here, every road bend, every trail. It proved very worthwhile later on, when I was leading my brother from here, almost forcibly. I used to be familiar with most of these villages throughout my career as an official, assisting Mikhail K during his visits on behalf of the Sokołów-Podlaski district committee (*Kreisleitung*).

Leshek Kotter, who, upon my father's request, traveled in 1961 to Treblinka to photograph what had been left of the camp site, was appalled by the cackles of human hyenas who combed the earth filled with the victims' mass graves looking for gold. After returning to Warsaw, he initiated a public scandal demanding that the camp perimeter be guarded and designated as an extermination and national memorial site. This was a quite hazardous move back then on the part of a civil servant—almost on the verge of rebellion. But Leshek insisted. He conducted an elaborate correspondence with various institutions, all of which were, of course, governmental. This was a one-sided correspondence, with no replies, that is, no replies with any significant content.

Someone once pinned this common phenomenon as "grass-talk" (*mowa-trawa*), but eventually, Leshek reached the head of the ministers' committee, Minister Wierczorek. And since he did so through close associates and because it probably coincided with the then-current agenda, it all amounted to a quite surprising acknowledgment of the place as a national memorial site.

A tender for the architectural planning of the site and for erecting a monument had been published. The lucky initiator, who did not expect it to get that far, tells us today that he almost had to beg them to first and foremost cover the camp's grounds in concrete in order to stop the desecration and looting of the graves.

After quite a few letters and meetings, they finally acknowledged this plea as just and took action.

We arrived there with high emotions, fueled by our own memories and Leshek's stories. That is probably why I dropped the video camera upon getting out of the car, which left it out of order until our return home. Since we'd left the regular camera in Warsaw, there was only Leshek's camera left, which used to be good, but regretfully, no more. And I had wanted to commemorate our visit—especially there!

We crossed the campsite in all directions more than once. It was before we saw Auschwitz-Birkenau, but we were quite surprised by the Treblinka memorial site. The stones scattered all over the area best resemble the gray and beaten masses who had been expelled to martyrdom. The victims' utter anonymity together, with their ascription to the Jewish people, inspire feelings of appreciation and gratitude to the monument's creators while enabling you to feel like a living part of this commemoration.

Here and there are small placards attached to some nameless stone. The placards inscribe first names and surnames, names of family members, all who perished in this camp. They were installed by a son or a brother who had miraculously survived and are nowadays living on the other side of the world.

From a time and distance perspective, one can clearly see that Treblinka's stones stand there shivering.

Compared to Treblinka, Auschwitz's "sterilized" barracks are almost insulting. This does not apply, of course, to the museum exhibitions of the murderers' plunder, the crematoriums, the execution plazas, the dungeons, and gallows.

It's about the long corridors filled with carefully suited photos. I dare claim that they were fitted in order to somehow balance, equate the amount of ashes on the other side of the camp, of victims whom no one cared to photograph, to personally identify; that other side of the camp consists at the most of numbers, silent numbers. I am aware that Auschwitz was a camp for Poles. It was not at all established with the Jews in mind. The site honors and respects the memory of the victims who perished there and had the privilege of being registered with their full names as well as the duration of their tortured period in the camp until they were sent to their families in urns. This cannot change the impression, as if one is witnessing a staged setup of what should have been left real, "unorganized," and authentic.[15]

One cannot say that about Brzezinka—named Birkenau. On the contrary. It is much neglected, even in a criminal way. (*These words had been written in 1991. These opinions were an effort not to be too harsh so as to remain objective. Our next visit in 1999 allowed us to change our opinion regarding the management's efforts on this memorial site*).

Except for the two barracks located right on the entrance of the camp, which still contain remnants of the original content of the barracks, only the first line of barracks remained standing. The only thing that remained from the rest of the barracks were walls and roofs. All the other barracks were entirely dismantled and left a forest of brick chimneys and a "mosaic" of mortar. Did the Germans leave it this way? As far as I remember, part of the camp had been demolished in 1945. I don't know whether all should have been left as it was the day of liberation. Probably not. But minimal preservation of the remaining relics is really not too much to expect. None of the barracks had even one door left on its hinges. Not even one of those famous three-tiered wooden bunks, on which the prisoners laid and turned from one side to the other upon order because otherwise, there wouldn't have been enough space for all of them. Not even one such row of bunks was left in its entirety, all along the barrack. Not even one fireplace out of two in each barrack that were supposed to heat the whole "block" was left complete. Not even one toilet to display how the prisoners lived. Or rather, died.

All the camp grounds were covered with wild and overgrown vegetation, some the height of a human, out of which protruded the tall, lonely chimneys. Nonetheless, all this begs precisely the impression one gets. Hundreds of chimneys across miles of empty space are, most likely, the only possible monument to the endless tragedy of millions—millions of human beings who were exterminated with diabolical decisiveness. Not just by gas and crematoriums but also by famine, disease, cold, and despair. God almighty! We stared at these endless spaces and thought that a person confined here seeing nothing but barbed wire and barracks that stretch to the horizon must have stopped believing there was some other world, a normal one.

But why now, 45+ years after the liberation of the camp, do they allow the remaining barracks to rot away like that? Why must we enter them through decaying and falling-apart doorposts stuck on the ground? Why are these barracks sinking, drowning in vegetation and weeds two meters high, so that one cannot see through them and must look for a way out like in a jungle?

It is insulting, outrageous, even more than in the "martyrs and Jewish fortitude" block (what a phrase full of pride, and it does not only relate to Polish Jewry, but to worldwide Jewry), where they emphasize and exaggerate the help bestowed upon the Jews by the Polish people, their organizations and resistance groups.

We both know the truth, especially about the noble Poles who, thanks to their help (or at least their silence), we survived, but also the truth about the hyenas who lurked waiting to murder Jews. For the sake of my peace of mind, and in order to spare the honor of the first ones, let us not measure the quantitative ratio between the two.

One cannot help asking whether those who have worked to erect the Jewish martyrdom memorial block, without having the means to do it (God knows what their motives were) and dedicated the entire limited space to testimonials about rescuing Jews by the Provisional Committee to Aid Jews (Zegota) and even by the Armia Krajowa (Home Army, AK)–do they even consider the fact that many of those who actually went through this period, who remember it and cannot ever forget it, are still alive?[16]

We were glad to be on our own in Birkenau. It allowed us to feel again our personal bond to the Holocaust. We were glad not to be with company like in Treblinka, that decent people like Leshek and his wife did not witness our highly agitated emotional state.

Upon leaving that block, I was given a feedback form. I wrote what I felt; I had no reason to feel uneasy about it. I noted politely the outrageous state of Birkenau and the eminent disproportion of the "distribution of credits." To make it clear that the writer was impartial, I signed as "an AK soldier–a citizen of Israel." I suppose with almost certainty that the form would have made its way to the garbage bin.

We were in Auschwitz again after some years, this time with Eva, so she would see for the first time the graves and the camps—so she would see with her own eyes this "issue" we had been telling her so much about. The site at Birkenau was in a rather satisfactory shape. Indeed, they had not restored what already could not have been restored, but at least they cleaned up the place. No more bushes and weeds, but most of all, the place was filled with visitors, both domestic and overseas groups. Undoubtedly, someone had discovered the tourist value of the site since our last visit. We did not go into the "martyrdom and fortitude of the Jews" block. Even if it still exists, why get upset for no reason?

In the Polish army, 1947

REVIEW REQUEST

Dear Reader,

If you have enjoyed reading my father's memoirs,
please do leave a review on Amazon or Goodreads. A few kind words
would be enough. This would be greatly appreciated.

Alternatively, if you have read my book as Kindle eBook you could
leave a rating.
That is just one simple click, indicating how many stars of five you
think this book deserves.
This will only cost you a split second.
Thank you very much in advance!

Eva Tidhar

NOTES

Prologue

1. https://photos.yadvashem.org/index.html?language=he&displayType=image& strSearch=3960

My Family

1. As they were named in Germany: Deutschen Mosaischen Konfession.
2. Yiddish for minor, unnecessary objects. שמונצעס
3. A graduation certificate one acquires after 10 years of school.

September 1939

1. The German army deployed mustard gas in 1917 near Ypres in west Belgium.
2. Westerplatte was the Polish army stronghold in the port of Danzig.
3. The Polish–Soviet War February 1919–October 1920.
4. https://www.yadvashem.org/untoldstories/database/index.asp?cid=1076
5. Graf (male) is a historical title of the German nobility, usually translated as "count."
6. Ledóchowski is the name of a Polish and Austrian noble family originated from Volhynia.
7. Menahem Mendel Beilis was a Russian Jew who was accused of ritual murder in the Russian Empire in a notorious 1913 trial, known as the "Beilis trial" or "Beilis affair."
8. Kutno, where my father's mother's Kutnowski family originated, was historically the center of a large Jewish community.
9. Többens and Schultz was a Nazi textile manufacturing company, producing German uniforms and garments in the Warsaw Ghetto and elsewhere during the occupation of Poland in WWII. It was owned and operated by two war profiteers: Fritz Emil Schultz from Danzig, and a convicted war criminal, Walter C. Többens.
10. In the fall of 1941, creative activity within the ghetto had increased significantly, particularly following the arrival of German entrepreneurs who hoped to exploit the Jewish labor force that was available. Alongside the German-owned factories that were established in the heart of the ghetto by entrepreneurs, Jewish workshops also increased their production and began to supply their products to Polish companies, and to the Wehrmacht.

https://www.yadvashem.org/yv/en/exhibitions/
warsaw_ghetto/workshops.asp

October and Afterward

1. A person exploiting the diminishing supply of goods in order to raise its prices above its true value.
2. The project was nicknamed "complet" consisting of groups of 5 to 6 students, illegally studying at the students' homes. Each meeting was dedicated to a different subject and teachers were changed accordingly. The method was officially acknowledged after the war.
3. The Diary of Mary Berg, *Growing up in the Warsaw Ghetto*.
4. The Germans also forbade Jews to play works by non-Jewish composers.
5. A two or three-wheeled passenger cart, which is generally pulled by one man carrying one passenger. A mode of transportations that was widely used in the ghetto, which lacked other means of public automated transportation.
6. The name the Nazis applied to the occupied regions of Poland that were not annexed to the Reich following the 1939 invasion. Most of the Jewish genocide was conducted in these regions.
7. Bohdan Khmelnytsky was a Ukrainian Cossack leader who revolted against the Commonwealth and its magnates (1648–1654). Throughout the uprising he conducted brutal pogroms against the Jewish population of Poland, Ukraine and Belarus.
8. Moryc Kohn and Zelig Heller, refugees from Łódź, joined Group 13, a Jewish-Nazi collaborationist organization in the Warsaw ghetto, but soon broke away to form other enterprises, including the horse-drawn wooden trolleys that transported passengers within the ghetto.

The Ghetto, 1941-1942

1. The Group 13 network (Polish: Trzynastka, Yiddish, ‎דאָס דרײַצענטל) was a Jewish Nazi collaborationist organization in the Warsaw Ghetto in WWII. The Thirteen took its name from the address of its office at 13 Leshno Street in Warsaw. The unit reported directly to the Gestapo office. The group vied for control of the ghetto with the Judennat, infiltrating the Jewish opposition within the ghetto, and running its own prison. There were about 300-400 uniformed Jewish officers, wearing caps with green bands. Its head branch was the Office to Combat Usury and Profiteering in the Jewish Quarter of Warsaw. It was supposed to establish supervising weights and measures in the Warsaw Ghetto bakeries, and to prevent the production of luxuries, like white-flour bread, but the main thrust of their activities was to bully and blackmail people.
2. Carbide lamps, or acetylene gas lamps, are simple lamps that produce and burn acetylene. Portable acetylene gas lamps were widely used in the ghetto due to cuts in the electricity supply.
3. My aunt Sala (Sara), her husband Zalman Jacobovitz, the children: Genia, Lipa and Rachel, and grandmother Neha Gitla.

4. Gęsiówka is the colloquial Polish name for a prison that once existed on Gęsia ("Goose") Street in Warsaw, Poland, and which, under German occupation during WWII, became a Nazi concentration camp.
5. Sidolówka was an unofficial name of the R wz. 42 hand grenade, produced by the Polish resistance organization Armia Krajowa in occupied Poland during WWII.
6. Following the 1939 German invasion of Poland, the Pawiak Prison (on Pawia–peacock–street) became a German Gestapo prison.
7. Pidyon Shvuyim (Hebrew: פִּדְיוֹן שְׁבוּיִים or Redemption of Captives) is a religious duty in Judaism to help release fellow Jews captured by slave dealers, or imprisoned unjustly. The release of the prisoner was typically secured by a ransom paid by the Jewish community. It is an important commandment in Jewish law.
8. In Frank Stiffel's book, *The Oxymoron Factor 2*, it is noted that every ghetto knew the phrase when it was appropriate. "Then, after a night of the breakfront's play, there was bread... on the black market. If the breakfront's play didn't go right, there were dead bodies of smugglers under the wall, and the food was scarce in the ghetto, and the hunger abounded" (p. 78).
9. In Frank Stiffel's book, it is noted that the poor inhabitants of the ghetto had a hard time surrendering their deceased relative's food stamps: surrendering the coupons meant losing the food rations, but not reporting the death could mean they'd have to hold the corpse at home. Many solved the dilemma by abandoning a naked, nameless corpse in the street, often with genitals covered by newspaper, to be pulled by Pinkert's burial service workers the next morning. (p.76).
10. *Khapper* was originally ascribed in Yiddish to an 18th-century Russian phenomenon, where the Jewish community employed kidnappers of Jewish boys to fill out a quota of Jews required for service in the Russian Army, where such quotas were not filled legally. In the ghetto it was ascribed to usually desperately starving young men who did not care if they were caught and beaten as long as they could grab a passersby's food and shove it into their mouths to succeed in eating something.
11. *Muselmann* was a term used among prisoners of WWII Nazi concentration camps to refer to those suffering starvation and exhaustion and who were resigned to their impending death. *Primo Levi* tried to explain the term in a footnote of *If This Is a Man*, his autobiographical account of his time in Auschwitz: "This word 'Muselmann', I do not know why, was used by the old ones of the camp to describe the weak, the inept, those doomed to selection."

End and Beginning

1. Maliniak is not the true family name. For reasons that will become clear later on, my father preferred to use an alias resembling the true name, and to keep the family's identity confidential. [E.T.]
2. The administrative territory designated by the Germans as General Governorate included much of central and southern Poland, western Ukraine, as well as the major cities of Warsaw, Krakow, and Lvov. The town of Węgrów (pronounced *Wengrow*) is located in the Warsaw district, about 80 kilometer northeast of Warsaw. In order to get from Kalisz to Warsaw or Węgrów, one had to cross the

border between the "Reich" in the east and the General Governorate in the west. (*See map further on*).

3. Throughout his life, my Father kept reminiscing of these moments: how he held his mother for the last time; the look on his uncle's face and his tears. It haunted him even more in his last years. [E.T.]

4. Also known as Vilnius or Wilno (in Polish), Lithuania's capital.

5. On 22 July 1942, Germans announced the launch of a resettlement "to the East" action in the Warsaw Ghetto. In reality, transports of Jews were heading towards the newly established Treblinka death camp where they were sent straight to gas chambers. Liquidation of the Warsaw Ghetto was part of the Reinhardt Aktion whose aim was to exterminate all Jews residing in the General Gouvernement. (Information from: Polin—Museum of the History of Polish Jews). Starting in July 1942, an area in the Ghetto began to be used by the Germans as place of selection, referred to as Umschlagplatz. Jews were gathered and held there before deportation to Treblinka. Between July and September 1942, approximately 300,000 Jews from the Warsaw ghetto were deported to the Treblinka II killing center.

Ksawerów

1. A morgen was a unit of measurement of land area in Germany, the Netherlands, Poland, and the Dutch colonies, including South Africa and Taiwan. The size of a morgen varies from 1/2 to 2 1/2 acres (2,000 m² to 10,100 m²).

2. The Kennkarte was the basic identity document in use inside Germany (including occupied incorporated territories) during the Third Reich era. Every male German citizen age 18 and older, and every Jewish citizen (both male and female) was issued one and was expected to produce it when confronted by officials.

3. *Volksdeutsche* were "people whose language and culture had German origins but who did not hold German citizenship". After Germany occupied western Poland, it established a central registration bureau, called the German People's List (*Deutsche Volksliste*, or *DVL*), whereby Poles of German ethnicity were registered as Volksdeutsche. Many Polish families of German ancestry faced the dilemma of registering and being regarded as traitors by other Poles, or not signing and being treated by the Nazis as traitors to the Germanic "race". Volksdeutsche enjoyed privileges and were subject to conscription, or draft, into the German army.

In Warsaw Again

1. RWD was a Polish aircraft industry active between 1928 and 1939. It was established by three young engineers, Stanisław Rogalski, Stanisław Wigura and Jerzy Drzewiecki, whose names formed the RWD acronym.

2. Hauptmann is a German word usually translated as captain when it is used as an officer's rank in the German army. Hauptmann literally translates to "'head-man,'" which is also the etymological root of captain. It equates to the rank of captain in the British and US armies.

3. A brand of military boots worn by German NCO's (non-commissioned officers), which were commonly sold on Warsaw's markets.
4. In 1943, in the mop-up operation following the liquidation of Warsaw Ghetto, the hotel was used by the Germans as bait for Jews hiding in Warsaw. There, the German agents and their Jewish collaborators pretended Jews could buy foreign passports and other documents, and then as foreign citizens, leave territories occupied by Nazi Germany. Approximately 2,500 Jews fell for this trap, with most subsequently arrested, moved to Nazi concentration camps (mostly Auschwitz and Bergen-Belsen), and perishing in The Holocaust. This case is known as Hotel Polski Affair.
5. In Poland under German occupation, especially in Warsaw, official Polish musical activity was allowed only in cafes and only with special permission. Illegal events were organized in private apartments.
6. *Vltava* is part of *Má vlast*, meaning "My homeland" in Czech, which is a set of six symphonic poems composed between 1874 and 1879 by the Czech composer Bedřich Smetana. In a borrowed Romanian form, it was also the basis for the later Israeli national anthem, *Hatikvah*.
7. The Deutsche Volksliste was a Nazi Party institution, classifying inhabitants of Nazi-occupied territories (1939-1945) into categories of desirability according to criteria systematized by Himmler.

1943

1. Józef Andrzej Szeryński was the commander of the Jewish Ghetto Police in the Warsaw Ghetto. Szeryński was viewed as a collaborator and traitor by the Jewish underground in the Ghetto. In August 1942, the Jewish underground attempted to assassinate him, unsuccessfully. Jakub Lejkin was a Polish Jewish lawyer, deputy commander subordinate to the Germans at the Warsaw Ghetto. Lejkin played a leading role in the deportation of local Jews to extermination camps. In 1942, he was assassinated as a result of the execution carried out by the Jewish Combat Organization.
2. The Polish Blue Police was a police force during WWII in German-occupied Poland protecting public safety and order in the General Government.
3. The Reichsgau Wartheland (also: Warthegau) was a Nazi German Reichsgau formed from parts of Western Polish territory annexed in 1939. The name was derived from the capital city, Posen (Poznań), and later from the main river, Warthe (Warta). *See map further on.*
4. Breslau is the German name for the western Polish town of Wroclaw.
5. The Annunciation is the Christian celebration of the announcement by the Archangel Gabriel to the Virgin Mary that she would conceive and become the mother of Jesus, the Jewish messiah and Son of God, marking His Incarnation.
6. *Kielbasa* is any type of meat sausage from Poland, and a staple of Polish cuisine.
7. Oberfeldwebel (OFW or OF) is the fourth-lowest non-commissioned officer (NCO) rank in German Army and German Air Force; equivalent to a sergeant in the British air force or staff sergeant in the US air force.
8. During the German occupation, 25 Szucha Avenue was in the center of the so-called police district which had the status "for Germans only", "and the street's

name was changed to Strasse der Polizei (Police Street). The Office of Security Police and the Security Service of the Warsaw District were placed in that building. A Gestapo detention center was working there—a place of interrogations of prisoners brought in from Pawiak jail and captured during street roundups. https://sztetl.org.pl/en/towns/w/18-warszawa/116-sites-of-martyrdom/51902-Gestapo-detention-centre-25-szucha-avenue

Life is not Always Gloomy

1. Because of its German majority, the Sudetenland became a major source of contention between Germany and Czechoslovakia. In 1938 as a result of the Munich Conference, it was transferred to Germany.
2. Waffen SS was the military branch of the Nazi Party's SS organization. Its formations included men from Nazi Germany, along with volunteers and conscripts from both occupied and unoccupied lands.
3. Unterscharführer was the most junior rank and most common non-commissioned officer rank of the SS.
4. The Home Army (Polish: *Armia Krajowa,* or AK), was the dominant Polish resistance movement in Poland, occupied by Nazi Germany and the Soviet Union, during WWII, formed in February 1942. Its allegiance was to the Polish government-in-exile.
5. Hans Heinrich Lammers (27 May 1879–4 January 1962) was a German jurist and prominent Nazi politician. From 1933 until 1945 he served as Chief of the Reich Chancellery under Adolf Hitler. During the 1948–1949 Ministries Trial, Lammers was found guilty of war crimes and crimes against humanity and sentenced to 20 years' imprisonment.

Memories with no Bravery

1. A popular name for the BBC World Service in Nazi-occupied Europe during WWII.
2. The National Armed Forces were a Polish right-wing underground military organization of the National Democracy (a Polish political movement) which operated from 1942. NSZ troops fought against Nazi Germany and communist partisans. They were antisemitic nationalists.
3. Józef Sigalin was a renowned Polish architect, born into a Jewish family of Warsaw industrialists, survived the Holocaust in the USSR and returned to rebuilt and renovate the demolished Warsaw. In his memoire of that time he wrote: "The city was a cemetery (...) There was no one. Only on the outskirts of Służewiec, Okęcie and Bielany did people–ghosts–appear. There were no tears of joy. These people had lost the ability to cry." https://culture.pl/en/artist/jozef-sigalin
4. Kulak, meaning "fist" or "tight-fisted," was the term used towards the end of the Russian Empire to describe peasants with over 8 acres (3.2 hectares) of land.
5. Świdnik is a town in eastern Poland, 10 kilometers (6 miles) southeast of the city of Lublin.

Instead of an Ending

1. The Cross of Valor (or *Krzyż Walecznych*) is a Polish military decoration awarded in wartime to an individual who "has demonstrated deeds of valor and courage on the field of battle." Until 1947, some 40,000 medals had been awarded to Polish soldiers fighting alongside the Red Army.

Annexe

1. *Organization Todt* or OT was a civil and military engineering organization in Nazi Germany from 1933 to 1945, named after Fritz Todt. The organization was engaged in many engineering projects in Nazi Germany and in occupied territories, using forced labor. Between 1943 and 1945, OT administered all constructions of concentration camps to supply forced labor to industry.
2. Polish participants of the Warsaw Uprising of 1944 in their testimonies and memoirs often incorrectly refer to 'Ukrainians' or the 'Vlasov Army' as the German collaborating forces who were guilty of pillage, rapes, and murders committed against the Warsaw civilians. However, in most cases the reference is to 1,700 soldiers of the Waffen-SS Brigade RONA (Russkaya Osvoboditelnaya Narodnaya Armiya), a Russian collaborating force headed by Waffen Brigadeführer Bronislaw Kaminski, an anti-communist Russian subject. The RONA brigade, at the time of the Warsaw Uprising, was comprised mostly of Russians with Belorussian and Ukrainian minorities. Most were volunteers, ex-POWs, and Red Army deserters. In addition to RONA, German forces included some units formed with volunteers and ex-POWs from various Soviet Union ethnic groups: e.g. Cossacks, Kalmucks, and Azerbaijanis - Bergmann Battalion). http://www.warsawuprising.com/paper/rona.htm

Epilogue

1. Jan Karski (24 June 1914–13 July 2000) was a Polish soldier, resistance-fighter, and diplomat during WWII, acting as a courier in 1940-1943 to the Polish Government-in-Exile and to Poland's Western Allies. He was reporting about the destruction of the Warsaw Ghetto and its operation of extermination camps on Polish soil murdering Jews, Poles, a.o.
2. The Warsaw W-Z Route (East-West Route) is a major traffic route. It was one of the first major post-WWII infrastructure projects, carried out during 1947-1949.
3. MDM stands for Marszałkowska Housing District located in the heart of Warsaw.
4. Royal Baths Park 17th-century gardens and palace is the largest park in Warsaw.
5. Eva Woidat was my mother's aunt, her mother's sister, who married a distinguished Polish community leader and converted to Christianity before the war. Just before the ghetto uprising, my mother, her mother and her brother fled the ghetto and hid in the Woidat home in Mokotow neighborhood in Warsaw. Only Eva's husband was aware of this, so whenever strangers came to the house,

the three had to go down to the cellar. My grandmother hid inside a closet and my mother and uncle hid under the potato sacks.

6. Kercelak was a famous market in the Wola neighborhood, not far from the Jewish Cemetery, which was destroyed in 1947.

7. Order of Lenin is the highest civilian award of the U.S.S.R.

8. A gymnasium is a type of school with a strong emphasis on academic learning, and providing advanced secondary education in some parts of Europe.

9. Cirankevitch were the leaders of the Polish Communist Party in the 40s and 50s.

10. *Tempora mutantur* is a Latin adage that refers to the changes the passage of time brings.

11. Wilanów Palace is a royal palace located in the Wilanów district, Warsaw.

12. The national radical camp (ONR) refers to at least three groups of far right ultranationalist Polish organisations, known to be violent toward Jews.

13. "Ghetto benches" was a form of official segregation in the seating of students, introduced in Poland's universities from 1935, widely adopted by 1937 and continued in force until the invasion of Poland in 1939. Under this system, Jewish university students were forced to sit in the left-hand side section of the lecture halls reserved exclusively for them. This official policy often involved acts of violence directed against Jewish students by members of various Polish fascist organizations (namely ONR). The "bench Ghetto" marked a peak of antisemitism in Poland between the world wars.

14. The National Radical Camp (Polish: *Obóz Narodowo-Radykalny*, ONR) refers to at least three groups that are far-right and ultranationalist Polish organizations with doctrines stemming from pre-WWII nationalist mindset. In the early 30s of the 20th century, they had been known to be violent towards Jews.

15. My father's reference here is to the exhibition in Auschwitz museum, of mostly non-Jewish victims, as opposed to the thousands of nameless Jewish victims in the "other side of the camp," meaning Birkenau, who remained anonymous to this day. [E.T.]

16. Żegota (The Polish Council to Aid Jews with the Government Delegation for Poland) was the codename for the underground Polish resistance organization active 1942–45 in German-occupied Poland, and established specifically to save Jews. Thousands of Jews were saved from death as a result of the systematic work carried on by the Council.

AMSTERDAM PUBLISHERS FURTHER READING

The Series **Holocaust Survivor True Stories WWII** consists of the following biographies:

1. Among the Reeds. The true story of how a family survived the Holocaust, by Tammy Bottner

2. A Holocaust Memoir of Love & Resilience. Mama's Survival from Lithuania to America, by Ettie Zilber

3. Living among the Dead. My Grandmother's Holocaust Survival Story of Love and Strength, by Adena Bernstein Astrowsky

4. Heart Songs - A Holocaust Memoir, by Barbara Gilford

5. Shoes of the Shoah. The Tomorrow of Yesterday, by Dorothy Pierce

6. Hidden in Berlin - A Holocaust Memoir, by Evelyn Joseph Grossman

7. Separated Together. The Incredible True WWII Story of Soulmates Stranded an Ocean Apart, by Kenneth P. Price, Ph.D.

8. The Man Across the River. The incredible story of one man's will to survive the Holocaust, by Zvi Wiesenfeld

9. If Anyone Calls, Tell Them I Died - A Memoir, by Emanuel (Manu) Rosen

10. The House on Thrömerstrasse. A Story of Rebirth and Renewal in the Wake of the Holocaust, by Ron Vincent

11. Dancing with my Father. His hidden past. Her quest for truth. How Nazi Vienna shaped a family's identity, by Jo Sorochinsky

12. The Story Keeper. Weaving the Threads of Time and Memory - A Memoir, by Fred Feldman

13. Krisia's Silence. The Girl who was not on Schindler's List, by Ronny Hein

14. Defying Death on the Danube. A Holocaust Survival Story, by Debbie J. Callahan with Henry Stern

15. A Doorway to Heroism. A decorated German-Jewish Soldier who became an American Hero, by Rabbi W. Jack Romberg

16. The Shoemaker's Son. The Life of a Holocaust Resister, by Laura Beth Bakst

17. The Redhead of Auschwitz. A True Story, by Nechama Birnbaum

18. Land of Many Bridges. My Father's Story, by Bela Ruth Samuel Tenenholtz

19. Creating Beauty from the Abyss. The Amazing Story of Sam Herciger, Auschwitz Survivor and Artist, by Lesley Richardson

20. Painful Joy. A Holocaust Family Memoir, by Max J. Friedman

---

The Series **Holocaust Survivor Memoirs World War II** consists of the following autobiographies of survivors:

1. Outcry - Holocaust Memoirs, by Manny Steinberg

2. Hank Brodt Holocaust Memoirs. A Candle and a Promise, by Deborah Donnelly

3. The Dead Years. Holocaust Memoirs, by Joseph Schupack

4. Rescued from the Ashes. The Diary of Leokadia Schmidt, Survivor of the Warsaw Ghetto, by Leokadia Schmidt

5. My Lvov. Holocaust Memoir of a twelve-year-old Girl, by Janina Hescheles

6. Remembering Ravensbrück. From Holocaust to Healing, by Natalie Hess

7. Wolf. A Story of Hate, by Zeev Scheinwald with Ella Scheinwald

8. Save my Children. An Astonishing Tale of Survival and its Unlikely Hero, by Leon Kleiner with Edwin Stepp

9. Holocaust Memoirs of a Bergen-Belsen Survivor & Classmate of Anne Frank, by Nanette Blitz Konig

10. Defiant German - Defiant Jew. A Holocaust Memoir from inside the Third Reich, by Walter Leopold with Les Leopold

11. In a Land of Forest and Darkness. The Holocaust Story of two Jewish Partisans, by Sara Lustigman Omelinski

12. Holocaust Memories. Annihilation and Survival in Slovakia, by Paul Davidovits

13. From Auschwitz with Love. The Inspiring Memoir of Two Sisters' Survival, Devotion and Triumph Told by Manci Grunberger Beran & Ruth Grunberger Mermelstein, by Daniel Seymour

14. Remetz. Resistance Fighter and Survivor of the Warsaw Ghetto, by Jan Yohay Remetz

---

The Series **Jewish Children in the Holocaust** consists of the following autobiographies of Jewish children hidden during WWII in the Netherlands:

1. Searching for Home. The Impact of WWII on a Hidden Child, by Joseph Gosler

2. See You Tonight and Promise to be a Good Boy! War memories, by Salo Muller

3. Sounds from Silence. Reflections of a Child Holocaust Survivor, Psychiatrist and Teacher, by Robert Krell

4. Sabine's Odyssey. A Hidden Child and her Dutch Rescuers, by Agnes Schipper

---

The Series **New Jewish Fiction** consists of the following novels, written by Jewish authors. All novels are set in the time during or after the Holocaust.

1. Escaping the Whale. The Holocaust is over. But is it ever over for the next generation? by Ruth Rotkowitz

2. When the Music Stopped. Willy Rosen's Holocaust, by Casey J. Hayes

3. Hands of Gold. One Man's Quest to Find the Silver Lining in Misfortune, by Roni Robbins

4. The Corset Maker. A Novel, by Annette Libeskind Berkovits

5. There was a garden in Nuremberg. A Novel, by Navina Michal Clemerson

CPSIA information can be obtained
at www.ICGtesting.com
Printed in the USA
LVHW090532090122
708053LV00004B/200

9 789493 276024